THE GRIDLOCK ECONOMY

THE GRIDLOCK ECONOMY

*How Too Much Ownership Wrecks Markets,
Stops Innovation, and Costs Lives*

MICHAEL HELLER

BASIC
BOOKS

A MEMBER OF THE PERSEUS BOOKS GROUP
NEW YORK

Books published by Basic Books are available at special discounts for bulk purchases in the United States by corporations, institutions, and other organizations. For more information, please contact the Special Markets Department at the Perseus Books Group, 2300 Chestnut Street, Suite 200, Philadelphia, PA 19103, or call (800) 810-4145, ext. 5000, or e-mail special.markets@perseusbooks.com.

Designed by Timm Bryson

Library of Congress Cataloging-in-Publication Data
Heller, Michael, 1962–
    The gridlock economy : how too much ownership wrecks markets, stops innovation, and costs lives / Michael Heller.
        p. cm.
    Includes bibliographical references and index.
    ISBN 978-0-465-02916-7 (alk. paper)
    1. Right of property. 2. Transaction costs. I. Title.
    HB701.H45 2008
    330.1'7—dc22
                                    2008011912

10 9 8 7 6 5 4 3 2 1

For Debora and Ellie

Contents

List of Figures

Preface

A few years ago, a drug company executive presented me with an unsettling puzzle. His scientists had found a treatment for Alzheimer's disease, but they couldn't bring it to market unless the company bought access to dozens of patents. Any single patent owner could demand a huge payoff; some blocked the whole deal. This story does not have a happy ending. The drug sits on the shelf though it might have saved millions of lives and earned billions of dollars.

Here's a second high-stakes puzzle: What's the most underused natural resource in America? The answer may be a surprise: it's the airwaves. Over 90 percent of it is dead air because ownership of broadcast spectrum is so fragmented. As a result, our information economy is hobbled. Wireless broadband coverage in America lags far behind that in Japan and Korea. The cost of spectrum gridlock may be in the trillions of dollars.

And another: Why do we waste weeks of our lives stuck in airports? The answer here is real estate gridlock. Since air travel was deregulated thirty years ago, the number of fliers has tripled. But how many airports have been built in America since 1975? One: Denver. You can't build new airports, not anywhere, because multiple landowners can block every project. Twenty-five new runways at our busiest airports would end most routine air travel delays in America.

What caused the potato famine that resulted in a million people starving to death in Ireland in the mid-nineteenth century? Why is African-American farm ownership 98 percent lower—*98 percent lower*—today than it was a hundred years ago? How come we can't get clean wind energy from Texas, where it's windy, to the coasts where people actually want green power?

All these puzzles share a common cause. Private ownership usually creates wealth. But too much ownership has the opposite effect—it creates gridlock. Gridlock is a free market paradox. When too many people own pieces of one thing, cooperation breaks down, wealth disappears, and everybody loses.

There has been an unnoticed revolution in how we create wealth. In the old economy—ten or twenty years ago—you invented a product and got a patent; you wrote a song and got a copyright; you subdivided land and built houses. Today, the leading edge of wealth creation requires assembly. From drugs to telecom, software to semiconductors, anything high tech demands the assembly of innumerable patents. And it's not just high tech that's changed. Cutting-edge art and music are about mashing up and remixing many separately owned bits of culture. Even with land, the most socially important projects, like new runways, require assembling multiple parcels. Innovation has moved on, but we are stuck with old-style ownership that's easy to fragment and hard to put together.

Fixing gridlock is a key challenge for our time. Some solutions are entrepreneurial; for example, people can profit from finding creative ways to bundle ownership. Philanthropists can assemble patents for disease cures. Political advocacy will also be necessary. But the first and most important step to solving gridlock is to name it and make it visible. With the right language, anyone can spot links among gridlock puzzles, and all can come together to fix them.

I first glimpsed the paradox of too many owners with my forehead frozen to a Moscow shop window and my mind desperately casting about for something halfway intelligent to report to Igor Gaidar, Russia's deputy prime minister for economic reform.

Back when the Soviet Union was crumbling, I flew to Moscow for the World Bank. Standing on a podium before billowing red bunting and an oversized statue of Lenin, I addressed Moscow's Supreme Soviet on how to create markets in land and housing. Destroying private property was simple; re-creating it from scratch, much trickier. As the joke went, anyone can turn an aquarium into fish soup, the challenge is turning soup back into an aquarium. First you define private ownership, then create owners, then. . . .

The transition from Marx to markets went quickly but not always well. At one point, Gaidar posed a puzzle to my team. A year after his government had privatized storefronts, shelves still remained bare. By contrast, on the freezing sidewalks, thousands of flimsy metal kiosks offered everything imaginable. Gaidar asked, "Why don't the merchants come in from the cold?"

Moscow was cold that winter: it reached minus forty degrees, the only temperature at which the Fahrenheit and Celsius scales converge. Still, Muscovites lined up at kiosks for bread and flowers while I peered into empty stores and talked with merchants. I learned it was easy to set up a kiosk. Just bribe a few officials and pay a Mafia gang for protection. In contrast, opening a store was far more difficult. When Russia privatized commercial enterprises, it split ownership among too many parties, any one of whom could block use—and did. One new owner was given the right to sell the store; a second, the right to lease the same store; a third, the right to occupy it. Looking into those empty stores was my first glimpse, quite literally, of a gridlock economy.

In the years since I discovered this market dynamic, a thousand scholars have tested, verified, and extended the concept. The gridlock paradox is a simple idea that explains a lot. Empty Moscow stores may seem far away, but missing drugs, slow wireless, air travel delays, and a near-infinity of everyday puzzles share this common cause—one whose solutions could jump-start innovation, release trillions in productivity, and help revive our slumping economy.

For example, as this book goes to press in the spring of 2008, the subprime mortgage crisis is in the news. The big investment bank Bear Stearns has collapsed. Falling real estate prices may tip the economy into recession. The gridlock angle hasn't been reported.

Not long ago, mortgage bankers sized up borrowers before making loans; lenders were a phone call away if home owners had trouble repaying. Not anymore. Investment banks engineered new mortgage instruments that gave larger loans on riskier terms to people with weaker credit. Banks pooled these new mortgages together, then split the pools into bonds with varying risk levels. The details were complex, but the results were magical: financial engineering seemed to transform dodgy mortgages into safe bonds. So long as interest rates stayed low and house values high, everyone made money.

But not for long. Fragmenting mortgage ownership broke the link between borrower and lender. When rates rose and prices dropped, the gridlock features of the new financial instruments came to the fore. There were so many partial owners of pooled mortgages that no one cared to act like an old-fashioned mortgage banker with careful underwriting and loan servicing. Until recently, foreclosure had been the banker's last resort because it's costly for everyone, including the lender. But in the new world of too many owners, widespread foreclosures became inevitable. Scattered owners of pooled mortgages could not easily reach agreement to restructure troubled loans. Today, there's no one for a borrower to talk to at the other end of the phone.

There's a regulatory gridlock story here as well. Mortgage regulation is still based on the old one-mortgage, one-banker model. (It's the real estate analogue to the one-product, one-patent model that makes high-tech innovation so difficult.) New financial instruments fall between multiple federal and state regulators. No single agency can protect the integrity of the financial system as a whole, but each is powerful enough to block the others from stepping on its bureaucratic turf. Regulatory gridlock meant that no one checked as hundreds of billions in dangerous mortgage bonds were created and sold.

By the time you read this, the mortgage crisis may have been sorted out. My point is not to focus on yesterday's story but to say that what is in the news often has a surprising gridlock angle. Too many owners mean too little prosperity.

In the following chapters, I'll take you on a tour of gridlock battle-grounds—from medieval robber barons to modern broadcast spectrum squatters; from Mississippi courts selling African-American family farms to troubling New York City land confiscations; and from Chesapeake Bay oyster pirates to today's gene patent and music mash-up outlaws. Each tale offers insights into how to spot gridlock in operation and how to overcome it.

This book is for anyone who wants to assemble resources for positive change, get a jump on next-generation innovation, or simply understand the hidden workings of everyday life. Nothing is inevitable about gridlock. Every example results from choices we make, and can change, about how to control the resources we value most. We can unlock the grid once we know where to start.

THE GRIDLOCK ECONOMY

one

THE TRAGEDY OF
THE ANTICOMMONS

B ig business is acting strangely. IBM recently donated five hundred software-code patents to the public for free use. Explaining the gift, a company executive said, "This is like disarmament. You're not going to give away all your missiles as a first step."[1] But why would IBM voluntarily disarm at all?

Celera Genomics, meanwhile, invested hundreds of millions of dollars to decode the human genome, then donated its massive DNA database to the public. A Celera spokesman said, "I feel like ultimately we did the best for science."[2] Sure. But science doesn't vote at board meetings or drive share prices. Wouldn't Celera's shareholders prefer that the firm try to profit from its investment rather than give it away?

Here's another puzzle: Drugmaker Bristol-Myers Squibb announced that it would not investigate "more than 50 proteins possibly involved in cancer." The patent holders, it explained, "either would not allow it or were demanding unreasonable royalties."[3] Why wouldn't these patent owners agree with Bristol-Myers Squibb to cure cancer now and divvy up the profits later?

These mystifying corporate behaviors are linked. Each results from a principle I call the *tragedy of the anticommons*. What's that? Start with something familiar: a *commons*. When too many people share a single resource, we tend to overuse it—we overfish the oceans and pollute the air. This wasteful overuse is a *tragedy of the commons*. How do we solve such a tragedy? Often, by creating private property. Private owners tend to avoid overuse because they benefit directly from conserving the resources they control.

Unfortunately, privatization can overshoot. Sometimes we create too many separate owners of a single resource. Each one can block the others' use. If cooperation fails, nobody can use the resource. Everybody loses. Consider the example of a brother and sister who jointly inherit the family home. "All of us as parents want to believe our children will be friendly when we're gone," says an estate-planning expert, but leaving the house to the kids is "a sure recipe for disaster."[4] One wants to rent the house out; the other, tear it down. If they can't strike a deal, neither can move forward.[5] The house sits empty. That's gridlock.

Now imagine twenty or two hundred owners. If any one blocks the others, the resource is wasted. That's gridlock writ large—a hidden *tragedy of the anticommons*. I say "hidden" because underuse is often hard to spot. For example, who can tell when dozens of patent owners are blocking a promising line of drug research? Innovators don't advertise the projects they abandon. Lifesaving cures may be lost, invisibly, in a tragedy of the anticommons.

Gridlock is a paradox. Private ownership usually increases wealth, but too much ownership has the opposite effect: it wrecks markets, stops innovation, and costs lives. Savvy companies such as IBM, Celera, and Bristol-Myers Squibb already understand some of the hidden costs of gridlock. Rather than waste time and money trying to assemble fragmented ownership rights that might profit them and benefit us all, many of the world's most powerful businesses simply abandon corporate assets. They redirect investment toward less challenging areas, and innovation quietly slips away.

But this debacle has a flip side. Assembling fragmented property is one of the great entrepreneurial and political opportunities of our era. We can reclaim the wealth lost in a tragedy of the anticommons. After you learn to spot gridlock, you will become convinced, as I am, that the daunting costs it imposes can be reduced or even reversed—not just in the business world but in our political, social, and everyday lives. You will want those who made the mess to clean it up. You may even find ways to profit from assembling ownership. But it takes tools to unlock a grid.

THE ORIGINAL ROBBER BARONS

During the Middle Ages, the Rhine River was a great European trade route protected by the Holy Roman Emperor.[6] Merchant ships paid a modest toll to safeguard their transit. But after the empire weakened during the thirteenth century, freelance German barons built castles on the Rhine and began collecting their own illegal tolls. The growing gauntlet of "robber baron" tollbooths made shipping impracticable. The river continued to flow, but boatmen would no longer bother making the journey.[7]

Today, the hundreds of ruined castles are lovely tourist destinations (figure 1.1 shows the location of a few of these castles along a short stretch of the river). They are bunched so closely together that you can easily bicycle from one to the next. But for hundreds of years, everyone suffered—even the barons. The European economic pie shrank. Wealth disappeared. Too many tolls meant too little trade.

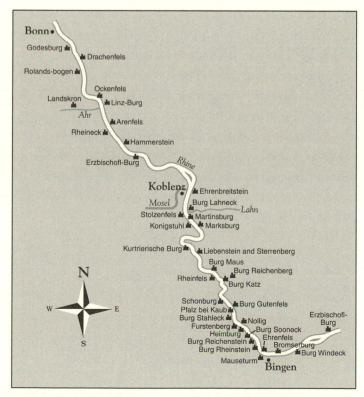

FIGURE 1.1: *Ruined castles on ninety miles of the Rhine—Bonn to Bingen.*[8]

To understand gridlock, we just need to update this image. *Phantom toll-booths* can emerge whenever ownership first arises—and property is being created all the time in ways many of us do not realize. Today's robber barons are public officials, ordinary companies, and even private individuals. Today's missing river trade takes the form of crushed entrepreneurial energy and forgone investment across the wealth-creation frontier. When too many public regulators or private owners can block access to a resource, or can separately set their terms for its use, they harm us all.

Here's a modern tollbooth example: In the 1980s, when the Federal Communications Commission first gave away licenses to provide cell phone service, it divided the country into 734 territories. According to one reporter, "Because the country was cut into so many slices, national service [was] difficult to establish, as if there were hundreds of little duchies, each with its own interests."[9] Today, the United States has less extensive wireless broadband service than a dozen of the leading world economies.

Phantom tollbooths in the airwaves mean that in America, "most of the spectrum is empty most of the time," says Dennis Roberson, Motorola's chief technology officer. "It's absurd." What's the hidden cost of spectrum gridlock? *Forbes* reporter Scott Woolley answers: "One of America's most valuable natural resources sits paralyzed, consigned to uses that time and technology have long since passed by. Old technologies are swamped with excess airwaves they don't use; newer technologies gasp for airwaves they desperately need; and promising industries of the future are asphyxiated."[10]

Americans live in the high-tech equivalent of the Middle Ages, with spectrum gridlock leading to slow wireless connections and dropped calls. Lost economic growth measures in the trillions of dollars; the harm from forgone innovation is incalculable. Gridlock dynamics, not spectrum dynamics, cause this "tragedy of the telecommons."[11]

GRIDLOCK IN LIFESAVING DRUGS

A tragedy of the anticommons can be a matter of life and death. For example, gridlock prevents a promising treatment for Alzheimer's disease from being tested. The head of research at a "Big Pharma" drugmaker told me that his lab scientists developed the potential cure (call it Compound X) years ago, but biotech competitors blocked its development. Had my informant's company and the biotech firms joined together, they might have earned a fortune; we might have limited Alzheimer's brutal human toll. But the head of research was frustrated by what was then a problem without a name. He found his answer in an article in *Science* that a colleague and I wrote on the paradoxical relationship between biomedical privatization and drug discovery.[12]

Around 1980, the U.S. government began allowing people to patent a wide range of the medical research tools and tests that underlie drug development. On the plus side, expanding the scope of ownership helped spark the biotech revolution. Private money poured into basic science because of the promise of profits. As biotech firms mapped the pathways in the brain affected by drugs like Compound X, they patented their findings. In many cases, the patents have led to better drug testing and safer drugs.

But the reforms had an unexpected side effect. As patents accumulated, they began to function like phantom tollbooths, slowing the pace of new drug development. Just as boatmen on the Rhine had to pay each baron's toll, the company developing Compound X needed to pay every owner of a patent relevant to its testing. Ignoring even one would invite an expensive and crippling lawsuit. Each patent holder viewed its own discovery as the crucial one and demanded a corresponding fee, until the demands exceeded the drug's expected profits. None of the patent owners would yield first. Biotech firms focused on their private gain, but the sum of their reasonable, individual decisions compromised the market for next-generation drugs such as Compound X.

The story does not have a happy ending. No valiant patent bundler came along. Because the head of research could not figure out how to pay off all the patent owners and still have a good chance of earning a profit, he shifted his priorities to less ambitious options. Funding went to spin-offs of existing drugs for which his firm already controlled the underlying patents. His lab reluctantly shelved Compound X even though he was certain the science was solid, the market huge, and the potential for easing human suffering beyond measure.

My informant asked me to keep confidential the name of his firm and the details of Compound X. He still hopes to assemble the needed intellectual property rights and does not want to tip his hand to competitors or regulators. But for the purposes of our story, his identity doesn't matter, because he's not unique. Every pharmaceutical firm operates in the same competitive environment. All are reluctant to disclose the patent thickets they struggle through; none will go on the record about the promising drugs they have abandoned.[13]

Biotech researchers are not evil. They are innovators who are doing exactly what the patent system asks of them. As individual property owners, they are behaving rationally. But from the perspective of overall social welfare, they might as well be robber barons. In sparking the biotech revolution, the federal government inadvertently created a property rights environment for basic medical research that can stymie collaboration and block the development of lifesaving drugs.

Compound X is not gridlock's only victim. Not only do research labs lose potential profits, but families lose loved ones and communities lose friends and neighbors. Research scientists have whispered to me about other potential cures blocked by a multiplicity of patent owners. These missing drugs are a silent tragedy. Millions have suffered and will continue to suffer or die from diseases that could have been treated or prevented, but no one protests. Where do you go to complain about lifesaving drugs that could exist—*should exist*—but don't? How do you mobilize public outrage about the gridlock economy in drug innovation?

THE QUAKER OATS BIG INCH GIVEAWAY

Phantom tollbooths capture one aspect of the tragedy of the anticommons. One after another, biotech patent owners demand their cut and block innovation. But there's another way to imagine gridlock. Multiple owners may appear before you all at once. Each holds one jigsaw puzzle piece. Unless you can buy up all the pieces, no one gets to see the whole picture.[14]

The World's Smallest Park?

Here's a small example. Readers of a certain age may recall the Quaker Oats Big Inch Giveaway.[15] In the late 1950s, Quaker Oats bought about twenty acres of scrubland in the Klondike and subdivided it into twenty-

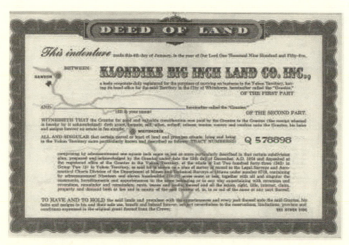

FIGURE 1.2: *My Quaker Oats Klondike Big Inch deed.*[16]

one million parcels of one square inch apiece. Then they put deeds to the square inches inside specially marked cereal boxes. After their fictional radio spokesman, Sergeant Preston of the Yukon, talked up the Klondike land on his weekly radio program, the "big inches" became a national phenomenon. Kids fought to get the deeds. I own the deed to square inch #Q578898 (fig. 1.2). You can buy your own big-inch deed on eBay.

The problem is that what's good for Quaker Oats is not necessarily good for the rest of us. Quaker Oats had little reason to focus on future use when it fragmented land for a marketing campaign. Suppose oil and gas were discovered under the big inches. If drillers required access to all the square inches, the oil would have remained underground even if every owner negotiated drilling rights in good faith. Just the cost of finding and bargaining with all the owners would have been prohibitive. Everyone suffers a hidden cost when legal rights diverge too much from the scale of efficient use and when simple tools to reassemble ownership do not exist.

In response to these hidden costs, legal systems have an odd assortment of rules that curb owners' freedom to divide their own property. Everyday annoyances such as real estate taxes and obscure laws such as the "rule against perpetuities" (a complex estate-planning law dreaded by generations of law students) all have an unappreciated role in overcoming or preventing gridlock.[17] These rules may run counter to our intuitions about individual liberty and freedom of contract. Why shouldn't we be able to use our property as we please? Who would possibly suffer if, for example, we subdivide it too much? Now you can glimpse a unifying reason for such rules: they serve as crude tools for reining in the impulse to create big inches.

Because Quaker Oats saw its big inches only as a marketing device, it did not worry about future land uses and did not bother registering the subdivision or paying land taxes. In time, the unpaid taxes mounted, the big inches were forfeited back to the territory, and the Yukon government auctioned the reassembled land to a single private owner. Almost everyone was happy: Quaker Oats sold a lot of cereal, the Yukon government returned the land to economic use, and my deed became a collectors' item. The disgruntled included a deed owner who tried to donate his three square inches to create the world's smallest national park, and a little boy who sent the local title office four toothpicks so that they could fence in his inch.[18] These disappointments aside, the law did the right thing. Real estate taxes were the hidden hand that gathered up the big inches and averted gridlock.

Fifty Miles of Concrete

There are weightier big-inch tragedies than those created by cereal companies. When you sit on the tarmac because the plane is delayed or circle waiting to land, a regulatory version of big-inch gridlock is a leading cause. Passenger travel has tripled since 1978 when airlines were deregulated. So how many new airports have been built in the United States since then? Only one: Denver's, in 1995. Local communities act like big-inch owners, blocking assembly of the land needed for new airports, both here and abroad.[19] Neighbors do all they can to delay or derail airport projects. Because of their ability to control the local land-use regulatory process, neighbors need not even own the underlying land to create gridlock and prevent needed development.

Neighbors block expansion of existing airports as well. Chicago O'Hare Airport has for decades desperately needed to realign its runways and add new ones. (Each new jet runway is about two miles long.) Neighboring home owners in Bensenville and Elk Grove Village have blocked the work. It's the same in New York City, Seattle, Dallas–Fort Worth, and Los Angeles: everywhere we need airport expansion, we get gridlock instead. According to the Air Traffic Controllers Association, "Fifty miles of concrete poured at our nation's 25 busiest airports will solve most of our aviation delays."[20]

Gridlock blocks new capacity in airspace as well as on the ground. In the New York City area, we could decrease air-travel delays by about 20 percent just by streamlining departure and arrival paths. Some of the existing approach routes date back to when pilots found the city by flying down the Hudson and looking out their windows for bonfires and beacons. Last year, regulators floated the first redesign plan in more than two decades. But the new routes would fly planes over well-organized home owners below. So Rockland County, Fairfield, Elizabeth, Bergen County, and suburban Philadelphia immediately filed lawsuits. Meanwhile, air-traffic delays in New York continue to radiate throughout the country.[21]

My all-time favorite news headline on big inches in air travel comes from the *Christian Science Monitor:* "Gridlock over How to End Flight Gridlock."[22] The underlying problem is that America currently lacks a fair and efficient way to assemble land for economic development—whether for new airports or any other large-scale land use. (In Chapter 5, I propose a solution.)

Gridlock in History and Culture

Big inches don't involve just deeds in cereal boxes or land for runways. They can also cut us off from our own history and culture. Think of the legacy of Martin Luther King, Jr. A few readers may have marched with him in Selma or heard his "I have a dream" speech on the steps of the Lincoln Memorial. Today, though, most of us know him indirectly, through writings, interviews, recordings, and videos.

For millions of Americans, Dr. King came alive through the Emmy Award–winning public television documentary *Eyes on the Prize.*[23] Clayborne Carson, a history professor at Stanford University, editor of Dr. King's papers, and senior adviser to the documentary, calls it "the principal film account of the most important American social justice movement of the 20th century."[24] To make this fourteen-hour documentary, filmmaker

FIGURE 1.3: *A public domain image of Dr. King.*[26]

Henry Hampton talked with hundreds of people who knew Dr. King—fellow activists, family members, journalists, and friends—and drew from many sources in a variety of media: video footage from 82 archives, almost 275 still photographs from 93 archives, and some 120 songs.[25]

To put these materials into the film, Hampton had to secure licenses from their copyright owners. Otherwise he faced possible lawsuits. Many of these licenses expired in 1987 after the film was first broadcast. Over time, rights to these video clips, images, and songs changed hands. Often, the original permission did not include rights to a television rebroadcast or use in new media such as DVDs. Because the *Eyes on the Prize* filmmakers lacked broad permission to use the underlying sources, the film could not be shown again. It sat unwatched for years.

When I talked with Professor Carson about *Eyes on the Prize*, he told me that the film could not easily be made today. Licensing all the pieces of intellectual property would be too daunting. Along with the film's other creators, Carson has spent many frustrating years trying to bring *Eyes on the Prize* out of the vault. The Ford Foundation donated six hundred thousand dollars to help buy licenses; other donors gave hundreds of thousands more. Even with these contributions, and a lot of volunteer efforts, the negotiations took nearly twenty years.

What caused the gridlock? Suppose the filmmakers used a film clip of an interview. People who were honored to appear in the original documentary can now demand payment for inclusion in the DVD. Owners of copyrighted songs sung in the background as Dr. King marched can demand compensation. So can the interviewer or narrator. And Dr. King's estate can request compensation for use of his likeness in the film.

To re-release the film, the producers had to jump through a thousand hoops, a process called "clearing rights" in the trade. Clearing rights is not cheap or fast. It has become a business that one practitioner describes as "half Sherlock Holmes and half Monty Hall."[27] While a merchant sailing on the Rhine could easily spot fortress tollbooths, the *Eyes on the Prize* team had to search hard for the many big-inch owners. Bringing the film to DVD meant identifying and locating each of the partial owners or their heirs, then negotiating payment to, or a release from, every single one of them. There is no convenient mechanism for bundling copyrights in the way that unpaid taxes can prompt the reassembly of fragmented, abandoned land.

Clearing rights is especially complex for music. When the *Eyes on the Prize* team could not get the rights to a song, the music had to be removed and replaced without "damaging the integrity of the sequence," according to Rena Kosersky, music supervisor for the project. "We're not talking about digital formats, we're talking about actual reels of material. It's difficult and very time-consuming."[28]

In 2006, the team effort finally succeeded in clearing the rights to (or replacing) each element of the film. *Eyes on the Prize* was re-released.

GRIDLOCK IN THE ARTS

James Surowiecki, writing in the *New Yorker*, argues that "the open fields of culture are increasingly fenced in with concertina wire."[29] He's right. The *Eyes on the Prize* DVD is one example among many thousands of potential new media creations that have been delayed or lost because of gridlock—a vast, unseen world of art and information.

Films and DVDs

Many documentaries are off the market or, worse, never made at all, and our collective history is lost. According to a 2004 study by the American University Center for Social Media, rights-clearance costs have risen dramatically, and clearing rights is now "arduous and frustrating, especially around movies and music."[30] Pat Aufderheide, a study coauthor, said, "Anyone who intends to make products for mass media is really hostage to the terms of copyright."[31] Copyrights may each be reasonable on their own, but together they add up to big-inch gridlock.

A recent *New York Times* story titled "The Hidden Cost of Documentaries" highlights a few other examples: *Tarnation,* a spunky documentary on growing up with a schizophrenic mother, originally cost $218 to make at home on the director's laptop.[32] It required an additional $230,000 for music clearances before it could be distributed. The adorable indie hit *Mad Hot Ballroom,* about eleven year olds in New York City who become passionate ballroom dancers, was almost not screened. Because of struggles to acquire clearances for music rights from multiple owners, many scenes had to be cut. Even having the law on the filmmakers' side didn't matter. The lawyer for *Mad Hot Ballroom* counseled film producer Amy Sewell that "honestly, for your first film, you don't have enough money to fight the music industry."[33]

To see how gridlock works in popular culture, consider *The Brady Bunch* sitcom from the 1970s. Creating a spin-off or sequel required agreement by, among others, each of the actors portraying the Brady kids (and their guardians while the kids were minors), the Brady parents, and Alice, the housekeeper. Getting simultaneous agreement from them all was, to say the least, a challenge.[34] To be fair, gridlock isn't always bad. Sometimes it's mined for comedy. In an episode of HBO's *Curb Your Enthusiasm,* actor Larry David discovers that the only way he can bury an ugly utility wire crossing his backyard is if all his neighbors approve. The deal collapses when one holds out.[35] No one loves the wire, but it stays. On balance, though, society's gains in comic plotlines don't outweigh our cultural losses.

Fans of the late-1980s classic television drama *China Beach* can't buy the series on DVD because the owner, Warner Brothers, cannot clear rights to all the expensive Motown music used in the show. Same with the late-1970s television show *WKRP in Cincinnati*—its owners have not been able to assemble rights to all the classic rock playing in the background.[36] Reporting in *Wired*, Katie Dean writes, "Serious fans want the whole show, not mangled scenes missing critical music."[37] Dean quotes David Lambert, the news director of a Web site covering TV shows released on DVD saying that fans "don't want the songs replaced. . . . They want to see it in the way they originally saw it broadcast, enjoyed it and fell in love with it. You can almost always count on some music replacement. We've got entire theme songs being replaced."[38]

Frank Sinatra's "Love and Marriage" is gone as the theme song on the third-season DVD of *Married . . . with Children*. On the *Wiseguy* DVD, the Moody Blues' "Nights in White Satin" is missing from a critical scene. When you buy DVDs of your favorite TV shows, you'll often find a small disclaimer on the box saying, "Music may differ from televised version," or more optimistically, "Features brand-new music selected by the executive producer."[39] Each of these DVD examples is small, perhaps trivial, but together they add up. The problem of big inches—too many rights in impossibly small pieces—breaks the link between the images and songs you love.

Music

Even hip-hop music is a victim of gridlock. Over the past generation, the sound of hip-hop has changed radically, in part because of a tragedy of the anticommons. Take the classic 1988 album by Public Enemy, *It Takes a Nation of Millions to Hold Us Back*. The album helped transform hip-hop by assembling a musical collage sound from small samples of hundreds of borrowed works. Over this wall of sound, Chuck D rapped:

> *Caught, now in court 'cause I stole a beat*
> *This is a sampling sport . . .*
> *I found this mineral that I call a beat*
> *I paid zero.*[40]

After the "Public Enemy sound" took off, the major record companies responded by asserting rights and demanding license fees for even the briefest samples. The 1988 album could not be made today. In a recent interview, Chuck D said, "Public Enemy's music was affected more than anybody's because we were taking thousands of sounds. If you separated the sounds, they wouldn't have been anything—they were unrecognizable. The sounds were all collaged together to make a sonic wall. Public Enemy was affected because it is too expensive to defend against a claim. So we had to change our whole style."[41]

If you are one of the millions of fans of the early Public Enemy sound, and if you wonder why hip-hop today often raps over just one primary sample, that's the reason. It's not only that musical tastes have changed. It's that song owners use their copyrights like big inches. The collage sound in rap is gone from the major music labels (though underground versions are still made). An online music activist writes, "It's becoming impossible for any producer—even the wealthiest producers like Puff Daddy—to make collage. . . . Albums like the Beastie Boys' *Paul's Boutique* would be totally impossible to make now. . . . If you take the hip-hop tradition seriously, then you have to acknowledge that the current situation has killed off part of that art form."[42]

Collage is gone; rap "mixtapes" may be the next to go. These compilations of unreleased mixes, sneak previews, and never-to-be released bloopers are often the only way for fans to keep up with the fast-moving genre. Today, mixtapes are a "vital part of the hip-hop world." The major record labels quietly rely on, and sometimes even bankroll, mixtapes to promote their artists. Recently, though, the Recording Industry Association of America had leading mixtape practitioner DJ Drama arrested. According to the *New York Times*, "Now DJ Drama is yet another symbol of the music industry's turmoil and confusion."[43]

Copyrighting a Single Note?

In short, copyright has veered off the rails. A court recently ruled that even an unrecognizable one-and-a-half-second sound clip was copyright-protected and permission was required before the clip could be sampled.[44] One commentator says, "The stories sound like urban legends, only they're true. . . . What's next, copyrighting a single note? We're almost there."[45]

Just as phantom tollbooths cost us Compound X, big inches impose a hidden loss on film, music, art, and history. By making culture too hard to assemble, we silently diminish our own collective wealth. And the greatest harm occurs along the frontiers of innovation, including artistic expression.

I believe that when Chuck D remixes short samples, much of it should be considered "fair use." Fair use is an old doctrine in American law that allows limited use of copyrighted material without permission or payment. It's not an exception or limitation to copyright. Fair use is part of our original compact with creators. Unfortunately, major copyright holders pressure Congress and the courts to shrink the zone of fair use. So what's the cost?[46] The answer is that an expansive sphere of fair use has a hidden value: it averts cultural gridlock.

The value we get from remixing tiny fragments of culture almost certainly exceeds the harm to individual creators. But Chuck D's record label won't defend this principle. Instead, it hopes to get paid when others sample its albums. The major record labels prefer an extreme version of copyright protection. We, as a creative society, are worse off. People will not stop making music even if their work is sampled.[47]

The fear of copyright lawsuits casts a shadow far beyond what the law grants—or should grant. Facing this shadow, almost everyone preemptively capitulates. As a professor, I run into Chuck D's sampling dilemma when I assemble course readings for my students. Scholars, like artists, tend not to have large budgets for teams of lawyers. Posting article excerpts on my nonpublic class Web site should be "educational fair use"— it's like holding a book for students in the library. Posting on class Web sites may indeed be fair use even under current law, depending on how we interpret some old cases.[48] But universities don't want to risk being sued. Instead of fighting to expand fair use, university lawyers demand that professors obtain copyright clearances and charge students for course readings. I don't want to burden my students with more debt, so I have two choices: either leave out excerpts that I think my students need or become a copyright pirate.

Copyright law has been unable to keep up with changing technological possibilities. In times past (less than a generation ago), the locus of value in the music industry was the individual song or album. Today, much value can be created from assemblies such as multimedia DVDs, mash-ups, and mixtapes. Documentary film or hip-hop music may not be your passion, but similar forms of gridlock affect what you see and hear, whatever your tastes in film, music, television, dance, or theater—or law school courses.

To circle back to the *Eyes on the Prize* documentary, at some point we might ask: who owns Dr. King's legacy—we the people or the scattered copyright owners who can hijack our collective memory? For now, filmmakers drop segments for which they cannot clear rights. They digitally mask background images. They cut out offending music. And they delete recalcitrant people.

THE COMMONS AND THE ANTICOMMONS

It's not that lawmakers set out to stop filmmaker Henry Hampton from telling Dr. King's story or prevent rapper Chuck D from creating the Public Enemy sound. Property rights respond to a real problem. Unless we provide some copyright protection, people might have too little incentive to invest in artistic expression. But if we protect ownership too much, we reach gridlock.

To understand the dilemma, it is helpful to start with commons overuse. Aristotle was among the first to note how shared ownership can lead to overuse: "That which is common to the greatest number has the least care bestowed upon it. . . . [E]ach thinks chiefly of his own, hardly at all of the common interest; and only when he is himself concerned as an individual."[49]

Why do people overuse and destroy things that they value? Perhaps they are shortsighted or dim-witted, in which case reasoned discussion or gentle persuasion may help. But even the clearheaded can overuse a commons, for good reason. The most intractable overuse tragedy arises when individuals choose rationally to consume scarce resources even though each knows that the sum of these decisions destroys the resource for all. In such settings, reason cuts the wrong way and gentle persuasion is ineffective. For example:

- We insist on antibiotics for minor illnesses without regard to the collective cost we suffer from the drug-resistant diseases that emerge.
- We blast our air conditioners on steamy summer nights knowing that the sum effect is to increase global warming, and create the need for more air conditioners.

- We drive alone to save a few minutes individually, but we collectively create congestion that slows us all.

In other words, I do what's best for me, you do what's best for you, and no one pays heed to the sustainability of the shared resource. Discussing "Easter Island's end," biogeographer Jared Diamond notes that the large statues of stone heads on a now barren island implicitly make a statement: this was once a lush land able to support a thriving civilization. He asks, "Why didn't [the islanders] look around, realize what they were doing, and stop before it was too late? What were they thinking when they cut down the last palm tree?"[50]

Ecologist Garrett Hardin captured this dynamic well when he coined the phrase *tragedy of the commons*. In 1968 he wrote, "Ruin is the destination toward which all men rush, each pursuing his own best interest in a society that believes in the freedom of the commons. Freedom in a commons brings ruin to all."[51] Since Hardin wrote these lines, thousands have identified additional areas susceptible to overuse and commons tragedy.[52]

In addition, Hardin's metaphor inspired a search for solutions. Most solutions revolve around two main approaches: regulation or privatization. Suppose a common lake is being overfished. Regulators can step in and decide who can fish, when, how much, and with what methods. Such direct "command-and-control" regulation has dropped from favor, however, partly because it fails so often and partly because of disenchantment with socialist-type regulatory control.

These days, regulators are more likely to look for some way to privatize access to the lake. They know that divvying up ownership can create powerful personal incentives to conserve. Harvest too many fish in your own lake today, starve tomorrow; invest wisely in the lake, profit forever. Extrapolating from such experience, legislators and voters reason—wrongly—that if some private property is a good thing, more must be better. In this view, privatization can never go too far.

Until now, ownership, competition, and markets—the guts of modern capitalism—have been understood through the opposition suggested by figure 1.4. Private property solves the tragedy of the commons. Privatization beats regulation. Market competition outperforms state control. Capitalism trounces socialism. But these simple oppositions mistake the visible forms of ownership for the whole spectrum. The assumption is fatally incomplete.

FIGURE 1.4: *The standard solution to commons tragedy.*

Privatizing a commons may cure the tragedy of wasteful overuse, but it may inadvertently spark the opposite. English lacks a term to denote wasteful underuse. To describe this type of fragmentation, I coined the phrase *tragedy of the anticommons.*[53] The term covers any setting in which too many people can block each other from creating or using a scarce resource. Rightly understood, the opposite of overuse in a commons is underuse in an anticommons.

This concept makes visible the hidden half of our ownership spectrum, a world of social relations as complex and extensive as any we have previously known (see fig. 1.5). Beyond normal private property lies anticommons ownership. As one legal theorist writes, "To simplify a little, the tragedy of the commons tells us why things are likely to fall apart, and the tragedy of the anticommons helps explain why it is often so hard to get them back together."[54]

FIGURE 1.5: *Revealing the hidden half of the ownership spectrum.*

Often, we think that governments need only to create clear property rights and then get out of the way. So long as rights are clear, owners can trade in markets, move resources to higher valued uses, and generate wealth. But clear rights and ordinary markets are not enough. The anticommons perspective shows that the *content* of property rights matters as much as the *clarity.* Gridlock arises when ownership rights and regulatory controls are too fragmented.

Making the tragedy of the anticommons visible upends our intuitions about private property. Private property can no longer be seen as the end point of ownership. Privatization can go too far, to the point where it destroys rather than creates wealth. Too many owners paralyze markets because everyone blocks everyone else. Well-functioning private property is a fragile balance poised between the extremes of overuse and underuse.

GRIDLOCK HERE AND ABROAD

In the chapters that follow, I will show you gridlock battlegrounds in business, politics, and everyday life. Once you know what to look for, you can spot gridlock all around. New stories crop up every day. Here are a few gridlock puzzles people have sent me:

- Why do so many people die of organ failure? One reason is gridlock in organ donation. Even when the deceased was in favor of donating his or her organs, any relative may be able to hold up the donation process. Organs go to waste, and potential recipients get sicker or die, while doctors make sure they have all the necessary permissions.
- What caused a deadly 2002 midair plane collision over Germany? In part it was Europe's air traffic control system, which has been described as "a patchwork, fragmented by national boundaries and differing technical standards." A one-hour flight from Brussels to Geneva requires pilots to make up to nine manual changes in radio frequencies. Besides the occasional collision, this system "wastes an estimated 350,000 flight-hours a year and costs travelers about $1 billion in flight delays and increased operating costs."[55]
- Why isn't there more clean wind power in the United States? Turbines work reasonably well now, but there is transmission gridlock. The highest wind potential stretches from Texas to the Dakotas; the strongest demand for clean energy is in dense

coastal cities. According to one industry advocate, "We need a
national vision for transmission like we have with the national
highway system. We have to get over the hump of having a
patchwork of electric utility fiefdoms."[56]

- What explains the 98 percent drop in African American farm
ownership over the past century? "Heir property" gridlock. Children inherit from parents. The number of heirs multiplies down
through the generations. As people scatter across the country,
family farms become impossible to manage. What happens next?
Often, an outsider buys a share owned by a distant heir and
forces a courthouse auction of the whole farm. As a result, the
locus of family reunions and cohesion is lost for a pittance.[57]

THE FLIP SIDE OF GRIDLOCK

Every tragedy of the anticommons contains the seeds of opportunity. Individual entrepreneurial effort, cooperative engagement, and political advocacy are the paths to fixing gridlock.

Let's return to gridlock on the Rhine. In 1254, the baron of Reitberg
went a little too far. He not only collected unjust tolls but also kidnapped
the queen of Holland as she sailed by. This uncivil act prompted the
burghers of Worms, a nearby city, to help bankroll the "Rhine League"—a
private collective effort to revive trade on the river. The league hired
knights, besieged Reitberg, rescued the queen, destroyed a dozen castles,
and reopened the Rhine to traffic. But the effort proved hard to sustain.
Freelance knights were costly. Neighboring towns, which benefited from
trade, failed to chip in. When the league collapsed, the robber barons proliferated anew, and river traffic shrank. More than five hundred years passed
with gridlock on the Rhine.[58] According to one boatman's plaintive song:

> The Rhine can count more tolls than miles
> And knight and priestling grind us down.
> The toll-man's heavy hand falls first,
> Behind him stands the greedy line:
> Master of tolls, assayer, scribe,—
> Four man deep they tap the wine.[59]

After the 1815 Congress of Vienna, the great European powers finally began removing the offending toll collectors. Then, in the mid-1800s, railroads emerged as a faster, cheaper, and more reliable substitute to river transport. Finally, gridlock eased.

This story illustrates the three distinct paths to overcoming robber-baron tolls: the creation of new markets, cooperation, and regulation. European railway markets eventually substituted for river transport. As a modern analogue, scientists may develop ways to work around patents that block biomedical research. The Rhine League's cooperation also has modern parallels: owners may create "patent pools" or "copyright collectives" to help assemble scattered rights. Finally, modern regulation can be seen as an analogue to the Congress of Vienna. Governments may modify industry regulations to make it more profitable to promote rather than block innovation, and advocacy groups may lobby for better-designed property rights.[60]

The point is that costly underuse can be fixed through individual, joint, and state effort. But first the problem must be identified and named. Because the harm that a tragedy of the anticommons causes is often invisible, we must train ourselves to spot a gridlock economy and then develop simple ways to assemble fragmented property. There is hidden treasure to uncover in business, politics, and even our daily lives.

Since I coined the term *tragedy of the anticommons,* the idea has taken root and started spreading. In 2001, Nobel Prize winner in economics James Buchanan and his colleague Yong Yoon demonstrated my anticommons hypothesis mathematically. They wrote that the concept helps explain "how and why potential economic value may disappear into the 'black hole' of resource underutilization."[61] In 2006, researchers discovered that people do worse negotiating anticommons dilemmas than identical tasks framed in tragedy of the commons terms.[62] Why? Perhaps because the dynamics of underuse are still so unfamiliar.

Now, business schools are starting to teach future MBAs how to recognize and resolve gridlock.[63] Policymakers are picking up the idea as well: both conservatives focused on misregulation and liberals concerned with excessive privatization. No matter where you stand, all can agree that grid-lock is a losing game.

How could such a fundamental law of economic and social life have es-caped our notice until now? There is a joke about two economists who are walking down the street when they see some hundred-dollar bills scattered on the sidewalk. As one of them bends down to pick up the money, the other says, "Leave them alone! If those bills were real, someone would have picked them up already." At times, simple truths are quite real, but we overlook them because they don't fit with our theories. Gridlock is such a truth, a feature of our everyday world that nobody stops to notice.

two

WELCOME TO
THE LEXICON

W hen I was drafting Chapter 1, my computer spell-checker kept underlining *underuse* with red squiggles. *Underuse,* it seems, is not a word in Word.[1] These squiggles are a signal: the nonexistence of a word can be as telling as its presence.

When we lack a term to describe some social condition, it is because the condition does not exist in most people's minds. When the opposite of overuse is not considered a word, it is unsurprising that we have overlooked the hidden costs of fragmented ownership. We cannot easily fix the problem until we have created a shared language to spot gridlock. You've already seen the key terms in the previous chapter, but there are still a few wrinkles. What follows will iron them out.

The Magical Parking Lot

So far, I've introduced the nutshell version of the commons and anticommons. To understand the concepts more fully, imagine you've discovered an empty paved lot near Times Square in New York City. At first, the parking paradise is free and open to all. No one tickets or tows. You park and go to the theater. No problem. Later, you tell friends, who park there too. No problem. But then others notice, and soon the lot is jammed. Cars are blocked in. Doors are dinged. Fights break out. The lot becomes a scary place. You pay to park elsewhere.

This overused lot is an example of a tragedy of the commons. It's a tragedy because every parker is acting reasonably, but their individual actions quickly sum to collective disaster. Similarly, if a single shepherd has access to a field, the result is well-trimmed grass and fat sheep. But open the field to all shepherds, each of whom may add sheep without regard to the others, and soon there may be nothing left but bare dirt and hungry animals.

Overuse tragedies are everywhere: species extinction, ozone depletion, and highway congestion. After Garrett Hardin popularized the "tragedy of the commons" metaphor in 1968, people gained a new language for a phenomenon that was widely experienced, but had been difficult to name. The concept helped people give voice to then-emerging concerns about environmental degradation.

Metaphors can be powerful. The tragedy of the commons concept revealed hidden links among innumerable resource dilemmas, large and small. Spotting this shared structure helped people identify shared solutions. Political scientist Elinor Ostrom created a global network of activists and scholars, the International Association for the Study of the Commons, with an online library that now cites about fifty thousand items related to the tragedy of the commons.[2]

How do we solve such tragedies? There are three distinct approaches: privatization and markets, cooperative engagement, and political advocacy and regulation. Bear in mind that each solution has an analogue on the anticommons side of the property spectrum. When I come to the pirate tales of the Chesapeake Bay Oyster Wars in Chapter 7, I'll discuss all these solutions in more detail. For now, I'll summarize them.

Private property and market transactions can solve overuse tragedy. Recall that in the parking example, you were the first to discover the empty lot. You might have claimed ownership for yourself based on your original discovery and first possession. Being first is a standard (but not necessarily fair or efficient) way to hand out rights in resources. Think about Internet domain names. For the most part, whoever wins the race to an online registrar owns the name.[3]

Another path to private ownership passes through state control. The state might reject your claim of original discovery and instead appropriate the lot and auction it to the highest bidder or transfer it quietly to a crony. However the lot arrives in private hands, it will likely be managed better than if it had remained open to all. Owners can profit if they spruce up the lot, repave it perhaps, paint lines, and keep it clean, safe, and well used. As a parker in a private property regime, you lose the freedom of the commons but gain order and access.

The moral justifications for private ownership are controversial for philosophers, but as a practical matter, moving to private property often does prevent overuse in a commons. The leading economic theory of ownership argues that this "conservation effect" is the main reason private property emerges in, and provides a benefit to, society.[4]

Because of our private-property focus, we tend to overlook cooperative solutions to overuse dilemmas. Cooperative solutions are often small-scale, context specific, local, and not reliant on legal structures—thus hidden. In the case of our magical parking lot, notes under windshields, gossip on the street, and other neighborly devices can coordinate the parkers. Parkers may figure out how to keep the parking lot running smoothly without state coercion or private ownership. In *Governing the Commons,* Ostrom demonstrated that close-knit communities around the world have succeeded in managing group property without tragic outcomes.[5] There are thousands of stories of successful cooperation that preserve contested resources and promote overall social welfare.

Finally, state coercion can solve overuse. Cooperative mechanisms may break down if there are too many strangers coming and going, if people don't really know each other, or if it is otherwise hard to discipline deviants. Then, parkers may move from polite notes under windshields to breaking antennae, purposely scratching cars, slashing tires, and fistfights. The state might assert ownership over the lot, put up a gate, and hand out or sell parking permits. But bureaucracy is costly and often capricious. Political pressure may lead to bizarre uses of the lot. States are rarely nimble or efficient parking-lot operators. Public ownership and management can eliminate the tragedy of the parking-lot commons, but they may create new costs and inconveniences for the parkers.

Privatizing a commons may cure the tragedy of wasteful overuse and lead to orderly parking, but it also may inadvertently spark the opposite—a lot that no one can use. The phrase *tragedy of the anticommons* describes this problem of wasteful underuse. Though the anticommons concept refers at its core to fragmented ownership, the idea extends to fragmented decision making more generally. Resource use often depends on the outcome of some regulatory process. If the regulatory drama involves too many uncoordinated actors—neighbors and advocacy groups; local, state, and federal legislators; agencies and courts—the sheer multiplicity of players may block use of the underlying resource. Throughout this book, I discuss both core ownership examples and regulatory extensions of the anticommons concept.

How could the parking lot become an anticommons? Recall that underuse in an anticommons is the mirror image of overuse in a commons. Much can go wrong when politicians privatize state-owned resources, when resources are owned for the first time, or when owners divvy up property later on. For example, in privatizing the lot, politicians might not want to annoy parkers who are also voters. So they might give free parking spots based on every parker's previous use of the lot. (This is approximately how U.S. regulators have allocated ocean fishing quotas and tradable pollution permits.) If there are thousands of parkers, but say one hundred spots, dozens might have to share each spot. Assembling the fractional shares back into a usable parking lot would require too many deals. Even if each parker behaved reasonably, bargaining is costly. And many of us are not reasonable, especially at seven o'clock in Times Square when shows are about to start. So the "privatized" lot may sit empty and unused—an anticommons.

Now substitute sheep in a meadow for the parkers in the lot. If a common field were privatized down to the square inch, no shepherd would be able to graze a single sheep. The same might happen if innumerable heirs separately owned scattered strips of an ancestor's farm. In an anticommons, the grass is lush and tall and unused; in a commons, it is picked bare. Either way, the pasturage is wasted and the sheep starve.

The parking lot and shepherd's field show that creating private property can solve the problem of overuse in a commons. But privatization can go too far. When it does, we can tip into gridlock, and again everyone loses.

Adding the concepts of underuse and anticommons makes visible a new frontier for private bargaining, political debate, and wealth creation. Our goal should be to find the sweet spot for property rights, between commons and anticommons.

TOLLBOOTHS IN THE AIR

Magical parking lots are improbable (especially in Times Square), but big inches can arise at any time. For air travel to exist today, the government had to overcome gridlock a century ago. There was nothing foreordained about this outcome. At the dawn of flight, both airspace and airplane manufacturing were primed to become tragedies of the anticommons.

The Lighthouse Beam

Think first about the airspace above your home. Ownership of air usually is attached to ownership of the land below. An ancient legal maxim reads, "Whoever owns the soil also owns to the sky and the depths."[6] The surface of the earth is just one plane in an infinite column of ownership. Because the surface of the earth is curved, the column is more like a pie wedge. In a 1928 poem "Legal Fiction," literary critic William Empson put the wedge image to good use:

> *Law makes long spokes of the short stakes of men . . .*
> *Your rights extend under and above your claim*
> *Without bound; you own land in Heaven and Hell; . . .*
> *Your rights reach down where all owners meet; in Hell's*
> *Pointed exclusive conclave, at earth's centre*
> *And up, through galaxies, a growing sector.*
> *. . . the lighthouse beam you own*
> *Flashes, like Lucifer, through the firmament.*
> *Earth's axis varies; your dark central cone*
> *Wavers, a candle's shadow, at the end.*[7]

No one can mine under your land or build an overhanging structure without your permission. If you control the air thirty-five feet below and

FIGURE 2.1: *Imagining the dawn of air travel.*[10]

above the ground, why not at thirty-five thousand feet down and up?[8] A century ago, this was an untested question. No one was exercised about the occasional balloon over-flight. Then came the possibility of air travel.

For an airplane to fly anywhere, it must cross innumerable columns of air. If you take the "lighthouse beam" idea seriously, then crossing each column without permission is a trespass. Each landowner could demand payment to pass through the airspace above. If that had been the law, airplanes would never have gotten off the ground. Air travel would be a missing market, and all the advances flight has brought would be difficult to imagine.

In the early days of flight, some landowners pressed the tollbooths-in-the-sky claim, and legal scholars could not agree on a way around it. Perhaps planes could fly over rivers and then pay for each necessary trespass over some thin corridor of land to an airstrip.[9] Alternatively, perhaps states could condemn overflight paths (just as they seized strips of land for railways and highways), pay compensation to landowners, and then be reimbursed by the airlines. Even children's books were concerned with the issue. In the 1910 book *Tom Swift and His Airship*, the author imagined airships over cities (fig. 2.1). Two years later, in *Tom Swift and His Great Searchlight*, the hero flew directly over his nemesis's home:

> "Hello Andy!" called Tom, as he swept slowly overhead. . . .
>
> "You get on away from here!" burst out the bully. "You are trespassing, by flying over my house, and I could have you arrested for it. Keep away."[11]

America averted gridlock in air travel by a timely adjustment in the legal meaning of the lighthouse beam of ownership. People may own "up to the heavens," but according to the 1926 Air Commerce Act, heaven ends one thousand feet above at night and five hundred feet up during the day, well below a plane's cruising altitude. Rejecting a trespass claim for overflights in 1936, a U.S. Court of Appeals wrote, "We will not foist any such chimerical concept of property rights upon the jurisprudence of this country."[12]

When a North Carolina chicken farmer sued to stop military training overflights during the run-up to World War II, the Supreme Court finally declared that the "lighthouse beam" doctrine "has no place in the modern world. The air is a public highway, as Congress has declared. Were that not true, every transcontinental flight would subject the operator to countless trespass suits. Common sense revolts at the idea. To recognize such private claims to the airspace would clog these highways, seriously interfere with their control and development in the public interest, and transfer into private ownership that to which only the public has a just claim."[13]

Courts and legislators got this one right. By legal fiat, we eliminated—er, adjusted—some sticks in the bundle of rights we call "private property" to accommodate a potentially valuable new technology. No compensation was due from the government or from fledgling commercial air carriers because nothing was "taken" from private landowners. Such property rights adjustment should not shock you. From a historical point of view, it is wrong to see private ownership as fixed and unchanging. Even the staunchest private-property systems are always adapting rights to manage new resource conflicts.

From Tom Swift to Google Book Search

The airspace debate is not a quaint historical curiosity. Internet guru Lawrence Lessig opens his book *Free Culture* by recounting the tale of shifting property rights to airspace.[14] The airplane overflight conundrum echoes through current debates over the assembly of digital databases. Google is trying to make tens of millions of copyrighted and noncopyrighted works searchable through its online database, Google Book Search. This could become the greatest library catalog in human history.

To protect authors' interests, Google makes only short snippets of copyrighted works visible, enough so you can make an informed decision to buy or borrow the original work. The Authors Guild nevertheless sued Google, claiming that the digital copies infringe their members' copyrights.[15] This claim sounds like the bully on his roof shouting at Tom Swift as he flies overhead through the column of air.

In his Web blog, Lessig lays out the connection between Google Book Search and airplane overflights.[16] The injury to each author is small or nonexistent, like the harm to each landowner from overflights. Also, the costs of negotiating consent with each copyright holder would doom the database, just as paying tolls to each landowner would prevent air travel. So Lessig argues that Congress and the courts should interpret copyright law to say that indexing of copyrighted books in searchable databases is fair use, just as overflights are not compensable trespasses. The precise doctrinal route to that solution matters less than the commonsense outcome: we should not let fragment owners create gridlock. Cutting-edge technology can be rescued from gridlock by creatively adapting property rights. This is nothing new. A century ago, at the height of laissez-faire capitalism, such adaptations got the airplane industry off the ground.

Gridlock in Airplane Manufacturing

A second form of gridlock almost ended flight in its earliest days—and has echoes in current tragedies of the anticommons. In 1906, the Wright brothers secured a basic patent on airplanes (fig. 2.2). Glenn Curtiss and other inventors improved on the design with better controls and engines. Everyone owned a piece of the plane, but they could not agree on licensing terms. In 1913, a court ordered the then-dominant Curtiss Company to stop making planes. Looking at the mess, the Federal Court of Claims reflected that "prior to January 1917, the development of the aircraft industry in the United States was seriously retarded by the existence of a chaotic situation concerning the validity and ownership of important aeronautical patents. . . . Various companies were threatening all other airplane and seaplane manufacturing companies with suits for infringements of patents, resulting in a general demoralization of the entire trade."[17]

Because of the patent tangle, the American aeronautics industry ground to a halt. European manufacturers, however, continued building more and

better airplanes. On the eve of
the U.S. entry into World War
I, Congress looked abroad and
saw warplanes flying around.
Domestic airplane manufacturing gridlock had become a national security crisis. In early
1917, Congress created a committee (including Franklin De-

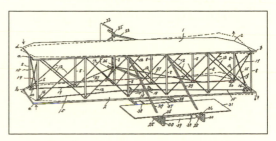

FIGURE 2.2: *An illustration from the Wright brothers'*
U.S. Patent No. 821,393.[18]

lano Roosevelt, then an assistant secretary of the navy) to "devise some plan
for remedying the current difficulties" in making planes.[19]

Committees back then worked fast. On March 24, 1917, FDR's group issued a report calling for creation of a "compulsory patent pool," a forcible
rearrangement of patent rights in plane manufacturing. The same day,
Congress passed legislation to create the Manufacturers Aircraft Association (MAA) that would control all the key airplane patents and pay a fixed
license fee to their owners. Three weeks later, the United States entered
the war. The MAA patent pool, formally created in July 1917, freed manufacturers from the threat of crippling patent litigation. Soon after, warplanes were being made en masse, and innovation in American airplane
technology resumed. The MAA pool lasted until 1975.[20]

We have air travel because of legal luck and political will. A tweak in obscure trespass rules, not breakthroughs in technology, redefined the "lighthouse beam" of ownership so that planes could fly. The imminent danger
of being outgunned in the "War to End All Wars" spurred Congress to
pool patent rights forcibly and quickly. Legislators could look to Europe to
see what airplanes could do if gridlock were solved. Without the conflu-
ence of these events, the world might look much less three-dimensional.

The tussle over airplane patents was not a special case. Henry Ford
helped the Curtiss Company finance its ruinously expensive defense in
patent litigation brought by the Wright brothers because Ford had survived
a similar threat to car manufacturing. Ford was worried about more such
lawsuits shutting down auto production. Patent thickets have threatened to
strangle emerging industries ranging from sewing machines to computers.[21] Today we can't imagine the absence of these technologies, but these
are the survivors. The technologies we rely on are the fortunate few for

which entrepreneurs were persistent, cooperation succeeded, and public officials got regulations right.

WHY *UNDERUSE* SHOULDN'T BE SQUIGGLY

My tales of the magical parking lot and column to heaven are a bit of a sleight of hand. They give a succinct overview of overuse and underuse, commons and anticommons—all the vocabulary you need to make sense of the gridlock dilemma. But *underuse* and *anticommons* are still squiggly. My spell-checker suggests *undersea* and *anticommunist* as replacements. The balance of this chapter explains why these words should enter our everyday lexicon. We need an easy way to bridge the language gap so that we can more clearly recognize the gridlock dilemma.

Besides highlighting the language problem, the squiggles prompted me to look around the Internet at overuse and underuse. Googling *overuse* yielded 3.5 million hits in early 2008, while *underuse* generated only 120,000. (*Commons* had 203 million hits and *anticommons* had 33,000.) The data immediately suggest two possibilities: either overuse is about thirty times more important a social problem than underuse, or we are only about 3 percent as aware of underuse as we should be. You will not be surprised to learn I believe the latter to be correct.

The Cure for Overuse

To understand the Google results, start with overuse. According to the *Oxford English Dictionary, overuse* entered the language as a verb in the early 1600s. One of the earliest usages is as apt today as it was centuries ago: "When ever we overuse any lower good we abuse it."[22] By 1862, the noun form was well recognized: "The oyster beds are becoming impoverished, partly by over-use."[23] Keep oysters in mind: that 1862 usage keenly observes a dilemma to which I return in Chapter 7.

Overuse continues to mean "to use too much" and "to injure by excessive force," definitions that have been stable for hundreds of years. Many of Google's top links for *overuse* come from medicine. Doctors diagnose "overuse syndrome" and dozens of "overuse injuries"—injuries from too much tennis, running, violin playing, book reading, whatever. So what is the opposite of overuse?

Ordinary use. The opposite of injuring yourself through too much use and excessive force is staying injury-free by using an ordinary amount of force. Instead of abandoning an activity, do it in a reasonable, sustainable way. In medicine as in everyday language, the goal is ordinary use (fig. 2.3). Since the 1600s, overuse and ordinary use have been an either-or proposition. Either you will feel pain in your elbow, or you will be able to play happily, if not well. When you overuse a resource, bad things happen. It is much better to engage in ordinary use.

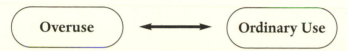

FIGURE 2.3: *Ordinary use as the end point.*

How do we achieve ordinary use? Recall the problem of the magical parking lot. The usual solutions to tragedies of the commons are, as I've mentioned, privatization, cooperation, and regulation. These three solutions map onto the traditional view that ownership can be organized into three basic types of property: private, commons, and state (fig. 2.4).[24]

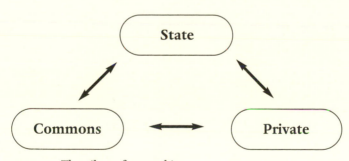

FIGURE 2.4: *The trilogy of ownership.*

We all have strong intuitions about private property, but the term is surprisingly hard to pin down. A good starting point comes from William Blackstone, the foundational eighteenth-century British legal theorist. His oft-quoted definition of private property is "that sole and despotic dominion which one man claims and exercises over the external things of the world, in total exclusion of the right of any other individual in the universe."[25] In this view, private property is about an individual decision maker who directs resource use.

Commons property refers to shared resources, resources for which there is no single decision maker. In turn, the commons can be divided into two distinct categories. The first is *open access,* a regime in which no one at all can be excluded, like anarchy in the parking lot or on the high seas. Mistakenly, the legal and economics literatures have long conflated the commons with open access, hence reinforcing the link between commons and tragedy. The second type of commons has many names, but for now let's call it *group access,* a regime in which a limited number of commoners can exclude outsiders but not each other.[26] If the ocean is open access, then a small pond surrounded by a handful of landowners may be group access. Group access is often overlooked even though it is the predominant form of commons ownership and often not tragic at all.

State property resembles private property in that there is a single decision maker, but differs in that resource use is directed through some process that is, in principle, responsive to the needs of the public as a whole. In recent years, state property has become less central as a theoretical category. The cold war is over, most socialist states have disappeared, intense state regulation of resources has dropped from favor, and privatization has accelerated. In a sense, state property has lost its special character. Today, for many observers, the property trilogy can be reduced to an opposition of private and commons property, what one scholar calls simply "all and none" (fig. 2.5).[27]

FIGURE 2.5: *The familiar split in ownership.*

I believe a substantial cause of our cultural blindness to gridlock arises from this too simple image of property. Note how the commons-private opposition tracks the overuse–ordinary use opposition. The former implies that there is nothing beyond private property; the latter suggests that we cannot overshoot ordinary use. Together, these oppositions reinforce the political and economic logic of the global push toward privatization. We assume, without reflection, that the solution to overuse in a commons is ordinary use in private ownership. This logic makes it difficult to imagine underuse dilemmas and impossible to see the uncharted world beyond private property.

Goldilocks' Quest

According to the *OED*, *underuse* is a recent coinage. In its first recorded appearance, in 1960, the word was hedged about with an anxious hyphen and scare quotes: "There might, in some places, be a considerable 'under-use' of [parking] meters."[28] By 1970, copy editors felt sufficiently comfortable to cast aside the quotes: "A country can never recover by persistently under-using its resources, as Britain has done for too long."[29] The hyphen began to disappear around 1975.

In the *OED*, this new word means "to use something below the optimum" and "insufficient use." The reference to an "optimum" suggests to me how *underuse* entered English. It was, I think, an unintended consequence of the increasing role of cost-benefit analysis in public policy debates. What happens when we slot underuse into the opposition in figure 2.3? Although the result seems simple, it leads to conceptual turmoil (fig. 2.6).

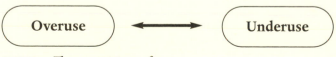

FIGURE 2.6: *The new spectrum of use.*

In the old world of overuse versus ordinary use, our choices were binary and clear-cut: injury or health, waste or efficiency, bad or good. In the new world, we are looking for something more subtle—an "optimum" along a continuum. Looking for an optimal level of use has a surprising twist: it requires a concept of underuse and surreptitiously changes the long-standing

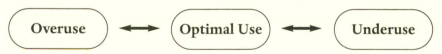

FIGURE 2.7: *Goldilocks' quest for the optimum.*

meaning of overuse. Like Goldilocks, we are looking for something not too hot, not too cold, not too much or too little—just right. Figure 2.7 suggests how underuse changes our quest.

How can we know whether we are overusing, underusing, or optimally using resources? It's not easy, and not just a matter for economic analysis. Consider, for example, the public health push to increase the use of "statins," drugs such as Lipitor that help lower cholesterol. Underuse of statins may mean too many heart attacks and strokes.[30] But no one argues that everyone should take statins; putting the drug in the water supply would be overuse. So what is the optimal level of use? To answer such a question, we engage in cost-benefit analysis. We estimate the cost of the drugs, assign a dollar value to death and disease averted, and quantify the negative effects of increased use.

Searching for an optimum between overuse and underuse sets us on the contested path of modern regulation of risk, an inquiry that starts with economic analysis but quickly implicates our core beliefs. To solve the equations, we have to put dollar values on human lives and on the costs of overuse and underuse behaviors. The process is filled with moral and political dilemmas. Should we assign different values to different people's lives—based on, say, age, earning potential, gender, occupation, or criminal record? Should we force people to take statins against their will if this reduces public costs and serves the common good?

This debate recurs in different guises throughout our daily lives. Driving faster gets you home sooner but increases your chance of crashing. Is the trade-off worthwhile? To answer that question, you need to know how to value life. If life were beyond value, we would require perfect auto safety, cars would be infinitely expensive, and car use would drop to nothing. But if there is too little safety regulation, too many will die. With auto safety, society faces another Goldilocks' quest: we strive to ensure that, all things considered, cars kill the optimal number of people. It sounds callous, but that's what an optimum is all about.

I raise this difficult topic to show that finding the optimum requires the idea of *underuse* and that this new word in turn transforms the meaning of *overuse*. Overuse no longer just means using a resource more than an ordinary amount. The possibility of underuse reorients policymaking from relatively simple either-or choices to the more contentious trade-offs that make up modern regulation of risk.

The Tragedy of the Anticommons

Adding the idea of "underuse" sets the stage for the anticommons. Looking back at figures 2.3–2.7, you can see there is a gap in our labeling scheme. We have seen the complete spectrum of *use*, but not the analogous spectrum of *ownership*. What form of ownership typically coincides with squiggly underuse? The force of symmetry helped reveal a hidden property form. Figure 2.8 shows my path to the anticommons.

FIGURE 2.8: *An ownership puzzle.*

I coined the term *tragedy of the anticommons* to help make visible the dilemma of overly fragmented ownership beyond private property. Just as the idea of *underuse* transforms the continuum of resource use, *anticommons* transforms the continuum of ownership. It shows that the move from commons to private can overshoot the mark (fig. 2.9). When privatization goes too far, resources can end up wasted in an unfamiliar way.

FIGURE 2.9: *The full spectrum of ownership.*

How Group Property Works

Seeing the full spectrum of ownership has another benefit. Our understanding of commons ownership may help inform solutions to anticommons gridlock. To start, consider the distinction between open access (anarchy open to all) and group access (property that is a commons to insiders and private to outsiders). This distinction can do some work on the anticommons side of the spectrum as well. The conventional wisdom has often overlooked group access, but we don't have to.

Under the right conditions, groups of people succeed at conserving a commons resource without regulation or privatization. Cooperation can get us to optimal use. Under what conditions does cooperation work, and what does that teach us about fixing gridlock?

Order without Law

Lobsters are loved too much. They can be overharvested in a tragedy of the commons. To conserve them, some Maine lobstermen have gone out-side the law to form "harbor gangs."[31] As *New York Times* writer John Tier-ney puts it, "The harbor gangs are built around the management principles of Tony Soprano." Newcomers who try to harvest lobsters don't experi-ence the ocean as a commons open to all. Rather, they face the discipline of the harbor gang. Tierney describes an escalating set of threats: notes in a bottle stuck in a trap, traps left open with lobsters removed, chain saws taken to traps, and buoy lines cut so the traps are lost. If the outsider "doesn't take the hint, his boat might be burned or sunk."[32] Excluding out-siders helps avoid harmful overuse.

But excluding outsiders is only half the battle. Harbor gang members must also watch each other, checking for cheaters. Because each gang re-turns to its own harbor to unload its catch, monitoring is relatively easy. Back in port, lobstermen can gossip at a dockside tavern about who is "pushing the lines," that is, dropping traps in another's turf. Reputation matters. In a small town, negative truthful gossip powerfully constrains people from taking so many lobsters that the catch becomes unsustain-able.[33] When gossip is not enough, though, insiders may employ a similar series of escalating threats as they use against outsiders, ranging from ty-ing hitch knots in offending lobstermen's buoy lines to cutting trap lines and torching boats. By limiting access to the resource—that is, policing each other and excluding outsiders—the gangs have created what legal the-orist Robert Ellickson calls "order without law."[34]

The net result is bigger lobsters in greater numbers where lobstermen aggressively defend their turf. Maine harbor gangs keep catches at a sus-tainable level in the offshore areas under their control. But there are costs to this illegal system of group property. The gangs inflict vigilante violence, discriminate against newcomers and outsiders, and sometimes fail to adapt to new environmental conditions.

Lobsters are not the only offshore resource conserved through order without law. Breaking waves are also a scarce resource. If you surf, you've learned (or should have learned) how order works on the waves. Drop in on a wave somebody else is riding, and you can expect swift retribution—punches, kicks, or another surfer riding over you on the next wave. Now, however, millions of poorly socialized newcomers are moving in, and long-established surfing codes may be breaking down. "You can just see that the use of surf breaks is growing by leaps and bounds," says Steve Pezman, publisher of the *Surfer's Journal.* "Meanwhile the resource has remained consistent, which at best has a kind of moderate carrying capacity for a quality experience."[35]

Surfers are having a hard time disciplining outsiders. Furthermore, they face new types of competitors for prime waves, such as kite surfers, sea kayakers, and others who may have their own competing norms—and may be faster, stronger, or meaner. Group property solutions can break down when pressure on the resource increases.

Hybrid Solutions to Open Access

At the extreme of open access, group norms don't stick. For example, anyone can fish for tuna on the high seas. Tuna fleets work in relative isolation, and their catches can be sold anonymously to diverse buyers. Conservation norms, such as voluntary limits on fishing seasons, may gain little traction. Gossip and other low-cost forms of policing don't work for wide-ranging international fleets. Unless states intervene, overuse is hard to avoid. Whales were saved from extinction more through naval powers enforcing international treaties than through gossip at the harbor bar.

The state can also sponsor hybrid solutions. What if the state asserted ownership over lobsters and fish, and then created private rights (such as licenses and tradable quotas) that complement cooperative solutions? Often, such hybrid regimes lead to fairer and higher-yielding results than informal group access can achieve. For example, in Australia, the government issues licenses for a sustainable number of lobster traps and enforces strict harvesting limits. Lobstermen can wait to harvest until the lobsters mature, or they can sell their government-created rights, secure in their markets and property. With far less fishing effort, this system yields more and bigger lobsters than U.S. lobstermen catch either in coastal harbor gangs or on the open ocean.[36]

The same distinction holds for tuna.[37] Fishermen off the U.S. and Canadian coasts are relatively free to fish, so they have fished many stocks to near extinction. U.S. policy is perfectly backward. Political pressure leads to fishing subsidies, so fishermen buy bigger boats, invest more effort, and end up with fewer and smaller fish—the worst of all conservation solutions for everyone, including the fishermen. By contrast, Australia has created "individual transferable quotas," which are basically property rights that amplify cooperation in managing free-swimming fish. Tuna fishermen make the most of "their" fish, penning, ranching, harvesting, and marketing them cooperatively. The result: less effort, healthier and bigger fish, and a much more valuable catch.

Although the long-term conservation outcome from Australia's approach is better, the initial creation of these hybrid rights is politically controversial—who starts out with what quotas? Should quotas be auctioned or given to insiders? It's this political thicket that keeps U.S. regulators from adopting the Australian solution. Hybrid systems are the cutting edge of natural resource management: examples include not only tradable fishing quotas but also carbon-emission markets and transferable air-pollution permits.[38] As we'll see, hybrid solutions can work far beyond lobsters and tuna, even beyond natural resources generally. They may reach to the edge of high-tech innovation.

Lessons from the Commons

Solutions to commons property dilemmas give clues to solving gridlock. For *open access*, like the high seas, states must command resource use directly or create hybrid rights, such as fishing quotas. The anticommons parallel to open access is *full exclusion* in which an unlimited number of people may block each other. With full exclusion, states must expropriate fragmented rights or create hybrid property regimes so people can bundle their ownership. Otherwise, the resource will be wasted through under-

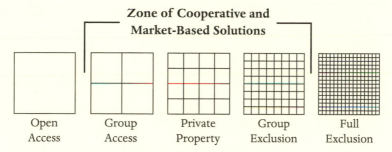

FIGURE 2.10: *The full spectrum of property, revealed.*[41]

use. There is, however, one important respect in which full exclusion differs from open access: an anticommons is often invisible. You have to spot the gridlocked resource before you can respond to the dilemma.

Group access in a commons also has an anticommons parallel: *group exclusion,* in which a limited number of owners can block each other. Recall the multiple owners of our magical parking lot. For both group access and group exclusion, the full array of market-based, cooperative, and regulatory solutions is available. Although self-regulation may be more complex for anticommons resources,[39] close-knit fragment owners can sometimes organize to overcome gridlock. For group exclusion resources, the regulatory focus should be support for markets that assemble ownership and removal of roadblocks to cooperation.

Group property on the commons or anticommons side of private ownership is exponentially more important than the rare extremes of open access or full exclusion. Much of the modern economy—corporations, partnerships, trusts, condominiums, even marriages—can be understood as legally structured group property forms for resolving access and exclusion dilemmas.[40] We live or die depending on how we manage group ownership. Now, for the first time, we can see the full spectrum of property, as shown in figure 2.10.

SYMMETRY IN THE COMMONS AND ANTICOMMONS

After I proposed the possibility of anticommons tragedy, economist and Nobel laureate James Buchanan, with his colleague Yong Yoon, undertook to create a formal economic model. According to their model, society gets the highest total value from a resource—say, the magical parking lot—when a single decision maker controls its use. As more people can *use* the lot independently, the value goes down—a tragedy of the commons. And as more people can *block* each other from the lot, the value also goes down symmetrically—a tragedy of the anticommons. Figure 2.11 shows their graphic summarizing this finding.

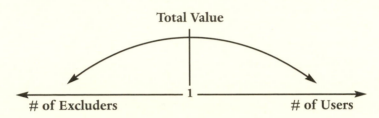

FIGURE 2.11: *Value symmetry in an anticommons and a commons.*[42]

After developing their proof and showing how the anticommons construct may apply to a wide range of problems, Buchanan and Yoon conclude that "the anticommons construction offers an analytical means of isolating a central feature of sometimes disparate institutional structures. . . . [People] have perhaps concentrated too much attention on the commons side of the ledger to the relative neglect of the anticommons side."[43]

The Economics of the Anticommons

In recent years, economic modeling of the anticommons has become quite sophisticated, and it keeps developing.[44] At the simplest level, anticommons theory can be understood as a legal twist on the economics of "complements" first described by Antoine-Augustin Cournot in his 1838 *Researches into the Mathematical Principles of the Theory of Wealth.*[45] Anticommons theory is a partial corrective for modern economic models that focus on "substitutes" and often neglect the role of "complements."[46] What's the difference?

In figure 2.12, Railways A, B, and C are substitute ways to get from here to there. Say the fare is 9. If railway A finds a way to provide service for 8, it will win riders. B and C must become more efficient to keep up. In markets with robust substitutes, competitors have incentives to innovate, lower prices, and thereby indirectly benefit society as a whole. By contrast, Railways D, E, and F are complements. So are toll castles on the Rhine, the thousands of transistors on a semiconductor chip, and the bundle of patents that enable a wireless network. When inputs are complementary, generally you want all or none of them.

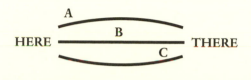

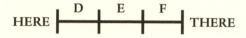

FIGURE 2.12: *Substitutes versus complements.*
Railways A, B, and C are substitutes. Railways D, E, and F are complements.

Again, assume the fare from here to there is 9. D, E, and F each charge 3. Railway D knows that if you want to ride, you must buy its ticket. So why innovate? Instead, D may *raise* its fare to 5, hoping that E and F lower theirs to 2 each. But why would E and F go along? More likely, they too would raise fares, so the total exceeds 9, and ridership falls below the optimal level. With complementary competition, incentives to innovate are blunted: if D did lower fares, then E and F just might raise theirs.

It's the same problem if D, E, and F are complementary patents instead of railways. Then innovators face what economist Carl Shapiro calls a "patent thicket," a lot of phantom tollbooths on the route to commercializing new technology.[47] Cournot proved that in markets dominated by complements—whether railways or patents—we can get higher overall social welfare if D, E, and F merge. Here, monopoly trumps competition. Anticommons theory, in turn, moves from railways and patents to ownership and regulation generally. All these concepts describe facets of the same dilemma: too many uncoordinated owners or regulators blocking optimal use of a single resource.

The Empirical Cutting Edge

Anticommons theory is now well established, but empirical studies have yet to catch up. How hard is it to negotiate around ownership fragmentation? How much does gridlock slow down technological innovation? Does the effect vary by industry? It is difficult to measure discoveries that should have been made but weren't, industries that could exist but don't. We are just starting to examine these conundrums.

In 2006, a team of law, economics, and psychology researchers published a paper reporting experimental findings that reject the presumed symmetry of commons and anticommons. They find that anticommons dilemmas "seem to elicit more individualistic behavior than commons dilemmas" and are "more prone to underuse than commons dilemmas are to overuse." The researchers conclude that "if commons leads to 'tragedy,' anticommons may well lead to 'disaster.'"[48] Another experimental team reports that "efficiency losses under the anticommons setting may be greater" than economic theory predicts.[49]

These preliminary findings of bargaining failure around gridlock may help provide some insight into otherwise puzzling economic phenomena. For example, some of the world's biggest energy companies have for years failed to agree on joint management of oil and gas fields they own together.[50] If one company pumps the oil too fast, it can wreck the pressure in the gas field; if the other extracts gas too fast, it traps the oil. American law has offered them an effective legal tool, called "unitization," to overcome gridlock and smooth joint management of divided oil and gas interests.[51] Yet firms block each other year after year.

How can this be? Oil units aren't a case of two spiteful neighbors arguing over a broken backyard fence. They involve arm's-length business negotiations between savvy corporations. Everyone has good information about the underlying geologic and technical issues. The gains from cooperation may be in the billions of dollars. Why doesn't one firm sell its interest to the other? Why don't the firms merge? What's going on? The experimental studies are beginning to give us explanations rooted in the psychology of gridlock.[52] Even the most sophisticated businesspeople can fail to reach agreement when a negotiation is framed in anticommons terms.

Rounding Out the Lexicon: A Few Caveats

A Caveat on Monopoly

In rounding out the gridlock lexicon, there are some caveats: first, this book focuses on one form of gridlock and one type of underuse, the tragedy that arises when ownership is too fragmented. Here, *multiple* owners can block each other from using a scarce resource. Underuse can also arise in the monopoly context, when a *single* owner blocks access to a resource. This situation may be tragic, but it is not an anticommons, and not gridlock in my sense of the term.

In the old economy, many companies held monopolies—Ma Bell, railways, local water utilities. Society gained the economic benefits of scale and scope from allowing these sectors to be monopolized. The state policed against abuse of monopoly power through complex rate regulation and oversight. Phone lines were cheaper and more available than in many other countries. The costs of these monopolies were often invisible, like deferred and dampened innovation. Why would a monopoly improve service if profits were regulated and innovation would render existing investments obsolete? The trade-offs inherent in managing monopolies are hard: Should private companies be allowed to compete with the U.S. Postal Service? Should national telephone companies be allowed to merge?

In an information economy, any piece of intangible property, such as a patent, is also a monopoly. We award patents because monopoly profits create incentives to invent and because patents give inventors incentives to disclose their discoveries (without patents people might prefer to invent things they could keep secret). On the other hand, drugs would be cheaper and lives could be saved if competitors could make generic copies at will. To balance the values of innovation, disclosure, and competition, Congress keeps shifting the bundle of rights that a patent confers. Managing patent law involves difficult policy questions: are there particular patents for which the social costs of monopoly are just too great?

The dilemmas of any individual monopoly in the old or new economy are a great topic—for another book. For better or worse, these quandaries are familiar. We do not, however, have much experience dealing with the interaction of ownership fragments or an array of blocking patents. The gridlock lexicon addresses not monopoly per se, but multiplicity.

A Caution on Absolutes

When talking about gridlock, stay away from absolutes.[53] First, you shouldn't assume that anticommons ownership is inevitably tragic. If we lived in a world where people had perfect information and could bargain with each other at no cost, they could avoid anticommons tragedy every time (just as, in a perfect world, there would be no commons tragedy, or for that matter, tragedy of any sort). In practice, however, bargaining is never free, people shirk duties and hold out for payoffs, and there are cognitive limits that shape owners' decisions. In the real world, anticommons ownership is not necessarily tragic, but it does tend that way.

Second, it's theoretically possible that an anticommons may face overuse instead of underuse. For example, consider real estate development along the California coast. It's a mess. Multiple community groups, environmentalists, neighbors, and government agencies may each prefer different versions of a project. Even in that regulatory morass, though, *overbuilding* may occur if it is sufficiently costly to exercise each right to veto development. Every opponent of development may prefer to go surfing and hope the others sit through the boring public hearings. If enough people opt for a free ride, a project might face *too little* opposition, not too much. It's an empirical question whether the California coast tips toward over- or underbuilding. That said, in most cases I've seen, anticommons regulation tends to be associated with gridlock, that is, with too little economic development, not too much.[54]

The Comedy of the Anticommons—or Gridlock by Design

The final caveat comes from legal theorist Carol Rose, who noticed the economic and social benefits of what she calls "the comedy of the commons."[55] Certain resources, such as roads and waterways, are sometimes owned most efficiently in common. As Rose points out, creating and enforcing private property rights is itself costly; sometimes these costs exceed the gains, not just economically but also socially. Village greens and town halls may strengthen communities in ways that are socially valuable but hard to quantify in monetary terms.

Rose's insight is equally useful on the anticommons side—there are both economic and social reasons that we may prefer group exclusion to sole ownership. For example, it's possible that creating multiple vetoes may help preserve a treasured resource against transient political pressures for development—for instance, Central Park in New York City or Indian burial grounds in Arizona.[56] Similarly, "conservation easements" intentionally use gridlock to foster environmental goals.[57] (With a conservation easement, the owner sells or gives away the right to develop land, gets a tax break, and retains the right to continue a current use such as farming.) The gridlock created by split ownership may be justifiable if the environmental gains exceed the fragmentation costs. On balance, though, I'm skeptical. What happens a generation from now when communities want to reduce sprawl but face a patchwork of easements that make "in-fill" development prohibitively difficult? Many conservation easements look to me like potential tragedies of the anticommons.

The real estate setting is a core example of an ownership anticommons. There are, in addition, extensions to the concept that may involve beneficial group exclusion. For example, a criminal jury usually requires unanimity; any juror can block a guilty verdict. This anticommons is justified (and thus not tragic) in a society concerned with avoiding wrongful convictions. Juries in noncriminal cases, on the other hand, usually do not require unanimity. We do not accept the same risk of gridlock there because we have no automatic preference for civil defendants over plaintiffs.

Similarly, the U.S. Constitution divides power among the executive branch, the legislature, and the judiciary and between the federal and state governments. As far back as 1788, when James Madison wrote *Federalist no. 51*, American constitutional theorists have justified "checks and balances" because they increase deliberation and protect minority interests—even though the fragmentation may create a political anticommons.[58]

Voters sometimes seem to prefer gridlock. So do investors. According to money manager John Davidson, "The market actually likes the executive and legislative branches under different leadership as it reduces any damage coming out of Washington." In 2006, Republicans controlled the White House, Senate, and House of Representatives. Then, in the November elections, Democrats won control of both houses of Congress. How did investors respond? "Wall Street rose . . . with the Dow Jones industrials reaching another record close as investors grew more confident that a huge victory by Democrats in congressional elections would result in grid-lock and keep lawmakers out of the way of business interests."[59]

How do you explain the veto power in the United Nations Security Council given to China, England, France, Russia, and the United States? It can be seen as an intentional use of an anticommons structure. When the big powers set up the UN, they feared collective action even more than inaction. Unless they could rely on gridlock to protect their national interests, the Big Five would not have agreed to give the UN its wide-ranging powers. The flip side of gridlock is that veto-holding nations can, and often do, block Security Council actions that could, for example, end wars and prevent genocides.

The "comedy of the anticommons" insight suggests that sometimes, for some resources, we should promote gridlock. Most of the time, for most resources, however, some positive level of use will be socially most valuable. Gridlock is rarely the optimum.

We have millennia of practice in spotting tragedies of the commons. When too many people fish, fisheries are depleted. When too many people pollute, we choke on dirty air. Then, we spring into action with market-based, cooperative, and legislative solutions. Similarly, we have a lot of experience spotting underuse caused by a particular monopoly owner. We have created regulatory bodies that know (more or less) what to do with such dilemmas.

But underuse caused by multiple owners is unfamiliar. The affected resource is hard to spot. Our language is new. A tragedy of the anticommons may be as costly to society as the more familiar forms of resource misuse, but we have never noticed, named, debated, or learned how to fix gridlock. How do we stumble into the problem of too many owners? How do we get out? As a first step, underuse in a tragedy of the anticommons should be squiggly no more.

three

WHERE ARE THE CURES?

You, or someone you love, may die because of a gene patent that should never have been granted in the first place. Sound far-fetched? Unfortunately, it's only too real. Gene patents are now used to halt research, prevent medical testing, and keep vital information from you and your doctor. Gene patents slow the pace of medical advance on deadly diseases.

—MICHAEL CRICHTON,
New York Times OP-ED,
FEBRUARY 13, 2007

W here are the lifesaving cures promised by the biotech revolution? Perhaps biomedical gridlock is blocking the way. Drugs that should exist are not being created. The stakes could hardly be higher.

On one side, advocates argue that Congress should limit patent rights generally or even bar new gene patents altogether.[1] At the other extreme, lobbyists for the biotechnology industry say there's no problem to speak of and pending legislation will make things worse.[2] The debate on Capitol Hill is a furious, life-or-death showdown over the public's health and the financial health of many leading industries. It's biotech versus telecom, big pharma against software. Everyone is struggling with the gridlock issue.[3]

As a *Los Angeles Times* editorial noted, "The legislative conflict reflects a growing sense in Washington that the patent system has lost its moorings. That's due in part to rapidly changing technologies that prompt patent holders to make novel and unanticipated claims. But it also reflects the nature of patents and intellectual property generally. With a plot of land or a string of pearls, it's easy to tell where one person's property ends and another's begins. With something as abstract as an invention, however, those lines are fuzzy and likely to shift over time."[4]

This chapter brings you up to speed on drug patent gridlock. A decade ago, Rebecca Eisenberg and I helped launch today's debate when we cautioned in *Science* that "privatization of biomedical research must be more carefully deployed to sustain both upstream research and downstream product development." Otherwise, we wrote, "more intellectual property rights may lead paradoxically to fewer useful products for improving human health."[5]

The danger we uncovered is that privatization can solve one tragedy (underinvestment) but cause another (an anticommons). These polar outcomes are not the only choices. Careful definition of property rights can make a difference. In recent years, private industry and public regulators have come up with many smart solutions and learned a lot about managing gridlock along the way. But progress remains partial and tentative. How many more lives could be saved if biotech property rights were better designed?

WHAT DRUG GRIDLOCK LOOKS LIKE

First, consider figure 3.1, in which the horizontal bars represent gene patents and the labels mark highly patented regions. Now imagine trying to create a medical diagnostic product that requires access to many patented areas on some chromosome. In the past thirty years, about forty thousand DNA-related patents have been granted.[6] Any discovery that relies on database creation is vulnerable.[7] Gene patents are not the only area at risk. More and more, invention requires assembling scattered bits of in-

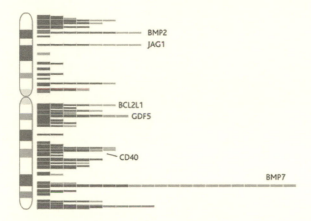

FIGURE 3.1: *Patent activity on a short stretch of chromosome 20.*[9]

tellectual property from across the biotech frontier—it's like trying to buy up all the original big inches.[8]

If gridlock blocks research, then what happens to the entrepreneurial energy in the drug industry? Figure 3.2 suggests part of the answer: firms spend resources threatening, initiating, responding to, pursuing, and settling litigation. Affymetrix, the firm at the center of the figure, is not an unusual case. Every pioneering biotech company sits in the middle of its own litigation web. According to Nicholas J. Naclerio, head of the BioChip Division at Motorola, the recent increase in biotech patenting has led not to more drugs but to "a bewildering web of lawsuits—and it may only get worse." He continues, "If we want to make a medical diagnostic with 40 genes on it, and 20 companies hold patents on those genes, we may have a big problem. It isn't at all clear how this is going to work out."[10] If everyone invests in the litigation merry-go-round, innovation is tossed aside, gridlock sets in, and we all lose out.

Keep in mind that this litigation snapshot covers only one corner of gene microarrays (a diagnostic tool in which multiple gene probes are attached to microchips and used to sift through the information contained within a genome). Whether you update the microarray story from 2000 to the present or look at other biomedical fields, the story is the same—a lot of innovation is being diverted to litigation.

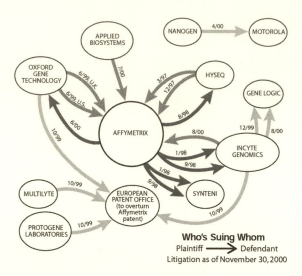

FIGURE 3.2: *A snapshot of gene-patent microarray litigation, 2000.*[11]

And note that litigation is only part of the story. The *process* by which patents are granted can cause gridlock just as easily as the *content* of the patents themselves. In the United States, for example, there are long delays between the filing and issuance of biotechnology patents. While patents are pending, no one knows what scope of rights will ultimately be given, if any. Pending patents do not by themselves create enforceable rights. Nevertheless, firms and universities will license rights to their research results before patents have been granted. Also, firms raise capital based on the prospective rights preserved by patent applications. In effect, each potential patent creates a specter of rights that may activate gridlock. Given the time crunch in biomedical research, the potential rights created by applications for patents may be more important than the actual rights, if any, eventually conferred by the U.S. Patent and Trademark Office (PTO).

A Revolution in Patenting

The exponentially rising level of patent applications in recent years means not only that delays are increasing but also that the quality of issued PTO patents may be decreasing.[12] Figure 3.3 shows all live patents from the founding of the United States to the present across all fields. As two leading patent theorists, Mark Lemley and Carl Shapiro, point out, patents are "probabilistic," that is, they are far less certain than people assume when they think about property.[13] The PTO grants most patent applications, then lets people fight over their validity later on. It's much easier to know if your neighbor is on your side of the fence than if a granted patent is valid or infringed. Almost half of patents litigated to judgment are invalidated; of those found valid, half are found not to be infringed.[14] But litigating each patent is expensive, time-consuming, and uncertain. Thus, an

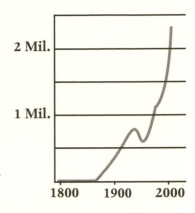

FIGURE 3.3: *Live U.S. patents by year.*

owner of a weak patent that may be invalid or not infringed nevertheless can use it to extract license fees and hold up innovation. The proliferation of weak patents can be a strong drag on innovation.

The most important cause of gridlock in biomedical research, however, is not any particular lawsuit or even uncertainty about patent scope or validity but the sheer multiplicity of rights that must be acquired to undertake innovation of any sort, including drug development. A firm might be confident that it will win a particular patent suit but not that it will prevail against every single one of a hundred weak claims. Fragmented ownership can be enough, by itself, to deter innovation.

For example, consider the potential gridlock effect of patents related to brain receptors (proteins in the brain that respond to particular molecules and stimulate brain-cell responses). Bennett Shapiro, Merck's vice president for worldwide basic research, explains that people who take "compounds for schizophrenia often develop other disorders some of which resemble Parkinson's disease, another disease involving the dopamine system. A rational approach to discovery of improved schizophrenia drugs would be to target specific dopamine receptors. But if different companies hold patents on different receptors, the first step on the path to an important and much needed therapeutic advance can be blocked."[15]

Suppose Merck finds a compound that shows promise against schizophrenia. The company then needs to uncover the compound's potential side effects before committing hundreds of millions of dollars to clinical testing and bringing the drug to market. But if the relevant receptors are patented and controlled by different owners, the research phase can quickly become prohibitively expensive. Before they can test their compound, Merck must strike a deal with every single patent owner of a relevant receptor. Each can block Merck's progress because the U.S. Food and Drug Administration (FDA) will require, quite reasonably, that the drug be tested for side effects against all known, relevant receptors.

From Merck's perspective, each patent or pending patent may act like a phantom tollbooth; together, the owners can be modern-day robber barons. If Merck calculates that it is too costly to overcome gridlock in schizophrenia research, the company simply reallocates its research funds to other areas where the property rights environment is less fragmented. In short, too many overlapping patents can push drugmakers away from the most medically promising lines of research to those that are least legally challenging.

Gridlock also can become a hot issue whenever lethal new diseases appear. For example, severe acute respiratory syndrome (SARS), a form of atypical pneumonia, emerged in southern China in late 2002.[16] Over the next six months, more than seven hundred people died from the new disease, including Carlo Urbani, the doctor who first identified SARS. Experts feared that the disease could become a global pandemic. Laboratories all over the world cooperated in a successful race to find the pathogen. This great public health achievement was soon marred by patent controversy: "It is likely that patent rights incorporating the SARS genomic sequence will be fragmented across several groups. Sorting out these rights will be complex and may require intervention of the law courts. . . . [For firms considering whether to develop a SARS vaccine], uncertainty over patent rights makes this decision even more difficult, because it is neither possible to determine the future cost of licensing the patent rights, nor whether all necessary patents will be available for licensing. . . . The incentive for vaccine manufacturers is therefore to delay the decision to invest."[17]

Concerned with preventing the next global pandemic, the World Health Organization (WHO) issued a statement in 2003, saying, "In the longer term, the manner in which SARS patent rights are pursued could have a profound effect on the willingness of researchers and public health officials to collaborate regarding future outbreaks of new infectious diseases."[18] Just a year later, in 2004, researchers became concerned that "patent rights are impeding efforts to prevent an outbreak of bird flu—avian influenza."[19] SARS and avian flu have not mutated into global killers, at least not yet, but potential superbugs are emerging all the time.[20] They won't wait for us to sort out fragmented ownership.

The Golden Rice Story

The threat of gridlock erodes the incentive to produce drugs particularly for diseases that afflict the poorest people with the least ability to fend for themselves. Here's a recent story I tell both as caution and inspiration. This tale involves a breakthrough in health technology that was invented some time ago but delayed on the path to saving lives because of a tragedy of the anticommons.

According to the WHO, dietary vitamin A deficiency causes some 250,000 to 500,000 children to go blind every year. More than half of those children who lose their sight also die within a year.[21] One early hope from gene research was to reduce blindness in developing countries by genetically modifying rice to produce vitamin A.[22] By 1999, a group led by Professors Peter Boyer and Ingo Potrykus had created a prototype of vitamin A–enhanced rice, an impressive scientific achievement. But after they invented this "Golden Rice," the project stalled.

To bring the rice to market and begin saving both sight and lives, Boyer and Potrykus had to negotiate licenses to as many as seventy U.S. patents (there were fewer valid patents outside the United States).[23] In addition, they needed access to fifteen other types of technical property. In total, they had to negotiate with more than thirty companies, universities, and other institutions. Identifying and negotiating with all these parties was time-consuming and expensive, even though all the owners understood that the final product may help avert millions of unnecessary cases of blindness and death. With Golden Rice, the humanitarian benefits were clear, moral outrage at patent gridlock was high, and the private owners could contribute their patents for third world health without imperiling profits in their first world markets. Potrykus describes well the complexity of the anticommons dilemma:

I was rather upset. It seemed to me unacceptable, even immoral, that an achievement based on research in a public institution and with exclusively public funding, and designed for a humanitarian purpose, was in the hands of those who had patented enabling technologies early enough or had sneaked in a MTA [material transfer agreement] in the context of an earlier experiment. It turned out that whatever public research one was doing, it was all in the hands of industry (and some universities). At that time I was much tempted to join those who radically fight patenting.

Fortunately, I did a bit of further thinking and became aware that "Golden Rice" development was only possible because there was patenting. Much of the technology I had been using was publicly known because the inventors could protect their rights. Much of it would have remained secret if this had not been the case. If we are interested in using all the knowledge to benefit the poor, it does not make sense to fight against patenting. It makes far more sense to fight for a sensible use of intellectual property rights.[24]

After much back-and-forth, the intellectual property owners involved in Golden Rice reached agreement to help bring this lifesaving crop to market. One company, Syngenta (then Zeneca), took the lead in assembling the rights, developing the technology, and donating the results to farmers in the afflicted countries. It arranged for intellectual property controlled by competitors such as Novartis, Bayer, Monsanto, and Japan Tobacco to be licensed free of charge for the sole purpose of promoting Golden Rice. In 2004, the first Golden Rice seed trials were harvested, and the project is now on its way to implementation in countries such as India and the Philippines.[25]

Is Golden Rice the future? Can its success be repeated with other diseases that primarily afflict the poor? Not easily, I suspect. Golden Rice is succeeding because it had forceful advocates who invented the product before they got permission and later cajoled owners into cooperation. Inspired leadership makes a difference, and shame can be a potent tool for forging agreement. Reputation matters: firms like to advertise their involvement in successful humanitarian ventures. For this high profile, nonprofit use, private patent owners were persuaded they should join. Their financial risks were relatively low because Golden Rice will be used primarily in poor, developing countries. Finally, American "land-grant" colleges owned much of the relevant intellectual property; these colleges have had a long tradition of public-spirited agricultural technology transfer.[26] This conjunction of factors is fortuitous and ad hoc. When the stakes are higher, then cooperation often fails and easy solutions give way.

The Anticommons in Agricultural Research

Biotech gridlock can slow not only lifesaving drug innovation but also life-sustaining agricultural development. The Golden Rice solution is not the norm at the cutting edge of agricultural innovation. A *New York Times* story illustrates the dilemma: "Once the realm of such public institutions like land-grant colleges, [agricultural research] is increasingly being controlled by private companies. This fundamental shift alarms some farming experts. . . . Now, these critics say, patent restrictions are choking the free exchange of seeds and technology that nourished the public system. Research on potential crop improvements has been delayed or abandoned."[27]

Industry leaders such as Monsanto may allow free licensing for research, but not for uses that may lead to commercial applications. Plant geneticists worry that agricultural biotech patenting is closing off a thousand-year-old tradition of hybridizing crops to improve health and nutrition. The *Times* story continues: "Scientists at the University of Costa Rica, for example, have genetically engineered rice to provide resistance to a virus that is a major problem in the tropics. But before the university can sell the seeds to farmers, it must get clearance from holders of as many as 34 patents."[28] A team of agricultural economists comments that "as agricultural research becomes increasingly complex, it depends more and more on access to knowledge and biological materials that have already been claimed as proprietary by others, and a thicket of blocking patents can choke the commercial 'freedom to operate' of any resulting agricultural innovation."[29]

Gridlock in plant genetics is as complex as in human drug development. We can't always expect to find competitors cooperating to solve a tragedy of the anticommons, innovators contributing discoveries to the public domain, or legislatures neutrally shifting patent law to accommodate the

public interest. This type of gridlock doesn't always announce or resolve itself. First, we must learn how to spot these problems.

FROM SHARING TO SUING

How does a biotech anticommons arise? Until the 1970s, much biomedical
research followed a "commons" model, under which anyone could use research results freely. Under this model, the U.S. government, universities,
and philanthropies paid for much "upstream," or basic, research and gave
away the results to the public. As late as 1975, scientists Georges Köhler
and Cesar Milstein decided it would be ethically wrong to patent the fundamental "monoclonal antibody" discoveries for which they later shared
the Nobel Prize.[30] Such unpatented biomedical discoveries provided much
of the raw material and knowledge that drugmakers later combined into
"downstream," or applied, products for diagnosing and treating disease.

An important transitional moment toward today's gridlock dilemmas
came in 1980, when Congress passed the "Bayh-Dole Act." This law encouraged universities and other institutions to patent discoveries arising
from federally supported research and then to try to commercialize these
technologies by transferring them to the private sector. In response to new
property rights promoted by the Bayh-Dole Act, patent filings and private
biotech investment increased. Billions in private equity funds began to
flow into biotech companies.

The new property regime helped shift biomedical research from the
commons end of the ownership spectrum toward a mix of private and anticommons elements. Nowadays, basic biomedical research may be supported by private funds, carried out in private institutions, or privately held
through patents, trade secrecy, or agreements that restrict the use of materials and data. The result has been a spiral of overlapping patent claims
throughout the biomedical sciences.[31] The culture of science has changed.
Nobody wants to be the last romantic contributing findings to the public
for free while everyone else is angling for a deal.

In this new environment, firms respond to rivals by ratcheting up their
own property-fragmenting activities, creating a spiral of "defensive patenting." As one drug company scientist told me, "Now we all have beads and
trinkets to trade." Merck's Bennett Shapiro explains, "Merck has felt the

need to become more energetic about patenting than it was years ago. For example, carrageenan footpad assays [a seaweed shot developed by Merck to lower the pain threshold of lab rats] were used to develop non-steroidal anti-inflammatory drugs. The assays were in the public domain, and many companies used them to develop new drugs. Today, Merck would patent such an assay and use its patent position to trade with other companies for access to other research tools."[32] This strategy of defensive patenting is also sometimes referred to by the cold war label "mutual assured destruction," or MAD.[33] For equally balanced competitors, a MAD strategy may lead to détente—firms cross-license their patents and forgo litigating. But in an asymmetric world, small biotech firms don't want beads and trinkets in trade from big pharmaceutical companies; they want cash.

The changing rights environment hasn't just affected the behavior of existing firms. It has catalyzed the emergence of its own brand of modern-day robber barons, firms often called "patent trolls." These firms do not invent or make anything; instead, they often seek out and buy control of relatively low-value, weak patents that may be infringed by valuable products.[34] MAD does not deter this last group. Their business model depends on leveraging defects in the patent system: trolls make money because litigation is chancy, court-ordered remedies exceed the probabilistic value of the litigated patents, and settlements can be coerced from successful product manufacturers desperate to avoid injunctions that shut down their businesses.[35]

The emerging structure of the biomedical industry would not be so worrisome if many more diseases were being cured. But this does not seem to be happening. According to economist Iain Cockburn, an acute observer of innovation in the pharmaceutical industry, "Notwithstanding extraordinary scientific achievements such as completing the sequencing of the human genome, the rate at which the industry generates new products appears to be shrinking. In 2002 the U.S. Food and Drug Administration (FDA) approved only seventeen new molecular entities (NMEs) for sale in the United States—a disappointing fraction of the fifteen-year high of fifty-six NMEs approved in 1996 and the lowest since 1983. Alarmingly, this decline occurred despite a doubling of research and development (R&D) spending by U.S.-based pharmaceutical companies between 1995 and 2002."[36]

In figure 3.4 you can see this discovery gap. R&D spending is rising, but new drugs are not forthcoming at the same rate. The figure has to be taken

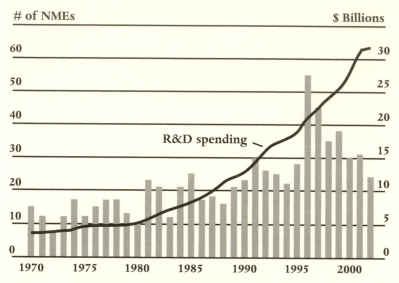

FIGURE 3.4: *U.S. drug R&D rises, drug discovery trails.*[38]

with a grain of salt: drug research takes years to come to fruition, so we may just be seeing a lag between investment and payoff. A few really important "new molecular entities" could more than make up for a low overall number. Maybe the easy discoveries have all been made. Still, investment in R&D has continued to increase, and discoveries that improve human health apparently have not kept pace.[37] Perhaps a tragedy of the anticommons helps explain why we're getting fewer bangs for more bucks.

How does gridlock arise? In our *Science* article, Eisenberg and I showed how fragmented property rights can inadvertently freeze biomedical innovation. You can picture an innovator entering an auditorium filled with owners holding their big-inch patents. Or you can imagine starting down a river, not knowing how many robber barons you'll encounter before you reach your drug-discovery goal. Either way, the multiplicity of fragment owners can cause gridlock.[39]

Gene Fragments

A decade ago, drug researchers faced the threat of big-inch gridlock in gene fragments.[40] Since then, luckily, the PTO and the big drugmakers successfully averted this particular anticommons. But gene fragments remain as a cautionary tale that has echoes in current biotech debates.

Throughout the 1980s, patents on genes generally corresponded closely to foreseeable commercial products: no product, no patent. Then, in 1991, the National Institutes of Health (NIH) started applying for patents on a type of "anonymous" gene fragment called an "expressed sequence tag," or EST. Although the NIH soon reversed course and took a hostile position toward such patents, its initial applications opened the door. Private firms began filing patent applications on newly identified DNA sequences, including gene fragments, before they had found corresponding uses.

Applications, however, are not the same thing as patents. The PTO could have easily created gridlock by issuing patents on thousands of ESTs, but in this case it managed to sidestep disaster. From the start, many people recognized the dangers of gene-fragment patents and argued that human genomic sequence data should remain freely available.[41] There was a widespread intuition among scientists and policymakers that issuing patents on gene fragments made little sense. Foreseeable commercial products, such as therapeutic proteins or genetic diagnostic tests, would likely require multiple fragments bundled together. A slew of separately owned gene-fragment patents would tangle firms in licensing negotiations before they could even begin to develop useful products.

Big drugmakers took what may seem like a surprising position in the EST debate: they decided they were better off donating gene-fragment data to the public than seeking patents. Although these companies may not have recognized the problem as a tragedy of the anticommons, they have long worried about competing ownership claims. By donating their EST findings, they hoped to prevent patents from stalling downstream research on projects that depended on access to large amounts of gene-sequence data. In 1995, Merck created the Gene Index, a public database of gene sequences, and announced that it would make its scientists' data freely available as quickly as possible. By 1998, Merck had published almost a million gene sequences. A subsequent evaluation suggests that "the Merck strategy has contributed to a significant easing of the anticommons threat in this area."[42]

In 2001, the PTO adopted new guidelines that raised the bar for patenting gene fragments. An applicant for a gene fragment patent needs to show that the discovery has a well-defined function or utility, a standard

that makes raw DNA sequences more difficult to protect.[43] On the litigation side, a U.S. court recently upheld the PTO's rejection of several such
patent applications.[44] Also, in 2001, the Human Genome Project published
a full genome, putting a large amount of raw genomic information into
the public domain and causing a sharp decline in gene-fragment patent
applications. In sum, a combination of drug-company activism, sensible
revisions to PTO guidelines, court decisions, and Human Genome Project
advances seems to have averted the gene-fragment version of big-inch
gridlock.[45]

Stacking Licenses

To picture "phantom tollbooths" on the route to drug discovery, consider
the case of "reach-through license agreements" (RTLAs) on patented research tools.[46] An RTLA gives the owner of a patented invention used in
upstream (or basic) stages of research rights in subsequent downstream
discoveries (the pills in the bottle). An RTLA might say something like,
"You can use my diagnostic tool for free now, but if you discover something valuable, you'll pay me 5 percent of your sales."

In principle, RTLAs offer advantages to both upstream patent holders
and downstream drug developers. They permit researchers with limited
funds to use patented research tools right away and pay only if and when
their research yields valuable results. Upstream patent holders may also
prefer a chance at larger payoffs from downstream product sales instead of
certain, but smaller, up-front license fees. That's the upside. The downside
is that RTLAs may lead to a tragedy of the anticommons if multiple upstream owners stack—or threaten to stack—overlapping and inconsistent
claims on potential downstream products.[47]

The threat of out-of-control RTLAs prompted public and private responses. The NIH reformed its licensing guidelines to benefit academic (but
not commercial) research. Shepherded in part by my coauthor Rebecca
Eisenberg, the guidelines suggest that NIH-funded genomic research tools
be licensed broadly and nonexclusively.[48] Universities have widely adopted
the new NIH approach and now also routinely reserve a "research exemption" for themselves and other noncommercial institutions.[49] In effect, research institutions are creating, license by license, their own limited,

royalty-free zone. Along with the NIH reforms, in 2001, the U.S., European, and Japanese patent offices decided that certain claims in DNA research-tool patents should not "reach through" to the drugs that are eventually created. Court decisions reinforced this policy change, but only regarding the patent claims themselves; they do not prevent parties from stacking burdensome contractual provisions in privately negotiated licenses.

On the corporate side, licensing practices are also changing. Sometimes patent owners prefer to keep their patents idle and use them to block competitors from developing better drugs. Generally, though, owners want to make money. To do so, they must offer reasonable licensing terms. For example, patent owners may set license rates that vary depending on how many other research tools must also be licensed. The overall royalty rate may be capped at a manageable level, such as a few percent of net sales. Then, as more tools are licensed, the amount for each license is adjusted downward to remain within the overall cap. There is now an array of such "antistacking" contract provisions available to firms when they draft licensing agreements.[50] Believe it or not, the easy availability and widespread use of legal "boilerplate" can have profound effects in sidestepping gridlock.

In sum, there has been some progress in avoiding phantom-tollbooth gridlock. Measuring the hidden costs that remain, though, is tricky. Commercial secrecy surrounds product development. If a particularly valuable product is in view, downstream product developers may be highly motivated to reach agreements with upstream owners. But if the prospects for success are more uncertain or the expected commercial value is small (even if the humanitarian benefit is high), then the parties may fail to bargain. According to one observer, the potential costs of gridlock remain high, "particularly in gene therapy, where the most promising advances now are related to rare genetic diseases that present small markets."[51]

Transition or Tragedy?

Is biomedical gridlock being resolved or getting worse? Some of the dangers caused by proliferating upstream patent rights appear to be receding as licensors and licensees gain experience and as institutions evolve to help owners and users reach agreements. Maybe the short-term costs from de-

layed treatments for disease are worth incurring if they allow upstream research to pay its own way and help ensure its long-term viability. Property
rights barriers to product development may be a transitional phenomenon, not an enduring tragedy.

On the other hand, try telling that to patients suffering from diseases that
could already have been cured. Three factors caution against an uncritical
deference to market forces.[52] First, high bargaining costs may be an enduring barrier to the efficient bundling of intellectual property. Bargaining
costs arise early in the R&D cycle, when the potential gains are the most
speculative. Because these rights are hard to value, it has been hard to
come up with standard licensing schemes. Research institutions have limited competence with this type of horse trading. Second, upstream biomedical intellectual property rights belong to a large, diverse group of
public and private owners.[53] Sometimes diversity makes deals easier to
reach ("You take the credit; I'll take the money"), but conflicting agendas
may make agreement difficult, especially for smaller biotech firms that depend wholly on licensing their patent portfolios. Finally, ambition and spite
often block negotiations that seem straightforward. Think back to the air-
plane-patent wars: Wilbur Wright went to his death in aggressive litigation
against Glenn Curtiss; there were no winners in that battle. When two or
more patent owners each hope to dominate a market, the history of
patent litigation suggests that bargaining will fail.

Three Markers in the Anticommons Fight

In an effort to move beyond theorizing about gridlock, teams of researchers have devoted themselves over the past decade to answering the
"tragedy or transition" question more concretely.[54] While the tragedy of
the anticommons threat is being debated, however, judicial and political
battles are overtaking the academic research. Once-in-a-generation patent-
law overhaul is working its way through Congress.[55] Key high-tech industries have recognized the anticommons threat to their bottom lines and are
now determined to reduce the cost. As one commentator notes,

> Intel, Microsoft, I.B.M., and Apple and others are increasingly finding
> the nation's patent system has become a minefield, and they are look-

ing for ways to limit the leverage of both small patent holders and patent "trolls," or speculators who buy hundreds or thousands of patents. . . . Opposed to big tech is a small group of high-profile inventors . . . [who] have joined forces with the pharmaceutical industry, which has traditionally relied on the protection of a strong patent system. The battle lines are now established, and legislators are being asked to grapple with the question of how best to protect innovation.[56]

In the political debate, three studies on the gridlock economy stand out as the most influential.[57] Reform proponents often cite the studies' conclusions; opponents argue that the underlying data do not warrant immediate legislation.[58] A fair reading of the three shows genuine—and justifiable—concern about gridlock in technological innovation, but the underlying empirical findings are indeed still inconclusive.

All three reports suggest that patents should be harder to get. In the first report, *To Promote Innovation: The Proper Balance of Competition and Patent Law and Policy,* the Federal Trade Commission (FTC) and the Department of Justice (DOJ) interviewed more than three hundred academics and high-tech industry representatives. Although respondents from biotech to software diverged on the anticommons threat, the 2003 FTC report concluded that "biotechnology patents might harm follow-on innovation through the creation of an anticommons." The FTC recommended reforms that would make it harder to obtain patents initially and harder to sustain them later on.[59] In the second report, *A Patent System for the 21st Century* (2004), the National Academy of Sciences (NAS) examined PTO operations, found that patent quality seems to be worsening, and made similar recommendations as the FTC report.[60] Finally, a 2006 study by the National Research Council (NRC), *Reaping the Benefits of Genomic and Proteomic Research,* focused more narrowly on biotech patenting. The NRC report concluded, like the other two reports, that the standard for patenting should be strengthened.

Since these reports were written, a series of Supreme Court decisions have started to rein in overly expansive lower court interpretations of patent protections. For example, the Court raised the bar for "obviousness" (a legal tweak that makes it harder to get a patent) and reduced the ease with which patent holders can threaten other innovators with business-killing injunctions.[61] It is too soon to know how these cases will play out, either in reducing gridlock on the ground or in shaping the congressional reforms.

How's Academic Research Doing?

The empirical debate has two distinct components: the threats to academic research and commercial drug development. The NAS and the NRC commissioned sociologist John Walsh and his colleagues to assess the dangers by surveying scientists. The first Walsh study, published in 2003, reported that academic scientists are surviving by acting outside the law: "University researchers have a reputation for routinely ignoring IP [intellectual property] rights in the course of their research."[62] All the respondents in government labs reported that they were flouting intellectual property law, whereas one-third of industrial researchers said they occasionally used patented research tools without a license.[63] Following the law is not easy. For example, to investigate ownership of the intellectual property used in a single campus lab, the University of Iowa had to contact seventy-one different entities and spend tens of thousands of dollars in background checks.[64]

This situation can't be good for drug discovery. Perhaps academic labs can tolerate what one study calls "scofflaw science" for a while, but not indefinitely and not without risk.[65] Ultimately, a property rights regime that turns researchers into patent pirates is corrosive. Scientists may be reluctant to publish results that would disclose their infringements of others' patents, open academic exchange is stifled, and everyone feels vulnerable and uncertain. Honesty and integrity are important at every stage in scientific discovery; deception and secrecy around patent rights undermine open inquiry. When new findings are hidden away, the innovation cycle is disrupted. The trend is toward more patenting, more secrecy, less cooperation, and less accumulation of the information needed for drug discovery.[66]

A second Walsh study in 2005 (with different colleagues) surveyed academic biomedical research scientists in more depth.[67] They found that 29 percent of recently executed material transfer agreements had reach-through claims, 16 percent provided for royalties, and 26 percent imposed publication restrictions. In areas with intense commercial interest, 30 percent of researchers surveyed did not receive the last biological research materials they requested.[68] Increasingly, diagnostic tests with commercial uses are being withheld, and researchers are more likely to abandon research that involves infringing activities. On the other hand, though, a substantial majority of respondents still deny facing delays from patent thickets and fragmented ownership.

How should we interpret these survey results? The second Walsh group goes in one direction. They conclude that there is "little evidence of routine breakdowns in negotiations over rights, although research tool patents are observed to impose a range of social costs and there is some restriction of access."[69] Although survey respondents reported that negotiations for licensing or material transfers are time-consuming, they rarely halt work. Walsh points out that respondents also deploy a range of ad hoc solutions: they may work around troublesome patents, move research out of the United States to offshore labs, pirate intellectual property, or even litigate.

Based on these findings, opponents of patent reform, including members of the Walsh team, have suggested a relatively hands-off regulatory response.[70] That strikes me as premature: researchers have noted design problems with some of the Walsh group's interview protocols.[71] Also, I don't believe U.S. innovation policy should rely on piracy and on moving research overseas to countries with more reasonable patent law regimes (which are becoming ever more restrictive under strong pressure from U.S. trade negotiators).

The more fundamental problem, though, is that surveying scientists just isn't likely to reveal systemic gridlock.[72] Scientists may simply gravitate away from congested fields. This is not a bad outcome if there are a large number of equally good research targets, but I'm skeptical that's the case for many diseases.[73] Another reason surveys won't capture potential gridlock is that academic scientists often behave as if there is a blanket research exemption to patent law. There isn't. A federal appeals court ruled in 2002 that no such exemption exists.[74] That may be a bad interpretation of Congress's intent in writing the patent statute, but for now, it's the law. The recent NIH guidelines encourage licensors to create a research exception only for a limited class of federally funded discoveries. Nevertheless, university scientists infringe broadly because they do not expect to be sued, for several reasons. Commercial patent owners may not want to disrupt re-lationships with academic counterparts, academic labs cannot pay big monetary damages, and, perhaps most important, commercial intellectual property owners hope someday to benefit from innovations that result from academic infringement. Thus, academics often use patents without permission.

The NRC report rightly cautioned that the current research setting could change "dramatically and possibly even abruptly" if research institu-tions try bringing their scientists into line with the law or if patent holders begin to assert their rights more forcefully.[75] One lawsuit could tip the bal-ance. Record companies have come after teenagers for downloading mu-sic; college deans hound professors who photocopy book chapters for students. It's hardly inconceivable that a biotech company or troll might decide to make an example of some university laboratory. Forbearance by biotech owners is not a stable solution to academic biomedical gridlock. A legal system that leads scientists to break the law routinely cannot be good or sustainable social policy.

How's Commercial Drug Development Faring?

Most of the empirical research on gridlock to date has tried (unsuccess-fully, in my view) to quantify its costs for academic research. This focus, though important, misses the bigger question of gridlock in commercial drug development—what potential lifesaving cures have commercial labs neglected because of biotech ownership fragmentation? The commercial side is where we create, or fail to create, the lifesaving tests and products that actually treat disease. "You really get ownership issues coming up when things get closer to market," says Barbara A. Caulfield, general coun-sel for Affymetrix, a leading maker of gene microarray chips.[76] Not surpris-ingly, her company has generally opposed the strongest version of DNA patenting because of its inhibiting effects on product development.

Commercial scientists cannot easily be patent pirates. The infringement is too discoverable, forbearance by competitors too unlikely, potential lia-bility too high, and the patentability of resulting discoveries too question-able. Why invest hundreds of millions of dollars in risky research if you might not be able to commercialize drugs later? Instead, commercial drug companies quietly abandon projects such as the Compound X case I discussed in Chapter 1. That example would not show up in surveys like Walsh's. It's not easy getting commercial scientists to reveal promising projects they have shelved because of licensing concerns. They may be subject to confidentiality agreements that prevent them from talking, and they prefer not to draw attention to potentially viable lines of business.

Philanthropists who step into this research void face daunting costs even before they get to the hard work of drug discovery. The Golden Rice story I told earlier is an unusual case because the product had already been discovered before the licensing began. In another instance, when starting work on a malaria vaccine, researchers found that one crucial component was covered by thirty-nine patent families—a multiplicity of rights that makes vaccine design costly and complex. Gridlock is a challenge even for the Gates Foundation, a well-off philanthropy that has committed substantial resources to overcoming tragedies of the anticommons in drug research.[77]

AN ARRAY OF SOLUTIONS

Gridlock does not have a single on/off switch. Anticommons ownership occupies half the property spectrum, ranging from limited to full exclusion. How gridlock operates depends on factors such as the number and type of players, the market structure, and the underlying resource. Just as there is a wide array of causes for drug-research tragedies, there are many potential solutions. Here, I gather together tools that can help overcome a biomedical anticommons. These tools are grouped into market solutions, "property-preventing institutions," pooling and other cooperative solutions, and regulatory reforms.

Market-Driven Solutions

The "transition not tragedy" camp notes that patents are wasting assets, which means they terminate after a limited period. Securing a patent is expensive; each can cost as much as tens of thousands of dollars. Private owners often have strong incentives to overcome gridlock, either to incorporate patents into valuable new products or to ward off litigation (the

MAD strategy). On the downside, patent portfolios are also valuable for shaking down successful innovators (troll-like behavior) or blocking competitors' innovations and improvements.[78]

Maybe we should leave the market alone and trust that sophisticated players can fend for themselves.[79] They can work out the deals they need. Downstream-product developers will buy licenses, negotiate material transfer agreements, or otherwise acquire the intellectual property rights they need.[80] On the academic side, university licensing offices may be getting better at managing their innovation portfolios, through experience and with NIH prodding.[81] To the extent that academic scientists need exemptions for research, the recent NIH guidelines are already creating a safe haven.

It would be great if downstream-drug developers could succeed under the current regulatory regime. Major changes to patent law risk unforeseen consequences. On the other hand, so does inaction. We've already seen reasons to doubt the "transition not tragedy" camp: widespread piracy and increasing secrecy among academic researchers, quiet concern by industry scientists that gridlock stifles innovation, and the decline of new molecular entities over the past decade. Although markets can help solve gridlock, they are not the only approach we need.

Property-Preventing Investments

Sometimes a company's best competitive strategy is to invest in *preventing* others from gaining property rights, even if the firm must give up rights itself. For example, this strategy can take the form of releasing hard-earned and proprietary research results to the public so that the discovery is no longer novel enough for others to get patents in that area.

Intellectual property theorist Robert Merges coined the term *property-preventing investments* (PPIs) to describe this unusual market behavior.[82] PPIs may seem odd, but they make sense when you look at innovation through the anticommons prism. PPIs help to answer a question I posed at the beginning of this book: why would profit-oriented companies such as IBM or Celera Genomics voluntarily dedicate proprietary research to the public?

PPIs are not motivated by altruism. Firms are trying to prevent gridlock from blocking their primary business lines. Drugmakers' competitive advantage—where they aim to earn their profits—is in developing and marketing drugs or diagnostic tests, not in untangling patent thickets that clog research. If, for example, they can ensure that raw genetic sequences are unpatentable, then products that build on sequence data are easier to create and become more valuable.

In addition to Merges's explanation, I believe there is a more subtle political motivation for PPIs in drug research. Big drugmakers are in a bind when it comes to patent law. Because of gridlock costs, they should be aligned with the rest of high-tech America. They should favor reforms that increase their ability to assemble patents and discover new drugs. Instead, they ally with biotech and other creators of basic research inputs. Why? It's because Big Pharma views the generic drugmakers as an even bigger threat than the biotech competitors. Billions in profits disappear overnight when patents expire, generics hit the market, and prices drop. Even a few extra months of patent protection can be worth a fortune.

Therefore, big drugmakers want the longest, strongest patent rights possible. They never want to be seen tolerating weaker patent protection anywhere, even on upstream research and even if biotechs and patent trolls can use those rights to crush future innovation. Against this political backdrop, PPIs play an underappreciated role for the big pharmaceutical companies. They are an indirect and partial way to undermine troublesome patents sought by biotech competitors without calling into question the drugmakers' commitment to strong patents on their core products, the pills in the bottle. This calculus helps explain a part of the motivation for the Merck Gene Index.

To give another PPI example, in the past decade drugmakers became worried about gridlock arising from patents on gene variants among individuals called *single nucleotide polymorphisms* (SNPs).[83] An SNP is a change in a single letter of the genetic code—an A becomes a C, for instance—so multiple variants may exist in a single mutated gene. In the 1990s, scientists began to recognize that particular variants could be associated with certain genetic diseases. SNPs can be markers for illness, but they could also create perfect gridlock: a company that wanted to devise diagnostic tests or therapies might need to license patents on multiple SNPs associated with a gene.

As with ESTs, drugmakers jumped in to block SNP patenting. The Wellcome Trust in England and many big pharmaceutical companies created the "SNPs Consortium" in 1999. By 2004, they had spent more than forty-five million dollars and placed almost two million SNPs into the public domain. Consortium members agree not to seek patents on the SNPs they contribute, but they remain free to patent downstream inventions derived from the data. Along with the SNPs Consortium and the Merck Gene Index for gene probes, there is now "Blueprint Worldwide," the "Protein Data Bank" for proteins, and "GenBank" for genes. Increasingly, biology journals require donation of gene and protein sequences to the public as a condition for publication (with the risk that researchers will delay publication to protect their commercial edge). Merck also provides the research community, at cost, with 150 types of patent-free "transgenic" mice without use restrictions—another type of upstream research tool donated to the public domain.[84]

Can we rely on PPIs generally to prevent gridlock? No. Sometimes, the interests of big drugmakers, philanthropies, and academic researchers align. Then, by hard effort, PPIs may be created that forestall gridlock. But just because firms mobilized to address ESTs and SNPs does not mean they will prevent all ownership fragmentation in biomedicine. Patents on SNPs are still being filed and may yet cause a tragedy of the anticommons.[85] On balance, I see no reason to expect that PPIs are likely to be the norm.

Patent Pools and Other Cooperative Solutions

PPIs stand between individual firm competition and cooperation-based approaches. There are other such intermediate solutions. Communities of intellectual property owners who interact a great deal will sometimes develop cooperative institutions to reduce the costs of bundling rights. Some of those institutions are legally sanctioned. In the music industry, copyright collectives known as ASCAP and BMI make it possible for radio stations to play what they want and make a single blanket payment instead of negotiating a fee with each recording artist (though the collectives do not license rights for DVD use, the source of the *Eyes on the Prize* gridlock I mentioned in Chapter 1).

In Chapter 2, I introduced another cooperative institution called a *patent pool* and showed how it can be used to assemble fragmented property rights. True, there was nothing cooperative when Congress forced the formation of the Manufacturers Aircraft Association pool in 1917—the Wright brothers and Glenn Curtiss were willing to see the airplane industry grounded rather than reach agreement. Other times, though, patent pools have emerged through the voluntary efforts of the competitive patent holders without government strong-arming.

The law and economics of pooling are complex and not well understood. Even after pools are created, their internal dynamics are fraught with peril for bargaining failure. Patent pools seem to work best when linked to an emerging technical standard designed to facilitate large-scale technology licensing. The greatest successes have come in the electronics industry, where, for example, pools ensure "interoperability" of MP3 or DVD players: you can download a song or video to any player, or stick a disc in it, regardless of brand. Even in such auspicious areas, however, pools are scarce and full of dangers for those who want to make products incorporating the pooled licenses.[86]

These pools risk being challenged on antitrust grounds. To qualify for antitrust approval, a pool must assemble "essential" complementary patents, but it is not clear that biotech patents could meet this requirement.[87] Interviews with biotech industry members suggest they still view patent pooling as a risky activity.[88] Even a remote prospect of facing triple damages in a private antitrust suit makes firms hesitate. In the past decade, only four major pools (MPEG-2, two DVD pools, and the 3G mobile wireless platform) have solicited and obtained business reviews from the U.S. Department of Justice that give innovators confidence they won't be sued on antitrust grounds.[89]

Adding to the industry's anxiety is variability in the antitrust climate from year to year. For example, in 1997, the DOJ allowed the pool that created MPEG-2 technology. But in 1998, the Federal Trade Commission filed a complaint that forced the laser-eye-surgery patent pool to dissolve. What was the difference? It's not clear. Both seemed to be procompetitive solutions to patent gridlock.[90] Today, the revenues from sale of devices based in whole or in part on patent-pool technologies are at least one hundred billion dollars per year.[91] Impressive, but there could be much more. For biotech pooling to have any chance, Congress may need to create special antitrust rules.

In any case, the FTC report discussed earlier concluded that patent pools are not likely to help in biotech: "It is not an industry in which defining standards is important. . . . A company's worth is tightly tied to its intellectual property and fosters a 'bunker mentality.'"[92] Patents matter more to the pharmaceutical and biotechnology industries than to other industries, so firms in these fields are less willing to participate in patent pools that undermine the gains from exclusive rights. Also, the lack of substitutes for certain biomedical discoveries (such as patented genes or receptors) may increase some patent holders' leverage, aggravating negotiation problems. Rivals may not be able to invent around patents in research aimed at understanding the genetic bases of diseases as they occur in nature. And patent claims in biomedical research tend to be narrower and held by more dispersed owners than in fields where pools have succeeded. A further complicating factor is that commercial products in which the licensed biotechnology is to be embedded usually do not exist yet. Even if owners were to incur the heavy costs of organizing a pool, licensees would still have to carry out extensive and risky R&D to invent an effective and safe diagnostic test or treatment.

On balance, I doubt the biotech industry is amenable to pooling, even if the antitrust environment were to become more favorable.[93] Patent pools may be a good solution to gridlock in some circumstances—for example, in telecommunications, semiconductors, or nanotechnology, where standard setting is important[94]—but it is doubtful they will do the same for biomedical research.

There are other cooperative solutions that can be ventured. Some research fields have tried to organize themselves to avoid fragmentation. For example, major players in computational biology (also called *bioinformatics*) have made an effort to retain the "open science" spirit by aggressively discouraging patenting and litigation. According to Cockburn, "lessons learned from the struggle over the human genome sequence have been effectively applied by public sector researchers."[95]

Other examples include "peer production" (online creations such as Wikipedia) and publicly minded licensing (like the Creative Commons).[96] These approaches can perform a kind of market jujitsu, adjusting existing ownership forms to sidestep gridlock. They can't get a drug through FDA trials, but peer production and publicly minded lincensing can get people working together for innovation or advocacy. In the agricultural research area, owners created the Public Intellectual Property Resource for Agriculture, a mechanism for collaborative management of agriculture-related intellectual property in the public interest.[97] Another group is Biological Innovation for Open Society, an analogue to the "open source" movement in software, that prohibits technologies developed with its tools from being privately appropriated in the later stages of development.[98]

Regulatory Solutions

Big pharmaceutical companies are willing to spend tens of millions on ad hoc solutions such as the Merck Gene Index or the SNPs Consortium, but they oppose legislation tweaking patents in upstream basic research for fear it will weaken rights in the downstream products where they earn their profits. That view may be fine from an industry perspective, but it makes for bad social policy.

On the public side, there are many experiments to consider, including variants on the legislative initiatives that are always pending in Congress. When Tom Swift flew through the column of air over the bully's house, we tweaked the law to say Tom was not a trespasser. Now that scientists are routinely ignoring intellectual property law, maybe it's time to redefine rights so that drug inventors are not forced to be pirates. We should make sure that the patent monopolies we bestow are giving us our money's worth.

Although there are pros and cons to each potential reform, we could consider proposals exempting research, experimental, and diagnostic uses from patent protection; expanding exclusions to what constitutes patentable subject matter; or adding "public order" and morality clauses to patent law.[99] Why not broaden the reach of the NIH licensing guidelines (creating a limited research exemption) to all research paid for by federal agencies? More generally, why rely on ad hoc guidelines when we could legislate that all federally sponsored research provides an exemption for research uses?[100]

We could also fix patent administration along the lines suggested in the FTC and NAS reports: something as simple as funding and training more patent examiners could help. Patent offices outside the United States have responded to specific concerns about a genetic anticommons (like our EST debate) through stricter limits on, and broader exceptions to, patentability.[101] Similarly, we could tinker with the arcane rules for patentability, which are very good for lawyers' bank balances but often less benign for the rest of us.[102] Finally, we could mandate creation of an office within the PTO responsible for studying the effects of the patent regime on competition and innovation—an internal institutional counterweight to the staff's pro-patent bias.

More forceful reforms are possible. Arti Rai and Rebecca Eisenberg have suggested making it easier to invoke "march-in rights" on federally sponsored but privately patented discoveries. ("March-in rights" can be understood as the drug-patent equivalent of eminent domain, more or less.)[103] Though patient advocates call for this solution, the NIH has never agreed, perhaps for the same reasons that condemnation of land is also infrequent: governments are not good at pinpointing the right property to condemn, and potential condemnees launch intense and effective opposition.[104] Rai and Eisenberg have also proposed empowering the NIH and other federal agencies to terminate patent rights specifically when they threaten to create anticommons gridlock.[105]

A CAVEAT: ONE PATENT DOES NOT CREATE GRIDLOCK

To be clear, I am not arguing against patents for drug research. The gridlock problem is distinct from the routine underuse inherent in any well-functioning patent system. By conferring a temporary monopoly on an invention, any single patent necessarily increases prices and restricts use. We willingly pay this cost to motivate invention and disclosure.

There may be exceptional cases, however, where the social cost of a single patent is too high. For example, the most widely cited recent controversy has concerned Myriad Genetics' patents on "BRCA1" and "BRCA2," gene mutations associated with breast cancer risk.[106] Because of Myriad's broad patents and restrictive licensing practices, much follow-on research has been blocked. For example, Myriad has prevented "major cancer centers from devising inexpensive 'home-brew' tests for the breast cancer genes."[107] Researchers cannot work around the patents: either you are working with the right breast cancer gene mutations or you are not. Outrage toward Myriad Genetics has been global.[108] It's not, however, an example of gridlock.

The trade-off between the private gain and social costs of any *single* patent is an old problem, and one that patient advocates, drugmakers, Congress, and the courts are already well equipped to handle. I have nothing to add to that debate. Today we face a distinct and unfamiliar problem: in the new world of cumulative biomedical innovation, progress increasingly requires access to *multiple* inputs to create a single useful product.

A decade after Eisenberg and I first hypothesized the tragedy of the biomedical anticommons, the empirical studies that would prove—or disprove—our theory remain inconclusive. This is no surprise. Gridlock is hard to quantify in part because it involves testing a counterfactual: what cures would we have if people could work together more easily?

Survey research can't easily answer this question. It's true that if you ask research scientists directly, many are not so worried about gridlock. However, if you had surveyed pilots in 1915 about gridlock in commercial aviation, they would have been puzzled too. Are patents preventing passenger air travel? Pilots would reasonably have replied that there's no such thing as passenger air travel and never could be. Would there be a market for faster, larger cargo planes if patents could be more easily cross-licensed? Again, the reply would be that no one would want to send cargo by air. Just as it's unrealistic to expect pilots to be aware of the future possibilities of commercial air travel, there's no reason to expect that scientists would be good observers of a systemic and hidden threat like the tragedy of the anticommons. Big drug companies are better positioned to notice gridlock, but their fight with the makers of generics gives them good reason not to talk about how patent proliferation threatens innovation.

The crucial point is that the emerging structure of drug discovery clashes more and more with old-fashioned patent law and competition policy. The risks of gridlock should, at the least, prompt hard thinking on how to carry out more penetrating empirical studies. Also, the dearth of blockbusters in the drug-discovery pipeline should prod the big pharmaceutical companies off the position that the existing patent regime must be defended at all costs. There must be room to strike a deal: we protect drugmakers' ability to earn a profit; they stop blocking reforms that high-tech innovators (including drug developers) need so they can fairly and efficiently assemble multiple patents into valuable new products.

Our goal should be, as it always is with patents, to grant the least protection possible without destroying robust incentives for private investment and innovation. In making this trade-off, we should stay alert to potential tragedies of the anticommons, even though their costs are and will remain hard to pin down. With a little tweaking, not unlike the tweaking that gave us air travel a century ago, we can unlock the grid and accelerate the search for cures.

four

YOU CAN'T HEAR ME NOW

The wireless telegraph is not difficult to understand.
The ordinary telegraph is like a very long cat. You pull
the tail in New York, and it meows in Los Angeles. The
wireless is the same, only without the cat.

—ATTRIBUTED TO ALBERT EINSTEIN

My grasp of the science behind telecom is rudimentary—about enough to get that Einstein was joking.[1] But I do know that in the United States, I can't watch TV smoothly over wireless broadband and my cell phone still drops calls. One analyst writes, "Most U.S. homes can access only 'basic' broadband, among the slowest, most expensive, and least reliable in the developed world, and the United States has fallen even further behind in mobile-phone-based Internet access. . . . Japan and its neighbors have positioned themselves to be the first states to reap the benefits of the broadband era: economic growth, increased productivity, technological innovation, and an improved quality of life."[2]

How did this happen? Figure 4.1 explains part of the story: we see a few narrow peaks of intensively used frequencies separated by deep valleys of dead air in the prime spectrum bandwidths. (Prime spectrum is the range of frequencies most useful for transmitting voice, data, and images.) Technological limits do not explain the peaks and valleys; telecom policy does.

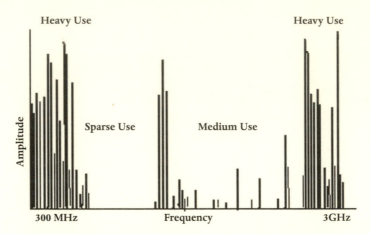

FIGURE 4.1: *Spectrum use (and underuse) in the United States.*[3]

Like the air we breathe or the water we drink, spectrum is a scarce natural resource. So even here we cannot escape Goldilocks' quest—the search for the socially optimal level of resource use I discussed in Chapter 2. Our quest is to avoid extremes of spectrum overuse and underuse in tragedies of the commons and anticommons.[4]

DIMENSIONS OF UNDERUSE

Not surprisingly, we already have a vocabulary for defining spectrum overuse: according to one definition, overuse occurs when a transmission device uses "more spectrum than is necessary to transmit the information it has to transmit, hence increasing its potential to conflict with other users."[5] At an aggregate level, overuse arises when too many users transmit on too thin a sliver of spectrum—users interfere with one another and reduce the quality of transmission all along the spectrum.

Defining underuse is trickier. The engineering and design of spectrum rights are, as noted by telecom analysts Dale Hatfield and Phil Weiser, "far more difficult than ordinarily suggested. Problems such as geographic spillover and adjacent channel spillover make it much more difficult to define rights to spectrum. . . . Unlike the case of real property, which is measured in two or three dimensions, there are as many as seven dimensions by which electromagnetic frequency can be measured, and the best way to measure these dimensions remains unsettled."[6] Even with that caveat, the valleys in figure 4.1 are "highly suggestive" of gridlock—though more technological and market data would be needed for a firm conclusion.[7]

To spot gridlock we must look at indirect evidence: slow broadband transmission rates, dropped calls, and the like. But we don't need engineering degrees to know something has gone wrong with telecom policy. For example, we know American consumers pay more for higher transmission speeds than do Japanese consumers.[8] If you visit South Korea, you can experience the future of telecom firsthand and ask, why can't I get these technologies in America?

One economist estimates that "perhaps as much as $1 trillion might be lost over the next decade due to present constraints on broadband development."[9] That represents millions of jobs and generations of innovation lost to what telecom economist Thomas Hazlett calls a "tragedy of the telecommons."[10] As a result of this tragedy, "The Japanese and the South Koreans will be the first to enjoy the quality-of-life benefits that the high-speed-broadband era will bring[:] . . . easy teleconferencing, practical telecommuting, remote diagnosis and medical services, interactive distance education, rich multimedia entertainment, digitally controlled home appliances, and much more."[11]

Because cell phones work (sort of), we overlook the regulatory causes and costs of unnecessarily dropped calls and limited service. Because broadband gets faster (by a little) every year, few people notice how policy mistakes have foreclosed growth. It's not that American telecom providers are behind their Japanese counterparts in technological ability. Poor service results, at least in part, from spectrum fragmentation and patent gridlock. As one commentator notes, "While the vast majority of TV airwaves goes unused, rampant cellular crowding causes blocked, dropped and tinny-sounding calls."[12] According to Patrick Gelsinger, chief technology officer at Intel, more than 90 percent of the airwaves are unused at any one time. He says, "If any other natural resource was this underutilized, it would be considered a national travesty."[13] Again, amplitude of use isn't necessarily a function of gridlock, but the amount of dead air is striking.

Why isn't there more of an uproar? Electrons are invisible and telecom networks intricate, so the issues may seem hard to grasp beyond the "cat versus no-cat" level. For voters and consumers, telecom is a classic "MEGO" issue, meaning "my eyes glaze over." Regulators struggle with technical challenges and political pressures. Established companies are happy to protect revenues from existing network investments rather than pursue new markets.

Our attention may wane, but fixing the tragedy of the telecommons could not be more crucial to economic growth. At the high-tech frontier, losses that you can't see really do harm you.

WHY SO MUCH SPECTRUM IS IDLE

Let's start with prime radio spectrum usage in the United States. What makes some spectrum "prime"? First, the ability to penetrate buildings, which is why radios and cell phones can work indoors; second, the ability to transmit long distances at low power, which means batteries can be small and radiation levels low.[14] Much of that prime spectrum, the range shown in figure 4.1, is little used.

Who is letting that happen? We need to know who "owns" what. Here, I put "owns" in quotation marks because of legal fictions the Federal Communications Commission (FCC) has long entertained. Legal fictions are often useful, but they structure thinking to highlight some policy concerns and hide others. One fiction is that spectrum is so scarce that it should not be privately owned; another is that licenses are not forms of ownership. Generally, an FCC license comes with severe restrictions on use and transfer, but gives its holder the exclusive right to broadcast over a defined slice of spectrum in a particular geographic area. Although this isn't ownership in the everyday sense, we can translate existing license regimes more or less into the familiar ownership categories.

Figure 4.2 shows roughly how prime spectrum is distributed among the basic types of ownership.[15] Notice that most spectrum is in anticommons ownership. Keep in mind that the numbers are always changing and the categories blur together (spectrum auctioned in 2006 and 2008 will raise the private wedge to about 12 percent when it comes online). With this figure,

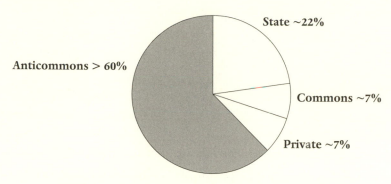

FIGURE 4.2: *How prime U.S. spectrum was "owned," as of January 2004.*

I'm offering a simple map of a baffling and intricate set of licensing arrangements. Together, figures 4.1 and 4.2 help explain why the United States has fallen off the innovation frontier.

State Spectrum

The first wedge in the pie chart is state spectrum. The United States has large swaths of it for airplane and maritime navigation and communication, the military, satellites, astronomy, and other public uses. At least 22 percent of prime bandwidth in the United States is state controlled (it could be more than 50 percent, depending on how you count bandwidth in mixed uses).[16]

Is this spectrum well managed? Not often enough. Is there too much of it? Yes. Public management of spectrum has all the pros and cons of public management of any resource, from open rangeland in Nevada to low-income housing in Brooklyn. Checks and balances on managers are weak; incentives for innovation and good performance are largely missing.

Cities control wide swaths for public safety and other uses (greater than 70 MHz), but they too often mismanage what they have, using ten times more spectrum per call than do private cell phone carriers, while providing much less reliable service—as attested by the tragic failure of the New York City Fire Department's network in the aftermath of the World Trade Center attacks.[17] Yet there continues to be pressure to allocate even more bandwidth to public uses. In early 2008, a block of prime spectrum for a hybrid private-public safety wireless network was put up for auction. Bidders did not meet the minimum reserve price.[18] Given the government's dismal record of spectrum management, the auction's failure is no surprise.

The U.S. military is the biggest holder of prime spectrum (roughly 500 MHz); its wasteful management is the most harmful to American prosperity and long-term economic security. Bands used by the military—for instance, at the Pearl Harbor naval base in Hawaii—may be left empty across the rest of the country. But go overseas, where wars are actually fought, and those bandwidths are in use—for example, for next-generation cell phones. Exclusive domestic access for the military makes little sense from a national security or economic growth standpoint. As senior Intel executive Kevin Kahn, notes, "You can't run out onto the battlefield and ask the enemy to turn their network off."[19] State spectrum can be a maddening mess. If we're going to solve the spectrum shortage, eventually we'll have to transfer some state spectrum into private control. But let's leave this trade-off aside. It's a topic for another day.

The Spectrum Commons

Ever hear your neighbor's conversation on your cordless phone? If so, then you've experienced the frustration of overuse in a "spectrum commons." These "unlicensed" frequencies are not a commons in the sense that the underlying property rights are vested with a group of users who jointly manage them. Rather, the spectrum commons is a special kind of state spectrum, governed by the FCC and set aside for low-power devices, without exclusive private property rights, and with no effective owner.[20] For example, your garage door opener is a tiny broadcaster operating on the spectrum commons. Neither you nor the equipment maker needs a license (though the radio equipment used must be approved for sale by the FCC). Depending on how you count, spectrum-commons frequencies amount to about 7 percent of prime bandwidth.

From the FCC's perspective, unlicensed uses are popular: they have spawned many appealing technologies, such as cordless phones, and have vocal, focused constituencies. Some unlicensed bands get little use, such as those allocated for ham radio. Some have been regulated into complete nonuse.[21] The most popular unlicensed bands, however, suffer a different tragedy: congestion and overuse. For example, a band in the 2.4 GHz range is available for the use not only of cordless phones but also baby monitors, wireless routers, garage door openers, and other transmitters, including microwave ovens. That's why your communication devices may endlessly search for a clear channel.

The usefulness of the spectrum commons decreases as more devices interfere with each other. To limit congestion, the FCC further restricts equipment, usage, power levels, protocols, and allowable business models. You can transmit to your garage door opener from fifty feet away but not from five thousand feet. You can't just broadcast as you please in the unlicensed bands. In addition, there may be unwritten codes of conduct—for example, shaming rituals that keep chatter down on ham radio and CB radio channels. With well-tempered "etiquettes" and "protocols," people may be able to share spectrum, just like "good neighbors."[22] In our ownership lexicon, the spectrum commons is "limited access."

These unlicensed (but heavily regulated) bands present a double-bind: FCC restrictions allow only relatively low-value local uses that may become congested over time, and they make it impossible to assemble and transfer the spectrum to high-value networks, technologies, and applications.[23] You and all your neighbors might be happy to sell your rights to garage-door-opener spectrum and get in exchange access to some next-generation network technology. But in a spectrum commons, there's no way to make that deal. Paradoxically, the hidden underuse on the most intensively used bands may be even more costly to society than the congestion.

Although the gridlock side of unlicensed spectrum remains invisible, regulators are familiar with managing overuse. This isn't surprising: as we saw above, it's relatively easy to define "overuse" in telecom markets. The FCC can repair overuse with the full tool kit of solutions to tragedies of the commons. For example, as congestion increases, the FCC may mandate more technical standards that limit interference. The easiest response politically to congestion, however, is to allocate even more bandwidth for unlicensed use. This is why your cordless phones may now operate in the 2.4 GHz range as well as the old 900 MHz band. The FCC recently opened even more spectrum to unlicensed uses, including, for instance, a block up in the 5 GHz range. Of late, the most popular regulatory proposals before the FCC have been calls to transfer ever more licensed spectrum from the gray wedge illustrated in figure 4.2 to the spectrum commons.

However, such transfers present new challenges. For example, using unlicensed spectrum for mobile wireless, as some advocates suggest, would still require coordinating available channels among users. Expanding the spectrum commons doesn't solve the need for a central organizer of signal transfers and the technological problem of "mobile handoff."[24] This technological problem, in turn, is related to the economic one: unlicensed spectrum can't operate outside of the law of commons tragedy. Private cooperative efforts don't necessarily work to overcome coordination problems if there are scattered anonymous users. When the FCC restricts uses further, it also dampens incentives to innovate and invest in the unlicensed bands. Why should innovators go to the effort of using spectrum more efficiently if they have no way to capture the benefit of less crowded airwaves? The lack of infrastructure investment is a fundamental and often overlooked consequence of the unlicensed bands.

The Promise of the Spectrum Commons

In the past decade, many leading information theorists have challenged this skeptical account of the commons spectrum.[25] For them, the goal of spectrum policy is to increase the amount of effective communication or, conversely, to reduce the costs from interference. One way to achieve that goal is to use technology to multiply the amount of prime spectrum. If usable bandwidth becomes plentiful, then congestion is not a problem. For them, the best solution to spectrum gridlock is to combine technology with cooperative norms.

To understand the spectrum-commons advocates' argument you need a smidgen of telecom policy history.[26] In a nutshell:

- From the earliest days, almost a century ago, centralized spectrum control was explained to the public as a way to manage scarce bandwidth and avoid airwave interference—just as the Soviets argued that central planning was needed to coordinate wheat production. Until recently, the FCC assigned spectrum for free to politically favored interests; the licenses were limited to highly specified uses and could be transferred only after FCC approval.

- Half a century ago, Ronald Coase, a Nobelist in economics, argued that spectrum and wheat were indeed a lot alike, but that market forces could better allocate both. Not surprisingly, politicians, FCC regulators, and existing license holders such as TV and radio broadcasters and the telephone monopoly preferred centralized allocation.

- Starting with the introduction of cellular service in the 1970s and 1980s, the FCC began experimenting with lotteries for "flexible-use" licenses—the forerunner of what I call *private property spectrum*. During the privatization wave of the 1990s, Congress finally required the FCC to begin auctioning cellular spectrum and making licenses yet more flexible. De facto private property rights were created, for a small range of spectrum allocated for cellular-type licenses.

- Now enter the spectrum-commons advocates. They argue equally against the old licensing system and the emerging private spectrum. They say that technological innovations can free the spectrum commons from tragic scarcity. Just at the moment the private-property model was embraced by the FCC, they argue, it became unnecessary and indeed counterproductive.

In a world of cheap computing power, commons advocates say we do not need a centralized "broadcast" model, with concentrated private ownership of spectrum and heavy-duty network investments. Instead, we can move to a decentralized "internet" approach in which smart, low-cost, dispersed consumer equipment endlessly multiplies the paths for communication—and nurtures a new peer-to-peer culture. Recall that a key reason we create private property is to encourage conservation of scarce resources and help direct them toward higher-value uses. If spectrum is no longer scarce, the major economic justification for privatization falls away.[27]

Commons advocates argue that, indeed, new technologies are making broadcast spectrum practically unlimited. Directional antennae and multiple other tools are emerging to subdivide and reuse spectrum along untapped spectral dimensions. For example, "agile" radio can transmit in unused frequencies and then switch away instantly when a licensed user starts up. Other sources may transmit "below the noise floor" heard by a licensed user on a band.[28] If the notion of discrete and limited broadcast "channels" is obsolete, then perhaps spectrum need not be licensed at all.[29]

Commons advocates also point to data like that contained in figure 4.3 to argue that unlicensed bands promote innovation, rather than stifling investment. Take a look at the unlicensed 2.4 GHz band: hundreds of companies have come to the FCC for authorization of thousands of new types of equipment (particularly after wireless-router standards were approved in 1999). By contrast, product authorizations for the licensed wireless bands haven't been appearing nearly so quickly. The widening gap in new equipment authorizations might imply that unlicensed uses are winning the innovation battle.

Not so fast. The FCC needs to approve all new devices in the unlicensed bands, but the wireless carriers police their own markets and equipment. For licensed spectrum, fewer than ten handset manufacturers control more than 99 percent of the U.S. retail market. New authorizations on the licensed bands are lower in number but greater in value. Also, note that spectrum commons innovations don't occur in a vacuum. They rely on pairings with private spectrum investments. For example, cordless phones and computer

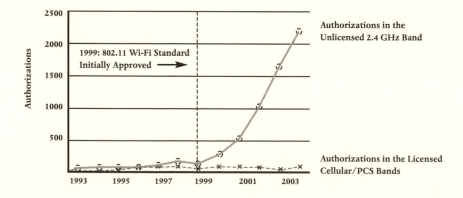

FIGURE 4.3: *FCC equipment authorizations, 1993–2004.*[30]

routers in the unlicensed bands don't have value apart from the private tele-com networks and the broadband carriers to which they are attached.

Before we celebrate the spectrum commons too much, we need a lot more information than charts like figure 4.3 provide. We need to under-stand how anticommons spectrum operates, and how commons and pri-vate spectrum innovations interact.

The Evolution of Private-Property Spectrum

After state and commons spectrum, we come to licenses that look a lot like ordinary private property. Bands are exclusively assigned. Licensees may manage this spectrum with a measure of autonomy. Flexible uses are al-lowed. License holders may change technology, services, and business models to maximize their own profits—much as ordinary merchants shift inventory in bricks-and-mortar stores.[31] For example, a licensee can switch cell phone customers over from analog to digital service without lengthy regulatory approvals. Today, big telecom players are willing to pay billions for this spectrum.

What I am calling private spectrum is of recent origin in the United States.[32] The technology for cellular service was first developed in 1947, but the FCC did not make spectrum available then. The FCC started making rules for cellular phone service in 1968, but did not begin issuing licenses until 1982. That period of regulatory gridlock was expensive by any esti-mate: each year of delay may have cost as much as thirty-three billion dol-lars in lost consumer welfare (measured in 1994 dollars).[33]

During the 1980s, the FCC eventually gave away two low-frequency (800 MHz band) licenses in each of 734 geographically defined U.S. markets—an instant anticommons because of the spatial fragmentation and license restrictions. Usually, one license went to the local Bell phone company; the non-Bell license went to a new competitor, first through a "beauty con-test," later by lottery in major markets. Initially, cell service was frag-mented and expensive. Overcoming the spatial anticommons took a decade of mergers and acquisitions.[34] During this period, the FCC was also loosening restrictions on the licenses—in 1988, for example, it allowed li-cense holders to upgrade to the digital technology of their choice. Verizon and AT&T eventually emerged with national wireless networks that consolidated many of the original cellular licenses.

In 1994, the FCC first auctioned flexible-use licenses, this time for high-frequency bandwidth covering personal communication services (PCS) and specialized mobile radio (SMR). Following these auctions, Sprint PCS emerged as a national network competitor. Similarly, Nextel assembled a national high-frequency network by buying thousands of gridlocked SMR licenses from local dispatch services for pizza delivery, taxis, and the like. Then the FCC waived some SMR license restrictions so that Nextel could offer wireless service to the general public. The emergence of these networks increased wireless competition nationally (though Sprint eventually bought Nextel): roaming charges dropped, flat-rate buckets of local and long-distance minutes were introduced, and the transition to digital service accelerated.[35]

By 2004, about 7 percent of prime bandwidth was in the most flexible form of license, what I am calling private-property spectrum. This private spectrum is the most heavily used, but it is also the most intensively shared. Because its owners enjoy relatively flexible and secure rights, they have been willing to make large complementary investments. Aggregate capital expenditure in cell infrastructure alone totals more than $150 billion. There are now almost 200,000 cellular base stations in the United States. Almost 250 million subscribers pay more than $140 billion annually for more than a trillion minutes of use (at an average charge of about 5 to 7 cents a minute). Thomas Hazlett estimates the consumer surplus created by this private-property bandwidth at about $80 billion annually (that's the difference between the price consumers are willing to pay and the actual price) and the total capitalized social value at more than $1.6 trillion.[36]

In terms of the economic activity it creates, private spectrum holds about a thirty-to-one advantage over commons spectrum: in 2003, private spectrum was associated with about $120 billion in direct economic activity. By contrast, commons spectrum generated about $4 billion in combined service revenue, equipment revenue, and network capital expenditure.[37] Looking back to figure 4.3, we see that unlicensed spectrum seems to create a lot of little innovations—but private spectrum is where the big-time innovation, investment, and economic returns have occurred so far.

New Spectrum Allocations

In 2006, the FCC carried out a big private-property auction for Advanced Wireless Services (AWS) spectrum, and another in 2008 for the 700 MHz spectrum auction.[38] For much of the last decade, however, a primary regulatory focus has been on expanding the spectrum commons. For example, in 2002, the FCC wrote that its "rules for unlicensed transmitters have been a tremendous success. . . . [This] shows that there could be significant benefits to the economy, businesses and the general public in making additional spectrum available for unlicensed transmitters."[39] But adding to the spectrum commons deflects attention from the economic problem revealed by figures 4.1 and 4.2: the vast swath of underused spectrum bracketed by overused slivers.[40] The premium that companies continue to pay for private spectrum (more than $13 billion for AWS licenses, $19 billion for 700 MHz licenses) suggests that privatizing more should be a higher priority now.

Scarcity of private spectrum, the limits of commons networks, and the waste of public spectrum go a long way toward explaining bottlenecks in U.S. wireless broadband in comparison with the global cutting edge. For example, private spectrum has been so scarce that T-Mobile, one of the big four national wireless networks, simply could not upgrade to a third-generation (3G) wireless network. (3G is the current global standard for high-capacity wireless broadband.) Finally, at the AWS auctions, T-Mobile was able to acquire the spectrum licenses it needed for $4.2 billion. Immediately after, it committed another $2.7 billion to build out its system. However, using high-frequency AWS bandwidth is technologically complex, so as of mid-2008, T-Mobile's 3G service is still not available.[41]

Keep in mind also that my phrase *private-property spectrum* is shorthand for a complex licensing scheme. Structuring property rights in telecom is at least as tricky as getting them right in the biotech field. The FCC can create "flexible-use licenses" that are no more useful than gene-fragment patents would have been. When rights are first auctioned, much depends on how bidding rules, exclusions, and subsidies are structured. In addition, the physical infrastructure, like cellular towers, has to be located somewhere. Every community wants good cellular service but none want the

towers. To create seamless national wireless coverage, the 1996 Telecom
Act partly overrode local restrictions on siting towers and reduced the anticommons threat to that piece of telecom infrastructure.[42] (Note the analogy to early air travel when Congress and the courts overrode local
trespass statutes so that airplanes could fly.)

Each choice in structuring auctions also shapes the private-property
rights, competition, and markets that will emerge. To avoid fragmentation
costs, the FCC might offer nationwide spectrum rights instead of localized
licenses; to get the most cash for the U.S. Treasury, they may allow anyone
to bid. For example, the 2006 AWS auctions were open to all. So, existing
players such as T-Mobile strengthened their positions, while potential
newcomers such as DirecTV and EchoStar were shut out. The consequence: T-Mobile could finally invest in a 3G network, but the satellite TV
broadcasters were not able to create a new national competitor to cable and
DSL. Creating property rights requires hard tradeoffs; it is never neutral.

The 2008 auctions for bands in the 700 MHz range also generated an intense lobbying effort to define the rules of the game. Because of its attractive physics, such as the ability to pass through walls, low-frequency
spectrum is especially valuable for broadband communications.[43] One
tower in the 700 MHz range could do the work of four comparable towers
at 1.9 GHz and ten towers at 2.4 GHz (fig. 4.4). Access to low-frequency
spectrum is part of what gives Verizon Wireless and AT&T their competitive edge on nationwide calling plans: their networks are built largely on
the 800 MHz bands given out in the 1980s. Sprint Nextel and T-Mobile
have to make do mostly with high-frequency spectrum they assembled
since the 1990s.[44]

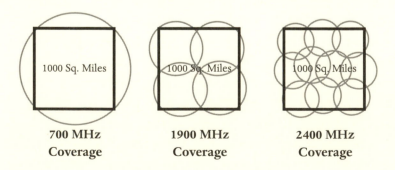

FIGURE 4.4: *Cell-tower coverage at varying frequencies.*[45]

The 700 MHz auctions have been described as "beachfront property" and the "last, great wireless auction."[46] With 700 MHz spectrum, a new competitor could build a (relatively) cheap, fast, powerful national network that would support next-generation high-speed wireless. Or existing providers could further entrench themselves. That's why the fight over the auction rules was so heated. Should the FCC maximize the financial take for the U.S. Treasury or the gains to the U.S. economy as a whole? Should there be caps on spectrum ownership so T-Mobile, Sprint, and others could catch up with, and provide more serious competition to, AT&T and Verizon? Should the FCC promote the creation of a national wireless competitor to existing cable and DSL pipelines? Should part of the spectrum be reserved for public safety uses? (Note: the hybrid private-public safety portion of the 700 MHz auction was the only one that failed—a caution perhaps about the dangers of fragmenting property rights.)

Whenever property rights are created for the first time, that's where the action is. If you think there's intense lobbying around health care or defense, try telecom, where trillions in potential producer and consumer welfare gains (or losses) are on the table and our high-tech future turns on the outcome.

The Zone of Agreement

Look back at figures 4.1 and 4.2. You can see there's a lot of room for improvement. Let's experiment with putting more spectrum to work. Many countries have moved successfully to flexible-use licenses—it's a matter of political will, not technological limits. Great Britain, for example, in 2004, adopted a plan that would shift prime spectrum from about 11 percent in private ownership to 69 percent by 2010.[47] As former FCC chair Reed Hundt and economist Gregory Rosston write, "To implement a good spectrum policy, the government should immediately make more spectrum available. The two key ways to do this are to increase the supply of spectrum outright and to get rid of use and eligibility restrictions on spectrum."[48] Both spectrum-commons and private-property advocates concur: end the gridlock. Larry Lessig puts it well:

> Liberating spectrum from the control of government is an important first step to innovation in spectrum use. On this point there is broad agreement, from those who push for a spectrum commons to those,

like [Thomas] Hazlett, who push for a fully propertized spectrum market. All agree that the only thing that government-controlled spectrum has produced is an easy opportunity for the old to protect themselves against the new. Innovation moves too slowly when it must constantly ask permission from politically controlled agencies. The solution is to eliminate the need to ask permission, by removing these controllers at least.[49]

We need to end the case-by-case regulatory allocation that entrenches nontransparent, highly restricted, low-value uses. What comes next? Fights over spectrum ownership parallel the arguments in biotechnology between advocates of a genetic commons (to support a scientific culture of sharing) and partisans of privatizing basic science (to spur biotechnology investment). In both economic arenas, the fight to end gridlock is lost in a swirl of pressing policy issues.[50] On balance, I am still agnostic as to how people ultimately should access spectrum. Should we have public "parks" amid private ownership? Probably yes, there is room for all, but first we must unify rights in spectrum into coherent, well-defined ownership bundles. Otherwise, we are stuck where we started, with spectrum wasted in a tragedy of the anticommons.

THE ANTICOMMONS SPECTRUM

My numbers are easy to contest—spectrum allocation is complex, with interwoven public, private, and unlicensed uses. Nevertheless, no matter how you slice it, more than half of prime spectrum is still licensed in what I would call anticommons uses. There are many stories I could tell about this spectrum. Here are two: "analog TV spectrum" has been held hostage by modern robber barons, and "wireless cable/educational television spectrum" has been owned like big inches.

The Analog TV Broadcasting Anticommons

For decades, underused analog TV broadcast spectrum has been a major cause of gridlock in telecom markets. About 400 MHz of prime bandwidth—67 channels of 6 MHz each—are allocated to over-the-air broadcasting in each of 210 television markets. In addition, each of these 14,000 potential local channels is bracketed by empty spectrum to avoid potential interference. There is more wasted "white space" between channels than there are occupied channels. Most channels in most places aren't used. There are only about 1,700 TV stations in the country, an average of about 8 stations per market.[51]

Virtually all of the 400 MHz reserved for analog television broadcasting is wasted in anticommons use, even the spectrum on which TV stations are actually broadcasting. How can I say that? Doesn't over-the-air local TV broadcasting provide some value? Not really. There are more than 100 million U.S. households with TVs; about 90 percent of them pay to receive multichannel TV and video via cable and direct satellite broadcast. That is, they pay to avoid relying on free transmissions. Still, about 15 million households rely on local over-the-air broadcasts. Thomas Hazlett points out that it would cost less than $5 billion to hook up every remaining over-the-air household with a cable or satellite connection.[52] If everyone could get local programming for under $5 billion, then that's all the social value we're getting from the 400 MHz of spectrum allocated to analog TV broadcasts.

By contrast, the 170 MHz of private spectrum (less than half the amount dedicated to analog TV broadcasting) contributes more than $1.6 trillion to the national wealth.[53] In other words, the best alternative uses of analog spectrum could be as much as *three hundred times* more valuable than broadcasting. This ratio suggests the scale of underuse in this anticommons tragedy. In a well-functioning private-property market, the underused resource would be reallocated overnight. Content from local channels would be distributed by cable and satellite. For years now, there would have been no analog broadcasting. The constraint to this value-creating reallocation is that the analog spectrum is as heavily state controlled as was Soviet direction of wheat production.

Analog spectrum has been stuck in gridlock. Having originally received the spectrum for free, TV broadcasters were not allowed to cash it out. So a vicious cycle started. Broadcasters kept allocated spectrum hostage.[54] They dragged their heels on giving back analog bands. One FCC chair called the television broadcasters "spectrum squatters." Senator John McCain, when he was chair of the Senate Commerce Committee, which oversees the FCC, called "the transition to digital television . . . a grave disappointment for American consumers and nothing short of a spectrum heist . . . by television broadcasters."[55] But Congress also shares in the blame: it pushed the FCC's analog termination dates later and later. Finally, Congress settled on a date: over-the-air analog transmissions will end in February 2009. This back-and-forth has wasted years of potential consumer welfare gains from spectrum reallocation.

Let's make a quick comparison between TV and cell phone conversion from analog to digital. On the broadcasting side, decades have passed waiting for TV to go digital. By contrast, cell carriers converted from analog to digital seamlessly and quickly. Because they could reap the profits, providers invested in more, better, and cheaper digital service. Getting value from scarce private spectrum was motivation enough. In 1995, virtually all 30 million U.S. wireless subscribers had analog service. By 2007, there were 240 million digital subscribers, as compared to 1 million who still had analog service (fig. 4.5).[56] To make this switch, cell phone companies required no public gifts of spectrum. What's the difference between cell and television performance? Private versus anticommons ownership of the underlying spectrum—not technological limits.

There's another unfortunate chapter in this gridlock tale. In the 1996 Telecom Act, Congress gave back to broadcasters 294 MHz of spectrum for digital TV broadcasting from the 402 MHz of analog spectrum that the broadcasters were to return to the public. Retrieving analog spectrum was

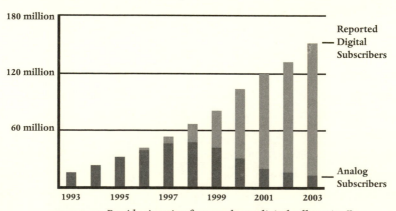

FIGURE 4.5: *Rapid migration from analog to digital cell service.*[57]

a good idea; granting free spectrum for over-the-air digital broadcast spectrum was not.

To be fair, there is something to be said for the broadcasters' position. The current owners paid to acquire the companies that control analog licenses—only the first licensees got them for free. Many people share an intuition that taking away "property" without compensation would be unfair (even though the original licenses stated that they were not to be considered private property). Also, providing a free, ad-supported means of over-the-air communication may benefit the public, including those who can't afford cable or satellite.

On the other hand, cable and satellite already provide near-universal digital service without using any spectrum at all. They could be made universal through a relatively modest government subsidy if access and cost were a concern. And the efficiency concerns we have regarding uncompensated government confiscations don't seem as compelling for television broadcasters. Even if some compensation were in order, it needn't be spectrum limited to *over-the-air digital broadcasts*. If broadcasters insist on delivering content over-the-air, they could buy spectrum like everyone else. The hidden cost of digital broadcast spectrum may be gridlock—prime spectrum trapped in highly restricted, relatively low-value uses that can't easily be redeployed. So the argument really comes down to whether one believes the public value of over-the-air digital broadcasting exceeds the value of alternative uses of that spectrum. Given the welfare calculations we've seen so far, I would opt for the alternatives.

The Wireless Cable/Educational TV Anticommons

Underused analog television bandwidth is just one wedge in the anticommons spectrum pie. I will mention another path through which spectrum wealth can be lost.

Above the unlicensed 2.4 GHz band, you'll find 190 MHz of spectrum licensed originally for "wireless cable" and local educational television. Wireless cable went through a boom-and-bust cycle, but never really got going. It was crushed by landline and satellite cable. Local educational stations never added much value, especially by comparison to the economic potential of this spectrum. Until recently, the spectrum was almost wholly wasted. How do we know? A data set of 2001 sales shows that licenses were typically valued at about 3 percent of the value of comparable PCS licenses on neighboring private spectrum. The disparity persists.[58] In 2004, when Nextel bought some of these licenses, they paid "1/200th the cost" of comparable PCS spectrum, according to one industry executive. "A lot of that has to do with how messy the process of being able to provide services in the spectrum [has been]."[59] The low value is driven partly by the laws of physics—building a network up at 2.5 GHz is relatively expensive—and partly by gridlock.

These wireless cable/educational TV bands could support wireless-voice or high-speed data networks. In 1998, the FCC amended the licenses to allow such high-demand "two-way" services, but left in place other old "one-way" broadcast-model rules. The resulting systems don't mesh. Licensing two-way wireless cells under the one-way broadcast rules is costly and complex—"in essence, the subdivision of spectrum space is heavily taxed."[60] The old rules also require that new wireless users leave swaths of spectrum dark on both sides of each old TV channel to avoid interference with broadcasts that don't and will never exist. Finally, many channels are "interleaved" with channels assigned to microwave users, again to avoid non-existent interference.

Now the mix of rules hampers the ability of individual "licensees to deploy broadband services by giving adjacent channel licensees a 'veto power' over any proposed offering."[61] To put spectrum to use, license holders need to negotiate "interference agreements" with neighboring owners and secure FCC approvals. But negotiating spectrum sharing is like getting past robber barons on the Rhine. Deals are so complicated that they often don't get done.[62]

In 2002, license holders petitioned the FCC to reconfigure rights in the band to avoid the pointless inefficiencies generated by rules aimed at obsolete uses. The owners reached a consensus on how to move from anticommons to private spectrum, essentially by "repacking" the band and allowing licensees greater freedom to figure out their own interference rules. If I own the black squares on the chessboard and you own the white ones, and neither of us can do anything, let's trade so you get the top half of the board, I get the bottom half, and we both have a workable space.

The solution sounds reasonable until you run into the politics of spectrum redistribution.[63] The assorted university, high school, and religious-group license holders on the educational TV band are lobbying to keep their spectrum subsidies—it would be much cheaper just to pay them directly to give back our spectrum. Sprint Nextel and Clearwire, which now control the use of most of these licenses, want a share in the windfall. Other wireless providers don't want more competition. And as with analog television spectrum, the public has a claim. There must be room to strike a deal. The current obsolete system punishes everybody. We all lose out when spectrum trades at around a 97 percent discount to neighboring private spectrum. What innovations are we missing because 190 MHz of prime spectrum (more than total PCS spectrum) is stuck in a gridlock economy?

The Invisible River

Spectrum flows like an invisible river through a modern economy, either speeding it along or slowing it down. Both Democratic and Republican administrations constrained the FCC to create spectrum policy that limited America's global competitiveness—in cell phones, television, broadband, the Internet, and industries yet to be invented. Because Congress missed the subtle costs of spectrum underuse, it backed the U.S. economy into a tragedy of the telecommons. Now, America's information infrastructure is unnecessarily slow, expensive, unreliable, and out-of-date.

A WIRELESS-PATENT BATTLE ROYALE

> *For want of a nail the shoe was lost.*
> *For want of a shoe the horse was lost.*
> *For want of a horse the rider was lost.*
> *For want of a rider the battle was lost.*
> *For want of a battle the war was lost.*
> *For want of a war the kingdom was lost.*
> *And all for want of a horseshoe nail.*
> —MEDIEVAL NURSERY RHYME

A single industry may face multiple forms of gridlock. As we saw in Chapter 2, in the early years of air travel, fragmented landownership threatened to prevent overflights while patent wars blocked airplane manufacturing.

Telecom is the same. The telecom equivalent of blocked overflights is idle spectrum. The analogues to the Wright versus Curtiss battles are the patent wars at the cutting edge of telephony.

Bet the Company

In the telecom kingdom, today's great wireless knights—AT&T, Sprint, T-Mobile, and Verizon—often must license thousands of patents to provide any one consumer product. Even in existing markets, if they miss a single high-tech horseshoe nail, a whole network may be threatened. Worse, the fear of missing one patent deters investment. Whether a new technology infringes any other patent is never clear. At any moment, wireless providers and their suppliers are involved as plaintiffs, defendants, or interested third parties in myriad lawsuits.

Many are bet-the-company battles. For a while, we worried that the BlackBerry patent-infringement litigation would shut down our service. Finally, Research in Motion, which makes the BlackBerry, settled the case by paying "patent troll" NTP more than six hundred million dollars to license contested patents (which may still be found invalid).[64] A similar patent battle has threatened to cripple Vonage's Internet telephony business.

In South Korea and Japan, technology leaders probably make as many mistakes as their American counterparts, but they have succeeded in keeping the regulatory and competitive focus on increasing network access and capacity. In the United States, by contrast, companies often aim to hobble their competitors. Lobbying or litigating may be a more profitable way to win market share than innovating and investing. When I was working in Russia for the World Bank, I often heard a joke about the difficulty of creating markets: "A genie offers a Russian entrepreneur one wish. Any wish. Big smiles. Then, the genie gives one condition: 'Whatever you wish for, your neighbor will get double.' Frowns. The entrepreneur thinks and thinks. Eventually, the smile returns. 'I wish that you blind me in one eye.'" Companies accept being blinded in one eye if regulators or courts will blind their competitors in both. Gridlock may be profitable for existing companies, but it is costly for consumers.

Here's a bet-the-company tale that may be less familiar than BlackBerry or Vonage but with even greater stakes. A few years ago, Richard Lynch, the chief technical officer at Verizon Wireless, helped commit his company to move toward 3G technology, a multibillion-dollar investment.[65] Third-party suppliers, such as Samsung, invested yet more on advanced handsets and other compatible products. In turn, companies such as Qualcomm assembled hundreds of patented technologies into the microchips that control the handsets for the new network.[66]

The easiest way for rivals to cash in or catch up was to put roadblocks in front of 3G networks. In this case, the Qualcomm chips proved vulnerable. Chip maker Broadcom bought a few minor patents (for managing battery power) and then sued Qualcomm, claiming patent infringement. If Broadcom won, it could seek an injunction preventing sale of the Qualcomm chips, thus freezing the handset market and in turn shutting down use of Verizon's 3G networks—all because of patents with trivial value compared to the network investments.

Each lawsuit is a tough battle, usually invisible to consumers. As Broadcom started down the patent litigation path, the Supreme Court in another case reduced the availability of injunctions as a remedy. Justice Anthony Kennedy, concurring in the Court's judgment, wrote: "When the patented invention is but a small component of the product the companies seek to produce and the threat of an injunction is employed simply for undue leverage in negotiations, legal damages [that is, an award of money] may well be sufficient to compensate for the infringement and an injunction may not serve the public interest."[67]

Broadcom switched gears. It took up its case before an obscure federal International Trade Commission (ITC) tribunal. The ITC administrative-law judge decided that some Broadcom patents were infringed and ordered the Qualcomm chips, and handsets incorporating them, excluded from import into the United States.[68] Although an appeals court temporarily suspended part of the ITC's order, Broadcom's point was made: ITC exclusion will bring competitors to their knees as surely as an injunction, especially because all the chips and handsets are made abroad. Broadcom opened a new path to telecom gridlock.

Why should the ITC be able to take jurisdiction over a key piece of U.S. innovation policy and sidestep the Supreme Court's limits on injunctions? As one commentator notes, the ITC let Broadcom "use an intellectual-property dispute as a cover for enmeshing competitors in the protectionist mazes of international trade law."[69] Now, as the Wall Street Journal points out, "the

ITC has emerged as the patent bar's venue of choice to evade [the Supreme Court's limit on injunctions]. . . . The ITC staff seem only too happy to expand their turf in this fashion; they think they've died and gone to bureaucratic heaven."[70]

According to Lynch, the ITC exclusion order threatened a "crippling impact on Verizon Wireless's ability to deploy advanced broadband services."[71] With the exclusion order in effect, Lynch continues,

> It would become unduly speculative and risky to acquire the significant amounts of additional spectrum that Verizon Wireless currently plans to acquire, because that spectrum may cost billions of dollars. Yet, without this additional spectrum, the related ability to upgrade Verizon Wireless's network . . . and future growth will likely be substantially circumscribed. . . .
>
> Verizon Wireless would be forced to revise—and substantially to curtail—its current technology development path. . . . [A Broadcom victory] would cripple Verizon Wireless's ability to innovate in the longer term. Lead times for the development of new network technology often run two or three years or more, [but this litigation] could have consequences well beyond the next three years. . . .
>
> In short, Verizon Wireless has staked its entire technology road map, capital spending, and business plans on its ability to offer its subscribers the ability to use [handsets incorporating these Qualcomm chips]. The disruption, dislocation, and lost revenues that would result if [Qualcomm loses] would be enormous—causing losses of tens of billions of dollars in forgone revenues and shareholder value.[72]

Faced with this threat, Verizon Wireless cut a deal with Broadcom. The wireless carrier agreed not to fight to overturn the ITC exclusion order and to pay Broadcom up to two hundred million dollars to license the disputed patents.[73] For Lynch, "this was a way to take the risk out of our business. I needed a resolution for my customers and my business." Other wireless carriers like Sprint face the same calculus and may strike similar deals. Qualcomm soldiers on, trying to get the underlying ITC judgment and exclusion order overturned.[74]

The Gridlock Tax

Who knows which side has the better patent- and trade-law arguments? I don't have a position. But I do care about avoiding the costs of a gridlock economy. Keep in mind that a single lawsuit does not create an anticommons. It's the sum of all the litigation and litigation threats that ratchets down innovation. Like the biotech industry, telecom depends on the underlying intellectual-property regime. Potential innovators must worry about overlooking one trivial patent out of the many they must license. Also, like drug development, every corner of telecom has knockout lawsuits pending or threatened.

Broadcom and Qualcomm have multiple lawsuits under way against each other; Qualcomm is suing Nokia and vice versa on infringement claims similar to those involving Broadcom.[75] After these lawsuits resolve, there will be dozens more like them, and then yet more. Everyone threatens everyone else up and down the supply chain and across the industry. Even when the Supreme Court tries to rein in the gridlock threat, aggressive tribunals like the ITC pop up to punish innovation.

Uncertainty in litigation, as in regulation, is like a steep tax. Everyone grows more cautious about investment as risks multiply. The litigation lottery is as crippling for blue-sky experimentation in telecom as in drug research. Long the leader in innovation, the United States by 2006 had dropped to fifteenth among industrialized economies in broadband penetration per capita and had fallen out of the global elite in broadband network speed.[76]

So-called 4G technology (allowing the download of a whole movie in a few minutes or streaming high-quality television) is starting up in Asia and but a glimmer in the United States. A patent can spur innovation, but it can also become the horseshoe nail that leads to the downfall of a technology kingdom.

UNBUNDLING AND THE REGULATORY ANTICOMMONS

Fragmented spectrum ownership and telecom patent thickets are traditional and costly tragedies of the anticommons. Here's a quick excursion into a regulatory version: America's complex experiment with unbundling landline telephone networks.

In the 1996 Telecom Act, Congress acted to promote local telephony competition by forcing the regional Bell monopolies to open up their networks.[77] The FCC required the old monopolies to break their integrated facilities and services into discrete fragments—"unbundled network elements"—and make them available to new competitors. The notion was that the newcomers would assemble the elements they needed, complement them with their own investments, and offer new services. Freeing network fragments was supposed to lead to new firms, new investments, new facilities, and competitive local phone markets.

At least that was the hope. In some countries, such as Japan, unbundling seems to have succeeded. But in the United States, competition hasn't emerged for most of us (though business customers have seen more options). The reasons are complex. It's partly a story of shifting political commitments, with the old guard regaining the upper hand against new entrants before Congress, the administration, the FCC, and the courts. For example, a federal appeals court agreed with the old guard that "each unbundling of an element imposes costs of its own, spreading the disincentive to invest in innovation and creating complex issues of managing shared facilities."[78]

Another part of the story involves regulatory gridlock. Given the forced nature of the exchange, markets couldn't price network fragments. So Congress mandated that the FCC create an elaborate and controversial government-run pricing scheme. Overlapping federal, state, and even local regulators became responsible for approving prices, uses, "interconnection agreements," and many more operational details. Twenty-two economists signed a letter to the U.S. president, noting that "the current regime allows state regulators to establish the critical rules, which means there will be 50 different and frequently inconsistent telecommunications policies with which to comply, rather than just one. The problem is that uncertainty deters investment."[79]

Regulators can become like tollbooths along the Rhine. To develop a product, one needs the approval of each baron. But every competitor is also seeking favor. A regulatory anticommons directs both newcomers and the old guard toward a downward spiral of lobbying and litigating rather than toward competition over better products and service.

The Gridlock Hypothesis, Revised

Telecom is a good arena for spotting gridlock because the economic sector is so sensitive to the property-rights climate. Telecom typically requires large up-front fixed-capital investments—for example, to lay fiber-optic cable or launch satellites—followed by less expensive marginal investments to extend those networks and add new users. In this sense, telecom resembles the pharmaceutical industry, with its massive initial investments to discover effective drugs, test their safety, and bring them to market, followed by trivial marginal costs to stamp out the pills.

For such high fixed-cost but low marginal-cost industries, incentives to invest and innovate depend greatly on the initial specification and security of property rights. Skittish credit markets compound this effect. How much telecom innovation can we expect without long-term lending to back capital investment? Banks won't lend billions to create next-generation networks unless they are confident of being profitably repaid far into the future. (By analogy, think how much housing you could buy if there were no long-term mortgage finance.)

Seeing how telecom falls short leads me to refine my original gridlock hypothesis: likely, there will be *multiple* paths into and out of tragedies of the anticommons in any cutting-edge economic sector. Lifesaving drugs fail to appear because of an array of big-inch and phantom-tollbooth tragedies. Similarly, the aircraft industry a century ago suffered intersecting underuse tragedies—patent wars blocked plane manufacturing and trespass law threatened to prevent overflights. Air travel today is limited by gridlock in building new airports, expanding existing facilities, and streamlining flight paths. I would be surprised if patent blockades were not keeping Boeing and Airbus from building new energy efficiency, safety, and other technologies into their planes. Multiple paths to gridlock seem to be the norm. There are, unfortunately, parallel stories across the high-tech frontier:

- Firms in the *semiconductor* industry "find it all too easy to unintentionally infringe on a patent in designing a microprocessor, potentially exposing themselves to billions of dollars in liability and/or an injunction forcing them to cease production."[80]

- In the *software* industry, "the owner of any one of the multitude of patented technologies constituting a software program can hold up production of innovative new software."[81]
- At the *nanotechnology* frontier, we may already have patent thickets in "quantum dots" and "carbon nanotubes"; insiders are growing worried about gridlock in "nanowires."[82]

The net effect in these sectors, as in biotech and telecom, is that investment sticks to safe paths. The passion for innovation is blunted. What's the result? New technologies may emerge outside the United States, if at all, and migrate here only after they have become obsolete by global standards.

Your cell phone drops calls, has scratchy sound, and lacks many useful services that you've seen in your travels abroad. Now you know why. Well-intentioned policies have led to gridlock. Although the FCC is an easy target, it does not deserve all the blame. Its professional staff is highly competent. But regulators can be captured, while campaign contributions rain down on the politicians who are supposed to be overseeing national communications policy.

Broadcasters embrace the FCC because it gives them protected access to valuable spectrum. Big telecom companies tolerate the FCC because it can lock out disruptive new technologies. Strategic litigation further entrenches gridlock: patent thickets can be great anticompetitive tools. Even when the courts rein in patent law, companies can shift to other venues, as Broadcom did with the ITC. In telecom, competitors know that often the most profitable approach is not to innovate, but to stop others from investing.

Few people noticed when U.S. broadband penetration slipped out of the top ten globally. Then it slipped out of the top fifteen. At some point, people may begin to ask what happened. The answer is that telecom policy has combined spectrum underuse with patent thickets and regulatory gridlock. Tragedies of the telecommons may be invisible, but they translate to lost wealth, wrecked markets, and missed entrepreneurial opportunities.

five

BLOCK PARTIES, SHARE CHOPPERS, AND BANANA REPUBLICS

Grab this land! Take it, hold it, my brothers, make it,
my brothers, shake it, squeeze it, turn it, twist it, beat
it, kick it, kiss it, whip it, stomp it, dig it, plow it, seed
it, reap it, rent it, buy it, sell it, own it, build it, multi-
ply it, and pass it on—can you hear me? Pass it on!
—TONI MORRISON, *Song of Solomon*

L et's move now to the most low-tech of resources: land. Unlike gene fragments and spectrum allocation, land is tangible and familiar. We all know what it means to own, trade, develop, and live on land. Surely, gridlock cannot destroy the value of land. But it does: some of the most costly tragedies of the anticommons I have uncovered—often hidden in plain sight—involve land.

I will tell three emblematic stories of gridlock in land, what I call *block parties, share choppers,* and *BANANA republics.* As with biotech and telecom, I want to alert you to the paths by which anticommons tragedy can affect you directly. It does not matter whether the resource is intangible or rock solid.

A Window into Real Estate Gridlock

When the *New York Times* wanted a new headquarters a few years ago, it persuaded New York City to confiscate a site in Times Square.[1] The city displaced fourteen landowners and fifty-five businesses using what's called *eminent domain*. Eminent domain is the process through which a government condemns a resource, takes it for a public use, and pays *just compensation* to the private owner. This can be a fast way to assemble land, but it can be quite unfair to those whose land is taken—just compensation, as we shall see, is not always so just. Unfortunately, the more equitable alternative, buying the land on the open market, is costly and often fails. The United States lacks a good, fast way to assemble land for needed economic development.

When the *Times*'s confiscation was in the news, many people saw it as an example of a big, powerful corporation bullying the little guys. I thought, this is a "big-inch" dilemma. Here's a seedy block in Times Square consisting of many low-value parcels—parking lots, peep shows, novelty stores— not worthless, but a substantial underuse of some of the world's most valuable real estate. The *Times* imagined the fragments combined, with a sleek new skyscraper unlocking hidden value. Even if the way they combined the parcels was self-serving and unfair, the new value was real. Standing in Times Square, it is a short mental step to notice that cost of big-inch land fragmentation—the problem of *block parties*—is national and general.

I identified the second form of gridlock in land when a student spoke up in a law school class I was teaching on co-ownership and partition law. My student told the class how gridlock caused her family to lose its farm. As land passes down through the generations, ownership can become quite fragmented. Once there are too many owners, cooperation fails, and the farm is sold. The big-inch image makes my student's dilemma clear. When ownership is fragmented to a small scale (such as a fractional co-ownership interest) and ordinary use is on a larger scale (such as a farm), then you have a *share chopper* dilemma.[2]

Later I saw Native American families facing this dilemma, and Irish Americans with the same story deep in their family histories. Much Native American–owned land sits idle because of how the government broke up tribal reservations a century ago. A recent Supreme Court decision noted that on the Sisseton-Wahpeton Lake Traverse Reservation in North and South Dakotas, "an average tract [of forty acres] has 196 owners and the average owner undivided interests in 14 tracts."[3] Often, fractionated land cannot be sold, mortgaged, or put to any productive use. When bad law creates gridlock in land, people suffer brutal cultural, social, and economic harms.

Block parties and share choppers are core examples of tragedies of the anticommons: multiple owners blocking one another from putting resources to their most valuable uses. The third form of gridlocked land arises in the real estate development business, and extends the anticommons concept into the regulatory arena. As a property law professor, I often talk with developers. I ask them how many regulators stand between their initial ideas and breaking ground. Many developers go bankrupt waiting for an endless list of regulatory approvals. They complain that the hurdles add up to a legal environment in which they can "build *absolutely nothing anywhere near anyone*"—that is, a *BANANA republic.*[4]

Across America, BANANA republics have ratcheted up the cost of buying housing and doing business. In the highest-cost cities, people worry about building "affordable housing," but the real problem is too much bad and uncoordinated regulation that drives up housing prices for everyone. When the gauntlet of regulators resembles robber barons on the Rhine, then you have a BANANA republic. BANANA republics don't involve fragmented ownership as such. Instead, they are a nice example of fragmented and gridlocked decision making: too many cooks spoil the broth.

Gridlock matters. Block parties, share choppers, and BANANA republics are an unnecessary drag on the economy and a major source of tragedy for so many families. But there is good news, too. Value can flow again if we can free up land stuck in gridlock.

BLOCK PARTIES

Let's take a closer look at the economic, political, and moral stakes in real estate gridlock, starting with *block parties*.[5] In the late 1990s, the *New York Times* told New York City that land on Eighth Avenue between Fortieth and

Forty-first Streets would be a good spot for a new headquarters—or else the paper might move 750 employees to New Jersey (as if!). Mayor Rudy Giuliani and Governor George Pataki agreed to hand the land right over, even though the city did not own the site. So it used eminent domain to take the real estate. When *60 Minutes* came to investigate, *Times* executives ducked its cameras and refused to comment.[6]

New York gave the site to the *Times* (and to developer Bruce Ratner, an important Giuliani fund-raiser) for the "fair market value" of about $85 million, a figure reached by adding up the separately appraised values of the underlying parcels and leases. But the real market value of the assembled land could have been up to three times higher, as much as $250 million.[7] The discrepancy in values for part of one Times Square block suggests how much value is frozen in gridlocked land.

Eminent domain is one way to unlock that value. But it's a crude solution. No one ever explained to Sydney Orbach, the owner of a well-kept sixteen-story building on the site, or his neighbors, why their land should be so capriciously sacrificed for a "public use" (fig. 5.1). Orbach was willing to sell, but the *Times* did not negotiate with him. Why bother with voluntary market transactions when you can get the state to take the land you

FIGURE 5.1: *The Times Square site (left) and Sydney Orbach (right) in his building taken by the* New York Times.[8]

want? In addition, the *Times* asked that the long-term leases in Orbach's building be broken. One tenant, Scot Cohen, had run his family's well-known business, B&J Fabrics, from the building since 1958. Cohen says, "You just don't think things like that can happen in this country. . . . You work hard to build something up, and then someone who is bigger than you can take it away."[9] Under U.S. law, compensation of tenants after confiscation is often negligible.

Stratford Wallace's family had owned another building on the site for more than a century. The city justified the condemnation on the grounds that Wallace's building was "blighted," but as far as I can tell that was just a legal fig leaf with no real content. "I challenge them," Wallace told *60 Minutes*. "This is not blighted property."[10] Challenging a "blight" designation, however, is a losing game, as I teach my law students. In this case, the "blight" designation was created after the *Times* had already struck its deal with the city.

The city slowly ground down the former occupants' remaining legal challenges.[11] Meanwhile, the new *Times* building went up. Today, the *Times* headquarters is an architectural delight. Staffers occupy a lovely and convenient new workplace. Up to $165 million in real estate assembly value was created as if by magic and generously transferred, off the books, from the city to the *Times* and to Ratner.[12]

The One-Way Ratchet

Land is much easier to break up than to put back together—land transactions work like a one-way ratchet. Land becomes more and more fragmented, times change, and the scale of ownership no longer matches the optimal scale of use. Imagine an ordinary residential community in decline. The city eyes the area for much-needed economic redevelopment. A private developer is willing to build on behalf of a shopping mall or auto factory (or the *Times*). But these engines of economic growth work on a fast timetable. They need assembled, available land right away. In my hypothetical (and all too common) neighborhood, the parcels are small and the buildings run-down, or "blighted" in development lingo. How is the investor going to bundle the land together?

Assembling the land through tax forfeitures, the solution to the original Quaker Oats Big Inches, is not the answer. Generally, people don't fail to pay taxes on contiguous valuable parcels. In parts of the Bronx or Flint, Michigan, mass forfeiture left a checkerboard of city-owned sites interspersed with failing private ones—the worst of all possible outcomes from an urban-development perspective. Even if the parcels were contiguous, run-down areas dominated by tax forfeitures are often unattractive sites for shopping malls, stadiums, factories, or residential subdivisions. Cities can't wait for large valuable parcels to be forfeited back.

How about prohibiting fragmentation? Outright prohibition on subdivision makes little sense. Usually an owner's decision to break up land creates value, at least for a while. That's the genius of individual decision making in markets. Regulating subdivision, however, can make sense. Cities have created "exaction schemes" that require developers to pay the added costs that fragmentation and development impose on the public—for example, extra policing, schools, infrastructure, roads, utilities, and environmental degradation. But in many cities, exactions have multiplied. For a politician, why not demand concessions far beyond the costs created by the subdivision? The high price of new housing falls on newcomers who don't yet vote in the area; the benefits accrue to existing home owners and voters. When subdivision and other land-use regulations become onerous enough, the result is fewer subdivisions and less construction, which in turn means less affordable housing. We can easily mistake overcrowding in existing units and illegal subdivisions for a housing-affordability crisis, but these social ills are just artifacts of overregulation.

You may be surprised to learn that up to half a million people across the United States (mostly in Texas, New Mexico, Arizona, and California) live in illegally subdivided *colonias*—substandard shantytown neighborhoods much like those found in parts of Latin America.[13] While working in Venezuela, Honduras, and elsewhere, I found that poor residents often tried valiantly to conform to the law, but subdivision rules and other urban regulations made it impossible.[14] Subdivision should be easier and more affordable to accomplish, not harder and more costly. The solution to fragmentation isn't to burden subdivision.

What's left for the investor who wants to redevelop run-down real estate? How *should* we assemble land and overcome block parties? As I'll discuss below, the best approach would be to offer people a simple land-assembly tool that they could use when they choose. Many countries offer versions of this tool. The United States, by contrast, has traditionally had only two routes for assembling large sites: private voluntary contracting and eminent domain. Neither does the job well.

Voluntary Assembly versus Eminent Domain

On the voluntary market side, developers try to buy land secretly over the course of years and even decades using dummy buyers and "shill" corporations.[15] Why the secrecy? Negotiations frequently collapse when owners discover that an assembly is in process. Each owner (much like a patent owner in the biotech industry) may try to capture all the gains from assembly, even though there is only one surplus available. If just a few neighbors ask too high a price or refuse to sell, the result is a block party—a minority of landowners with low- or medium-value parcels blocks the majority from benefiting from the sale of land into a high-value assembly.

Voluntary agreements are not impossible, but they rarely work in America and elsewhere in the world (fig. 5.2).[16] In the Times Square example, a few of the fourteen landowners had been trying for decades to assemble the block. But others held out. And the assemblers held out against each other. Block parties are a form of minority tyranny. In deciding whether to hold out, each lot owner does not have to take account of the costs imposed on others or on society at large.

If voluntary assembly risks failure because of minority tyranny (those holdouts), then eminent domain risks success through majority tyranny. That's what the city's

FIGURE 5.2: *A lone holdout in a Chinese real estate project, March 2007 (top). The holdout, bulldozed, April 2007 (bottom).*[17]

confiscation for the *Times* looks like. Developers now specialize in persuad-
ing politicians to condemn real estate on their behalf. For example, Bruce
Ratner, the *Times*'s partner in Times Square, also organized Atlantic Yards,
a seventy-three-parcel, twenty-two-acre project that has cut through local
opposition in downtown Brooklyn. To assemble the site, New York will
designate the area as "blighted" and condemn the holdout landowners, including some lovely old blocks where houses routinely sell for more than
$1 million.[18] Then Ratner plans to knock down existing buildings and
(eventually) build a $4.2 billion project with perhaps sixteen skyscrapers
and more than six thousand apartments, a twenty thousand–seat arena for
the (presently New Jersey) Nets, and much else besides.[19]

Columbia University, where I teach, is in a similar position as Ratner
and the *Times*. Space per student is low. Not a tragedy perhaps, but the
school needs new classrooms, science buildings, and dorms. Where to put
them? For years, the school quietly bought land a few blocks north of the
existing campus in Manhattanville (or "West Harlem"). But Columbia
ended up with "checkerboarded" parcels, like big inches in the magical
parking lot (and like the Native American lands I discuss below). Voluntary deals went only so far. So Columbia called on New York to condemn
the Manhattanville holdouts. The university wants to fill in the checkerboard and create a contiguous, buildable site for a new campus. To disarm
local opposition, Columbia has offered millions in inducements to
Harlem neighbors and the city—jobs, schools, and other benefits.[20] So far,
the university has jumped through the initial regulatory hoops, including
approvals from key city and state agencies, but even eminent domain
places many phantom tollbooths ahead of development.

Eminent domain can overcome the minority tyranny of holdouts, but it
routinely leads to lengthy political fights, corruption, and unfair redistrib-
utions of property. Why do people fight eminent domain so vociferously?
When their land is taken, owners get paid "fair market value." What's
wrong with that? The answer is that anytime you say your property is not
for sale, you are valuing it above fair market value. Otherwise, you'd have a
"for sale" sign out front. You may have private subjective value in the location of your home, the strength of your community, or the local goodwill
you've created for your business. Although these values are real, they are

hard to measure and none are compensable on condemnation. Nor are you entitled to any of the gains resulting from the assembly itself. Even if you could be fully compensated in a financial sense, you may still object if you are forced to leave on someone else's say-so—this is a harm to your sense of personal dignity and autonomy.[21] These financial and nonfinancial harms lead wealthier landowners to invest in deflecting condemnations to less politically organized areas—often lower-income and minority neighborhoods. The most vulnerable communities cannot push confiscations further down the road. The bulldozer stops with them.

Not surprisingly, these coercive transfers have become a controversy magnet. A modern, dynamic economy really needs to assemble land for economic development. Eminent domain, though, accomplishes this task through a frankly political process. To increase their tax base, local governments are essentially transferring land from private party A to private party B and driving off politically powerless citizens—all without serious legal constraint. Offering developers confiscated land becomes part of city-suburb competition for growth and creates a spiral of interstate giveaways. Conveniently, none of these transfers shows up in any public budget.

The pace of condemnation waxes and wanes, but it has been an important part of state power since the earliest days of the American republic. We love it when government assembles someone else's too fragmented land, especially when redevelopment spurs economic growth, creates jobs, and boosts tax revenue for our benefit. But we get furious when people we care about are expropriated for dubious redevelopment projects. Until we come up with a better solution, eminent domain is the best answer cities have to the costly problem of block parties.

Susette Kelo's Home

Maybe courts can police against eminent domain abuses. I doubt it. Consider Susette Kelo's story:

> In 1997, I searched all over for a house and finally found this perfect little Victorian cottage with beautiful views of the water. . . . I spent every spare moment fixing it up and creating the kind of home I always dreamed of. I painted it salmon pink, because that is my favorite color.

FIGURE 5.3: *Susette Kelo (left) and her home in New London, Connecticut (right).*[23]

> In 1998, a real estate agent came by and made me an offer on the
> house on behalf of an unnamed buyer. I explained to her that I was
> not interested in selling, but she said that my home would be taken by
> eminent domain if I refused to sell. . . . Her advice? Give up. The gov-
> ernment always wins.[22]

In 1998, the City of New London, Connecticut, condemned Kelo's
house and transferred it to a private developer (fig. 5.3). The Institute for
Justice, a libertarian public interest law firm, chose Kelo as a good plaintiff
for its test case on eminent domain. It filed suit on her behalf to stop the
city's development plans and managed to assemble an unlikely array of litigation allies, including the NAACP, AARP, and the Cato Institute. Such an
alliance is a testament to the muddled politics of gridlock.

Kelo v. City of New London went to the U.S. Supreme Court, which ruled
five to four against Kelo in 2005, concluding that this condemnation was
permissible.[24] Although unremarkable from a constitutional perspective,

the decision created a political storm. "We lost the Supreme Court case, but we're ultimately going to win in changing the way that eminent domain is going to be used in this country," says Dana Berliner, a senior lawyer for the institute.[25] Since the Court's ruling, there have been dozens of state legislative initiatives to curtail eminent domain for economic development.[26] Kelo's house was not demolished. Instead, New London agreed to move it to a nearby site, where it should have a plaque memorializing the institute's creative litigation (and fund-raising) strategy.

As a matter of routine constitutional law, the Supreme Court decided *Kelo* correctly even if the underlying facts may seem troubling. In every generation, a case like *Kelo* has come to the Court, and every time the Court has ruled that the Constitution allows states to decide how to use their eminent domain power. There is little room for federal or judicial supervision.[27] This is as it should be. State and local legislatures, not federal judges, are the experts in discerning the interests of local voters and promoting their general welfare. If people are unhappy with how eminent domain is being used, the right place to complain is at the legislative level.

Despite the hullabaloo raised by *Kelo,* eminent domain is little used these days compared with decades past. Think back to the heyday of highway construction in the 1950s. Large amounts of land were confiscated, but this was often justified as necessary for fighting communism. (President Eisenhower sold the interstate highway system in part as a national defense project.) Building networks such as highways and railways usually does not raise intense opposition to eminent domain as such, even if those directly affected fight to shift the route. People accept that networks are legitimate "public uses." It's hard to imagine how basic infrastructure such as highways and railways could get built without condemning land. But the 1950s, '60s, and '70s also saw less justifiable, massive "urban renewal" projects that condemned and bulldozed mostly poor, urban minority communities.

If it's not new, why has *Kelo* become a cause célèbre? By framing the issue as "eminent domain abuse," the case touched a cultural nerve. However, cutting down on eminent domain by increasing federal and judicial policing is not the answer. There must be a better way to respect the interests of the politically powerless and still assemble land.

A Solution: Land Assembly Districts

Despite what the anti-eminent domain activists would have you believe, there is far too *little* land assembly for economic development in the United States today, not too much. The enormous premium paid for assembled parcels—up to a $165 million markup for the *Times*'s land assembly—attests to the acute shortage of large buildable sites in this country. To rephrase the public policy dilemma: must we choose between voluntary contracting with its holdouts and eminent domain with its capricious destruction? No. This is a false choice. Our anticommons lexicon can help us get past the old debate.

The key to solving the puzzle is to notice that land assembly involves gridlock. Once you see that, you can begin to imagine alternative solutions that combine the best of voluntary assembly and eminent domain. Recall the hybrid solutions to "limited access" commons and anticommons dilemmas that I've shown you throughout the book. When fish were being overharvested, Australia created "tradable fishing quotas"—a new form of private property that gave fishermen reason to conserve scarce fish stocks. We also have patent pools, copyright collectives, and spectrum packing.

Even in a tradition-bound area such as land, sometimes we create new forms of property if we spot gridlock.[28] When the new forms stick, they let people overcome gridlock with minimal government intrusion. For example, fifty years ago, condos and residential associations were a novelty—they hopped from European law through Puerto Rico and across the rest of the United States, and they eventually revolutionized how we live. It was unimaginable in 1960 that condos would become the dominant form of new housing in America. Yet we went from less than 1 percent of Americans living in "common interest communities" in 1970 to almost 20 percent of the total U.S. population—more than fifty-seven million people—living that way in 2006.[29]

The meteoric rise in condo living reflects how powerfully this ownership solution unlocks hidden value. Condos permit dense, overlapping ownership in areas needing housing—with easy-to-administer tools for fixing tragedies of the commons and anticommons. Today, home buyers demand, and developers supply, condo boards or residential associations for most new housing in the United States. People want to control their neighbors even if they must suffer oversight in return.

Condos are not the only new gridlock buster for land. Have you ever wondered why some downtown blocks have extra-nice garbage cans, street benches, trees, and have their own security and maintenance staffs? Look closely at the garbage cans, and you'll see a plaque like "Provided by the Main Street Business Improvement District." Business Improvement Districts (BIDs) are a new property form that bounced from Canada to New Orleans in the 1970s. They were adopted by New York in the 1980s. Now, more than a thousand BIDs exist nationwide.[30]

In a sense, BIDs are like condos retrofitted onto a commercial area to create amenities beyond those publicly provided. After a majority of adjoining business owners vote to create a BID, it becomes mandatory for all owners in the district. No free riders here; everyone has to chip in to pay for the amenities. The BID collects and spends money to create a nicer shopping experience. Before BIDs, cities underprovided local public goods, but the loss was hard to see: a steady trickle of consumers deserting the area for suburban malls that had ample parking and a safe, clean environment. BIDs gave merchants a tool to solve invisible gridlock in provision of urban shopping amenities. Old downtowns can now compete with new shopping malls.

Can a similar strategy of property-form creation help us solve gridlock in land assembly? Yes. The best reading of *Kelo* is that the Supreme Court is telling states that land assembly is their problem, and they should experiment with solutions. Here is one experiment that states could venture.

In a recent *Harvard Law Review* article, my colleague Rick Hills and I proposed creation of Land Assembly Districts (LADs) that could be retrofitted onto existing neighborhoods.[31] The key to LADs is that they fix gridlock by giving neighbors a say in whether their land is assembled for economic development. Governments could authorize LADs just as they passed laws enabling condominiums and BIDs to spring up. LADs would then be available to neighbors who want a quick and easy tool for joining together, negotiating for a share of land-assembly profits, and selling their community. If LADs were handy, neighbors in "blighted" areas could decide for themselves whether to assemble their own land, and government would have no reason to confiscate their property. By ending gridlock, LADs would make eminent domain for economic development obsolete. (Eminent domain for highways and other networks would continue, but that practice has been less controversial.)

LADs solve the problem of block parties by giving decision-making power directly to those most affected. Neighbors would have a reason to support cost-justified development instead of only nay-saying and deflecting change. In a LAD, neighbors would create a board—organized like a condo board—to negotiate a neighborhood buyout with potential developers. If neighbors value staying put more than they value the assembly premium, they would vote against the proposed deal, and development would go elsewhere. But if the requisite majority accepts the proposed deal, then all are governed by it. Everyone would get a pro rata share of the assembly surplus. With LADs, most people would be better off, particularly those in poor and minority communities. No one whose land is assembled would be worse off than under the current system: dissenters could opt for ordinary condemnation (bulldozing them today and paying fair market value later on).

The details of LADs are messy, as is any new legal form in the moment of its creation, but they are designed to prevent rip-offs by insiders, developers, or the city; to ensure fair treatment of every neighbor in the LAD; and to respect local political variation. Many details of LAD design are lifted from solutions to gridlock found elsewhere. For example, LADs borrow from a complex legal tool called "land adjustment" that partly solves the problem of land assembly in Germany, Taiwan, Japan, Korea, and other countries.[32] We also take elements from corporate-takeover law, bankruptcy law, and class-action litigation—all legal tools that people have created to overcome other forms of gridlock. LADs are not one-size-fits-all but can be tailored to the needs of the cities that adopt them. For example, cities with large numbers of poor renters may want to give them extra protection in their LAD statutes—perhaps a vote on the proposed deal and a share in the assembly surplus.

Let's give neighbors the legal tools they need so they can decide what's best for themselves and for their communities. In time, LADs could become just another ordinary property form, like condos or BIDs, with many of the same features and limitations. Missing law can be fixed inexpensively—but only if you know what to look for. With block parties, half the battle is spotting the gridlock dilemma. The other half is having the confidence to try experiments on the anticommons side of the property spectrum. Condo law was missing before 1960, BID law before 1980; perhaps we will see LAD law that solves yet another tragedy of the anticommons.

SHARE CHOPPERS

Share choppers are a second costly type of gridlocked land.[33] We risk creating a share chopper dilemma whenever we give landowners strong reasons to divide land down to the big-inch level and provide no countervailing mechanism to bundle the pieces back into productive use. There are share choppers in every corner of the world where I've worked—rural Bangladeshi villages, burned-out Jamaican slums, struggling Venezuelan shantytowns, and postearthquake zones in Armenia. They are a global phenomenon.

The End of Black Farm Ownership

As a law professor, I often hear insightful stories from students who link their personal experiences with pressing legal debates. A few years ago, when I was teaching the law of partition of co-owned land—a dry subject—one of my African American students told the class the tale of her family's farm. As a child, she had attended wonderful reunions that brought together relatives from all over the United States. They would return to an old farmstead in Mississippi presided over by an elderly aunt who had never left the land. At one point, a distant cousin with a fractional ownership share in the farm wanted cash, so he sold his share. The buyer then forced a sale of the whole farm. The family farm was sold on the county courthouse steps to a local white lawyer. Since the sale, my student's family has not held another reunion.

This story brought co-ownership law to life for me. Several other black students later recounted similar experiences of southern farms that had been in their families for generations and were lost to "partition sales." These stories were one of my earliest encounters with the social costs of gridlock. Investigating further, I found that black farmland ownership in the United States has suffered from big-inch tragedy.[34]

Following the Civil War, black Americans began acquiring land in earnest. By 1920, almost 1 million black families owned farms; they formed an integral part of the southern rural economy up through the 1930s and 1940s. But today, black families own fewer than 19,000 farms nationwide—a drop of 98 percent in less than a century. (By contrast, white-operated farms dropped by about 50 percent, from about 5.5 million to 2.4 million.) Partial explanations include consolidation of inefficient small farms and intense racial discrimination in farm lending. But there is more to the tale: an extra cost imposed by gridlock.[35]

John Brown's Farm

Here is one family's story.[36] In 1887, John Brown bought eighty acres of land in Rankin County, Mississippi. He was part of the great wave of freed slaves who invested their life savings in farmland. John lived a long life, and when he died in 1935, he did not leave a will. So ownership of his land split among his wife and children. In time they all also died without wills, so the land passed to their children and grandchildren. One of these children, Willie Brown, began consolidating ownership in the land by buying the interests of five of John's nine children: Frances, Minnie, Adda, Joe, and Lizzie. By the time Willie passed away, he had accumulated a 41/72 share in the family farm, which he left to his wife, Ruth.

In 1978, Ruth asked a court to divide the farm so that she would own her share of the land outright. The other sixty-six Brown heirs would then own the balance, in shares ranging from 1/18 of the farm down to 1/19,440. The court refused to partition the parcel by drawing a line on the land; it was too complicated. Instead, the judge ordered the land sold and the money divided among the heirs. As often happens in such forced sales, a single outside company was the only bidder. In this case it was a local white-owned lumber company that wanted to cut the timber.

Even though the family collectively valued the farm far above its auction price, no Brown heir placed a bid. Why? Partly because U.S. law often requires cash paid in full at such auction sales, a rule that makes bidding impossible for most ordinary owners. No single Brown heir could top the lumber company's lowball bid. There was no simple mechanism through which the heirs could quickly organize a joint family bid—a missing legal tool that commonly affects scattered heir owners. Ruth got a little cash from the sale—not nearly enough to replace the farm and nothing like enough to compensate her family for losing the locus of its cohesion and tradition. Sound familiar? We saw the loss of "subjective value" in the eminent domain context, but here Ruth likely did not even get fair market value (forced sales generally yield amounts below what is considered ordinary fair market value).

The Brown family story tracks the arc of black farmland ownership in America. When John Brown bought his farm, black families were rapidly accumulating land. By the time Ruth Brown lost it a century later, black landownership in the United States was in rapid decline. The decline has continued since the 1970s. The 19,000 black farmers in America today constitute less than 1 percent of American farmers, and black Americans continue to abandon farms at a rate three times that of white Americans.

This is an example of a gridlock economy—here caused by the intersection of American land law and cultural practices surrounding the making of wills. Many poor black farmers had good reason to be suspicious of local lawyers and so died without wills. With each generation, the farm split among multiple heirs. Over a quarter of black-owned land in the Southeast is now "heir property" averaging eight co-owners, five of whom live outside the region. According to the *Washington Post,* "More Mississippi land was owned by blacks in Chicago than by blacks in Mississippi."[37] One report concludes that partition sales (like the one that transferred Ruth Brown's land) are "unquestionably the judicial method by which most heir property is lost."[38]

How do heir property and partition law interact to dispossess black families? When John Brown died without a will, each of his children received a 1/9 share in the eighty acres. Often the first generation can get along and manage their parents' property. But in the next generation and the generation after that, people move away and family members have ever weaker ties to each other and to the land, creating practical problems that become irresolvable. Under the American law of co-ownership, land often cannot be managed unless fractional owners unanimously consent. One report notes that "heir property is rarely improved or developed due to the threat of partition sales and the difficulty of obtaining credit on partial interests in the property. In fact, a third more heir than non-heir property is not being used at all." The report adds that "the sale of the land, usually precipitated by an heir who is more than one generation removed from the originating source, becomes inevitable."[39]

If any heir wants out, the law gives two options: a court can partition the land by drawing lines on the ground proportional to the share ownership, or it can order the entire land sold and then partition the proceeds among the co-owners. Although the law is often written to prefer physically dividing the land, that route is hard to implement. It's expensive to hire land surveyors and appraisers. The resulting lots are often too small to be economically useful. So in practice, courts usually order the land sold, especially if there are many heirs.

Often, with African American–owned farms, a non-family member will track down distant heirs and buy one fractional share for a small amount. Under American law, any fractional share owner can force partition at any time. One scholar says that because heir property is so common among rural blacks, "the black community is particularly vulnerable to the unscrupulous partition sale brought about by someone buying out the interest of a single heir and then demanding that the land be sold."[40] Partition sales often take place in rigged markets with little information and few buyers. According to one analyst, the purchasers at these sales "are almost always white persons, frequently local lawyers or relatives of local officials, who make it their business to keep abreast of what properties are going to auction and who attend the auctions prepared to buy."[41]

The costs to black families are high. They get little money for their generations of stewardship of the family farm. The sale often breaks the intangible web of connections within the family. With the farm intact, an older family member might let some children settle on the land, and, later, the children might care for the elders. Landless elders, less able to mobilize this support, are more likely to suffer lower living standards.[42] The hidden tragedy for the Browns was not only the lowball price but also the loss of the special value of their particular farm. Lost family cohesion is just as real a social cost as the missing Compound X or slow wireless broadband.

Recently, some solutions have been tried in a few places. One approach has been to shame outside buyers, not unlike our Maine lobster gangs that use cooperative norms to exclude newcomers from coastal fisheries. For example, media mogul Ted Turner got into a conflict with a group of black heirs over some South Carolina property. When the heirs took the dispute to the press, Turner agreed to give them the land after they agreed that he was indeed the legal owner. In some counties, local officials have gone to the land auctions and encouraged bidders to give black family owners a chance to bid first. Shaming, however, works in only a limited number of cases. Another approach has been to tweak the law. For example, South Carolina has given farm family members "rights of first refusal." When "heritage land" is auctioned for a low price, family members have forty-five days to raise matching funds to buy the land themselves.[43]

These solutions may slow the losses a bit, but black farmers have little left to lose. Also, none of the solutions address the core management problem for heir property. Some public-interest law groups have pioneered a more enduring solution that leverages an existing ownership form: the "limited liability company."[44] Creating a family corporation requires agreement from scattered owners and imposes up-front costs, but it makes the land manageable by the farm's new CEO—perhaps the elderly aunt who still lives on the land. For most black families, however, all these solutions are too little and too late.

Native American Allotment Land

The decline in black landownership is not an isolated example. Native Americans suffer gridlock in land as well. Everyone is familiar with stories of broken treaties, forced migration, and the creation of special reservations. Few are aware how American property law has created a tragedy of the anticommons on some of the remaining Native American landholdings. In the late 1800s, the federal government broke up many reservations by "allotting" land to Indian families. Federal Indian law prevented allotment lands from ever being sold. Over time, down through the generations, allotment ownership within a family has splintered and multiplied.

Like "heir property," "fractionated lands" are often wasted.[45] Because of this ownership structure, much Indian-owned land sits idle today, impossible to farm, mortgage, sell, or use in any productive way. When you read

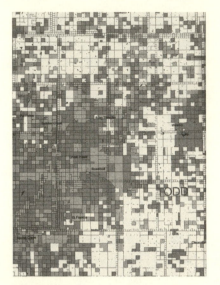

FIGURE 5.4: *Checkerboarding on the Rosebud Reservation in South Dakota. (Shaded areas are tribal trust land, blank areas are private land owned mostly by non-Indians.)*[46]

newspaper stories about judges holding Bureau of Indian Affairs bureaucrats in contempt of court, the underlying issue is often the bureau's disastrous accounting for the tangled web of Indian landownership. Allotment land does not inculcate market-based virtues. Nor does it help maintain the special relationship between Native Americans and their sovereign territory. Families feel disconnected from land that they cannot productively manage or control. Everyone loses, especially Native American allotment owners, who are locked into a dispiriting and pointless gridlock economy.

Just as fractionation causes gridlock for individual Native American families, "checkerboarding" causes gridlock for tribal self-governance (fig. 5.4). When reservations were allotted, land was distributed without concern for its effect on Native sovereignty. Now, many reservations contain a jumble of collectively owned trust land, individual allotment land, and privately owned non-Indian land.[47] These checkerboarded lands cannot be easily brought back into collective tribal ownership. Moreover, because of recent Supreme Court decisions, the checkerboarding can split tribal sovereignty, which doesn't reach in many cases to land owned by nonmembers. According to the Indian Land Tenure Foundation,

> Checkerboarding seriously impairs the ability of tribes or individual Indians to use land to their own advantage for farming, ranching, or other economic activities that require large, contiguous sections of land. It also hampers access to lands that the tribe owns and uses in traditional ways.
>
> Serious questions of jurisdiction also occur on checkerboard reservations as different governing authorities—such as county, state, federal, and tribal governments—claim the authority to regulate, tax, or

perform various activities within reservation borders based on whether a piece of land is Indian or non-Indian owned or whether it is fee-simple, in individual trust or tribal trust. Often these different claims to authority conflict, which sometimes creates economic uncertainty, racial tension, and community clashes within or near the reservation.[48]

The Path to Fractionation and Checkerboarding

How did Native Americans get stuck in this dismal land regime?[49] In the 1880s, Congress decided to break apart many Native American reservations. Legislators believed that individual farm ownership would speed the tribes' assimilation. Native heads of households were "allotted" 320 acres; individuals received 160 acres of tribal lands. Not coincidentally, allotment left large tracts of "surplus" reservation land that could be distributed to white settlers. To prevent the allotments from also ending up in the settler ownership, the United States held these lands in "trust ownership" with Native Americans as beneficiaries. The trust came with many restrictions on transfer. The parcels could not be sold or subdivided. Because no property taxes were owed, the land could not be forfeited back to the tribe.

At first, ownership of the lands could not be transferred at all, even through a will. Instead, when an owner died, the land was split among heirs. Children shared equally. If the owner had no living children, the property was split among grandchildren, parents, and other relatives. After one generation a parcel might have five owners, after two maybe twelve owners, after three, twenty-five owners. Even after transfers by will were allowed, most Native landowners did not make wills, so their shares continued to split among heirs. Try to imagine managing land with hundreds or even thousands of fractional heir owners. It's like building fences with toothpicks on acres of big-inch property.

As early as 1928, Congress realized that the allotment program was a disaster for Native Americans. One congressman, in a speech on the House floor, said that "good, potentially productive, land was allowed to lie fallow, amidst great poverty because of the difficulties of managing property held in this manner."[50] During a reform attempt in 1934, another member of Congress said, "The administrative costs become incredible. . . . On allotted reservations, numerous cases exist where the shares of each individual heir

from lease money may be 1 cent a month. . . . The Indians and Indian Service personnel are thus trapped in a meaningless system of minute partition in which all thought of possible use of land to satisfy human needs is
lost in a mathematical haze of bookkeeping."[51]

Amazingly, the fractionation problem still has not been solved. Since the
1930s, new lands have not been added to the system, but the millions of
acres already allotted have continued to fractionate. Congress made another attempt to fix the system in the 1980s by having tiny fractional shares
revert to the tribe when an owner died. Sadly, the Supreme Court struck
down this sensible reform.[52] The Court understood that fractionation had
become "extreme" and "extraordinary," noting that

> Tract 1305 [of the Sisseton-Wahpeton Lake Traverse Reservation in
> North and South Dakotas] is 40 acres and produces $1,080 in income
> annually. It is valued at $8,000. It has 439 owners, one-third of whom
> receive less than $.05 in annual rent and two-thirds of whom receive
> less than $1. . . . The common denominator used to compute frac-
> tional interests in property is 3,394,923,849,000. The smallest heir re-
> ceives $.01 every 177 years. If the tract were sold (assuming the 439
> owners could agree) for its estimated $8,000 value, he would be enti-
> tled to $.000418. The administrative costs of handling this tract are es-
> timated by the Bureau of Indian Affairs at $17,560 annually.[53]

Nevertheless, the Court rejected Congress's small-scale fix. The justices
made a mistake.[54] They missed the gridlock dilemma underlying allotment
land. Instead of assembling ownership to unlock value, they further entrenched the "meaningless system of minute partition." A significant portion of the Bureau of Indian Affairs budget is now consumed in tracking
fractional shares rather than supporting Native American education, em-
ployment, or infrastructure.

Even with the fractionation problem, the federal government has managed over the years to collect significant oil, mineral, and other royalty payments on allotted tribal lands. Paying out those funds to tribal owners is
another matter. Since 1996, five hundred thousand Indian allotment holders
have been pursuing a class-action lawsuit, *Cobell v. Kempthorne,* against the

Bureau of Indian Affairs and the Department of the Interior.[55] The suit aims to force the federal government to account for more than ten billion dollars in missing lease payments that the government, acting as allotment trust fiduciary, collected and never turned over to the trust's shareholders. "Trust fiduciaries," like the federal government in this case, have the highest duties of good faith and prudent management known to the American legal system. The case offers such a remarkable saga of federal government corruption, mismanagement, document destruction, retaliation, and perjury that a federal judge held Bruce Babbitt and Robert Rubin, then secretaries of the interior and treasury, in contempt of court for their departments' actions. At one point, the court described the government's conduct as "fiscal and governmental irresponsibility in its purest form."[56]

The saga continues. After a recent court ruling in the case, a *New York Times* editorial lamented that "the case of the mismanaged American Indian trust funds is Dickensian both in length—now 11 years before the courts—and inequity."[57]

The allotment tragedy represents not only a legal embarrassment but a failure of political will as well. Every so often, Congress tries to fix the problem, mostly to relieve the Bureau of Indian Affairs of the pointless and costly project of tracking allotment shares. Perhaps there is also some sense of the historic wrong that has been committed against Native American peoples. The latest tentative and partial legislative effort is embodied in the American Indian Probate Reform Act of 2004. But after a century of fractionation and checkerboarding disasters, millions of acres of Native land are still tied up. Weeds grow instead of crops. Native allotment owners can experience their land only as a frustrating liability, not as a source of livelihood and connection.

The Irish Potato Famine

Share choppers are not just an American phenomenon. They can arise anywhere people own and pass on land, which means everywhere. The Irish potato famine was partly the result of a tragedy of the anticommons.[58]

In feudal Britain, the eldest son inherited the family farm. Younger sons went to cities, joined the army, or entered the clergy; daughters were married off. Although this practice had high social costs, there were also benefits: British farms were kept together as they passed down the generations. With larger tracts, British farmers could safely diversify their crops and experiment with new ones.

The British applied a different law in Ireland. Small farms were physically subdivided among all male heirs. Average farm size thus shrank from generation to generation. By the early nineteenth century, many Irish farms were so small that they could barely support a family, and then only if they grew potatoes, the crop that provided the maximum nutritional payoff per acre. With just one viable crop, Irish farmers were particularly vulnerable to environmental shocks and disease.

When blight wiped out the potato crop in the late 1840s, many Irish had no alternatives, no safety net, and little help from the British. No mechanism existed through which poor Irish could have assembled farms back to safer scales that would have allowed more crop diversification. Had Irish property law been better designed, the nation might have avoided much of the suffering and dislocation brought on by the potato famine. As it was, up to a million people starved to death, and another million or two emigrated to America to avoid the same fate.

Rational Individuals and Group Tragedy

Though the precise legal mechanisms differ, the African American, Native American, and Irish cases all share a tragedy of the anticommons thread. The law encouraged farmers to fragment their resources down to the big-inch level and offered them no tool with which to aggregate land back to a usable scale. For all these groups, a gridlock economy imposed a brutal cost on the most vulnerable families and communities.

Notice that the individual black landowners, Native American allotment owners, and Irish farmers in each generation acted rationally, even as their increasing numbers made joint management impossible. The rational quality of their decisions parallels that of each baron on the Rhine, who built his castle and set up his tollbooth without any intent to harm overall European trade. We see corollaries today: each biotech start-up patents its discoveries heedless of the impenetrable patent thickets that may result. Every music label asserts its copyrights without thinking of the DVDs, mash-ups, remixes, or whatever else it might be blocking.

Whether you resonate more with the big-inch or the phantom-tollbooth image, the unifying theme is this: as owners multiply, there comes a point where rational individual choices add up to a collective tragedy of the anti-commons. If gridlock were a board game, it would be one in which you throw the dice, and whatever number turns up, everybody loses.

We need to change the rules. Share chopper gridlock requires policymakers to tweak legal and financial systems. These tweaks are not so complicated. For example, Germany has long faced the problem of fragmenting ownership and farm breakups as heirs move away. Given the desire of some family members to protect their ancestral farms, a regional German government created legal models and financial tools that allow one family member to get a mortgage, buy out the others at market prices, and stay on the farm. Share chopper gridlock can be solved. But it takes a proactive approach.

BANANA Republics

BANANA is my favorite bit of real estate lingo. It stands for "build absolutely nothing anywhere near anyone." *BANANA republics*, as I define the term, refer to settings with so many overlapping regulatory restrictions that new development seems impossible.

Although they are bad for society as a whole, BANANA republics, like most forms of gridlock, offer profit opportunities for savvy investors—in this case, regulatory arbitrageurs. As the *New York Times* noted a few years ago, "Some of the largest publicly held real estate investment companies say they would rather own property in Boston than in Atlanta and Dallas. Steven Roth, the chief executive of Vornado Realty Trust, says there is an easy way to explain this seeming paradox. It is difficult to build in Boston where land is scarce, residents are vocal, and zoning disputes can last years. The opposite is true in Atlanta and Dallas. 'Whenever it's almost impossible to add supply,' Mr. Roth said, 'that's where I want to invest.'"[59] The location of Vornado Realty Trust investments can guide us to America's worst examples of gridlock economies.

To understand BANANA republics, start with another real estate term, *NIMBYism*, perhaps the most primal of landowner instincts. *NIMBY* means "not in my backyard." Everyone wants the city to build homeless shelters, just not near them. Everyone agrees we need affordable housing. Yes, build it, but not on my block. Home owners don't want anything nearby that might lower the value of their homes—like affordable apartments, churches, halfway houses, or city dumps. If every home owner is able to get his or her particular NIMBY concern written into law, collectively we create a BANANA republic. This isn't an anticommons based directly on ownership of land. It's an anticommons based on fragmenting who directs the regulatory process and on how approvals proceed.

In American suburbs, home owners are the voting majority; in cities, renters may be the crucial pressure bloc.[60] Local officials, wanting to keep voters happy, create more and more mechanisms to restrict development: environmental impact reviews, architectural review boards, subdivision regulations, historic preservation districts, landmark commissions, building permit requirements, rent controls—all part of the multilayered gauntlet of American land-use controls. Think of each of these mechanisms as a phantom tollbooth along the path to real estate development. Each tollbooth may have made sense on its own terms when initially enacted. Collectively, however, regulatory layering adds up to gridlock with mind-boggling costs for society. Legal theorist Richard Epstein says of this gridlock:

> [Twenty] or more agencies—the number is not fanciful—are given the power to veto new construction on grounds such as environmental protection, antigrowth or sewage. In principle these permits do not allow the regulator to hold out as if he were a private owner of some portion of the resource, but the ability to force zoning officials to behave in accordance with the narrow dictates of their mission statement is a trick that few landowners have been able to consistently master. The value of the property gets destroyed because of the implicit anticommons power when multiple regulators each exert hold-out power.[61]

A Natural Resource BANANA Republic

BANANA regulations can arise in any setting, not just urban development. In 1996 the Alaska legislature created a "shallow natural gas" leasing program that bypassed the existing BANANA regulations governing deep-hole drilling

"We got a great buy on the apartment, but, unfortunately, it didn't include the mineral rights."

FIGURE 5.5: *The dilemma of split ownership.*[63]

for oil and gas.[62] For a short while, drillers could secure over-the-counter leases to extract shallow natural gas without local government interference and with only a day's notice to surface owners (fig. 5.5). The gauntlet of phantom tollbooths was replaced with one booth, right at the mouth of the river, and smooth sailing from there.

The program went too far for Alaska's purportedly pro-property rights electorate (people often style themselves as "property-rights advocates" until a neighbor wants to do something they don't like). In 2004, surface landowners rebelled and pushed the legislature to repeal the natural gas program. The pendulum swung the other way. Again, BANANA regulations govern extraction: new leases are put to a lengthy competitive bid procedure; each lease requires an administrative process that results in a "best-interest finding"; pointless local regulations are no longer subject to state override; lengthy public "notice and comment" periods have been added for each stage of exploration, development, and transport; and negotiations with surface owners are now required.[64] According to the president of the board of a surface owners' advocacy group, "Rather than reform the regulatory snarl over split-estate ownership, the new [state] standards complicate it. With federal, state, borough, and several types of private owners holding rights to subsurface resources, it's nearly impossible to determine who regulates what."[65]

Welcome to the world of BANANA republics in natural resource extraction, where politicians' self-interests intersect with their lack of attention to the costs of gridlock. Development of shallow natural gas in Alaska has ground to a halt. So much for the pro-property rights frontier. So much for energy independence.

Horizontal and Vertical BANANA Republics

A horizontal BANANA republic arises when a city requires developers to march from office to office collecting approvals. According to the *New York Times* story that accompanied figure 5.6 (one of my all-time favorite news pictures),

> On many a weekday morning at, say, 5:30 or 6, a visitor to the New York City Department of Buildings will step out of an elevator into a series of empty corridors and stumble upon briefcases, standing in lines like toy soldiers, with their owners nowhere in sight. . . . The briefcase line, marking the order of who gets first shot at seeing a building examiner, is just one of many tribal customs that have evolved over the years among expediters, to aid them in their daily battle with the Buildings Department.
>
> Now, what, you may be wondering, is an expediter? They are the people who are hired by architects and building owners to get permits for construction and renovation—by figuring out which forms to fill out, which lines to stand in and what will satisfy a particular building examiner.[66]

New York is not unique. In Washington, D.C., Jerald Clark, head of a lucrative building permit expediter service, says, "We never, ever get a set of drawings that can get a permit—there's always something missing."[67] In D.C., securing a building permit for a typical construction project requires eleven different approvals. Los Angeles has similar complexity. In 1995, former LA mayor Richard Riordan noted that "our Byzantine system . . .

FIGURE 5.6: *New York permit expediters' briefcases all in a row.*[68]

needs an overhaul or we're on the brink of an engine blow-out."[69] Los Angeles did succeed in passing reforms in 2000, but things are still a mess. Virtually every Los Angeles project is subject to discretionary review by multiple city decision-making bodies. For a building permit alone, a developer still needs approvals from thirteen city departments.[70]

The second type of BANANA republic is vertical. Permits must be secured from multiple layers of government, not just multiple departments within a single level. To build, you need not just a building permit but also city zoning approvals, a state environmental review, federal Clean Water Act clearances, and on and on. These requirements can directly conflict with each other. And the costs of compliance at each level of government can be high. For example, one process in California, the oft-required "environmental impact review" (EIR), will cost a developer at least one hundred thousand dollars, but the tab often runs to more than one million dollars.[71]

An EIR takes at least six months and often years, during which time the financial calculations underlying the development may shift. EIR requirements were enacted with the noblest of environmental intentions, but in practice they often serve as weapons for delaying, and thus killing, cost-justified projects that neighbors don't want, usually for some undisclosed nonenvironmental reason. It is not socially acceptable to object to having poor people living nearby, but it is fine to campaign for open space.[72] Environmental reviews can become phantom tollbooths; the victim is affordable housing.

There are a million stories of gridlock arising from BANANA republics. To give a New York example, consider the "Battle of the Mall at Oyster Bay." In the early 1990s, a big developer announced plans for a high-end shopping center in a wealthy Long Island suburb. "What has happened," the *New York Times* noted, "is something akin to Long Island's version of the Hundred Years' War . . . fought with the state-of-the-art weaponry of suburban land-use politics. Lawyers litigate. Civic groups agitate. Governments deliberate. More than $100 million has been spent by [the developer] alone. And nothing happens." The article quoted economist Clifford Sondock as saying, "On a scale of 1 to 10, with 10 the most difficult for development, Long Island is a 9 or a 10. It's like building in Cuba."[73] He's wrong—it's easier to build in Cuba. When an autocratic government decides to build, it builds.

BANANA republics take a toll. They bankrupt or scare off competitive new developers and leave the field to megaplayers. Reduced competition further drives up prices and shifts developers toward luxury projects where they face less opposition and can more easily recoup their investments. Although the direct cost of BANANA republics is high—forcing developers to hire expediters and land-use lawyers—it is the smallest part of the damage that gridlock inflicts. BANANA republics radiate harm throughout the economy, squeezing out affordable housing, crushing entrepreneurial energy, and deterring growth.

Worldwide BANANA Republics

James Buchanan, in his article with Yoon proving the mathematical symmetry of commons and anticommons, mentions an example from a trip he took to Sardinia, Italy, in 1999: "A potential entrepreneur seeks to invest in a combined seaside/hunting-preserve resort. Action is inhibited, however, by the necessity of getting permits from several regional agencies (for example, the tourist board, a hotel-restaurant agency, and the wildlife protection agency), each of which holds effective exclusion rights to the project that might, if implemented, be productive of value."[74]

Japan is famous for BANANA republics. Its urban residents live in some of the smallest homes per capita of any rich country, in part because of the "world-class tangle of real-estate laws, a thicket that makes New York's labyrinth of rent regulation look simple by comparison." The cost of these regulations became visible to me after the 1994 Kobe earthquake. Thirty billion dollars quickly flowed into the city, highways (held in undivided state ownership) were quickly rebuilt, but much of the city lay in rubble for years because "a single angry tenant can block urban renewal. And does."[75]

Anticommons ownership characterizes urban Japan in part because of laws enacted during America's postwar occupation. Urban-planning theory is not America's proudest export. Under these laws, some land in Kobe has become divided into "thousands of parcels the size of a U.S. garage," and a building "can be based on a plot that is actually dozens of smaller parcels thrown together by developers." More than three hundred renters, lessees, landowners, and subletters might own overlapping claims on a single block; each one had to agree before rebuilding could go forward. According to a city official, "It's like trying to get thousands of little corporate presidents to agree on one plan."[76] Rebuilding to pre-earthquake sizes was often illegal in any case because of additional BANANA republic regulations. One study of 107 condominium complexes that had suffered severe damage revealed that only 28 could be rebuilt in compliance with current regulations.[77]

After big inches and BANANA republics are created, it is difficult to find a way out. According to one reporter, "The city could conceivably evict any tenant or landlord and buy the land under laws of eminent domain. But Japanese authorities frequently decline to seize property because of the nation's preference for harmony and consensus." Instead, two years after the Kobe earthquake, 7 out of 10 buildings were still damaged or in rubble; rebuilding plans were set but blocked by owners. The effects spread beyond housing costs: "The whole system is a drag on the economy and can even pose trade barriers. Japan's bad loan crisis will take years to mop up, in part because squatters and deadbeat debtors have such strong rights to stay put. Tokyo's Narita Airport is still unfinished 18 years after opening, because farmers refuse to give up land on what would become a second runway."[78]

The Hidden Cost of BANANA Republics

In a recent *New York Times Magazine* story, Jon Gertner writes about Harvard economist Edward Glaeser's work on urban U.S. BANANA republics. Glaeser has shown what urban economists have always known: that scarcity of land never really explains the high cost of housing. Even cities like New York, Boston, and San Francisco have plenty of well-serviced, low-density land that is hardly built up. In New York, for example, Glaeser found that the average height of new buildings has steadily *decreased* over the past thirty years, though demand has been going up, and higher densities would be good from an environmental point of view. Gertner recounts how Glaeser and a coauthor "took a close look at Manhattan and estimated that one half or more of the value of condominiums in the borough could be thought of as arising from some type of regulatory constraint preventing the construction of new housing." According to Glaeser, "I'm not in any sense trying to suggest that we want a developer's paradise where you can build anything, anywhere. . . . But I sure as heck think the current situation happened by happenstance, happened by changing the legal norms, which in no sense is guaranteed to yield a socially desirable outcome."[79]

The sum of Glaeser's "happenstance" can take many forms, not just the horizontal and vertical types of gridlock introduced above. Cities vary in how they allow land-use and building-permit processes to accumulate over time. After every public outcry, cities pass some new restrictions. Environmental impact statements are expanded. So what if they cause delays without much improving the environment? We add lead-paint abatement requirements even though other cheaper programs would do more to improve kids' health. We mandate child guards on windows because you don't want kids pitching headfirst from apartments. We expand handicapped access rules because every bathroom should be equally accessible. These are all goods. And so is the statin drug Lipitor—it helps reduce cholesterol and save lives. But as we saw in Chapter 2, you wouldn't mandate that everyone in America take statins. That would be overuse. Instead, you'd look for the optimum level of use, just like we should be looking for the optimum level of health, safety, and other forms of regulation.

Few of these requirements are truly unreasonable. In isolation, even the most draconian land-use control rarely amounts to an illegal "taking" of private property. So there is little that courts can effectively do to police these regulations. Local regulators may start with good intentions, but a gauntlet of good intentions kills off all but the most politically connected developers. Legislators get trapped in a downward spiral of counterproductive programs such as rent control or "inclusionary zoning" (rules that force developers, at great cost, to build "affordable housing" in cities that are expensive only because of bad regulation). Constituencies grow up around each control scheme, and bureaucracies fight to justify their continued existence. Why simplify? The answer is that pervasive corruption, expediters, and pirate construction are real drags on the economy. Many developers just give up.

The BANANA republic dynamic is like the frog reflex (don't try this at home). Put a frog in a pot of boiling water, and it tries to jump right out. Put it in a pot of cool water and slowly turn up the heat, and the frog doesn't jump even as it boils to death.

Fixing BANANA Republics

Preventing BANANA regulations may be impossible. To do so, voters and the media would have to monitor regulators with extraordinary vigilance. On the other hand, sometimes curing BANANA republics is cheap. We don't need to abandon any particular area of environmental or health regulation. Instead, we should just coordinate approval processes better and check to see if the benefits of new regulation outweigh the hidden costs of gridlock.

For example, a city can mandate "one-stop shops" for permits. Developers can use one contact point within the city bureaucracy to get quick responses from all the relevant departments. Another approach is the "deemed-approved remedy" for developers. If regulators fail to object within a set time, the developer's proposal is automatically approved. This approach makes regulators, and ultimately legislators and voters, bear some of the cost of uncoordinated regulatory hurdles. A third approach is "antisnob zoning acts" used in several New England states to streamline approvals for proposed affordable housing developments.[80]

The difficulty with these cures is that politicians first must be able to identify gridlock and, second, must want to end tragedies of the anticommons they currently tolerate, even quietly embrace. Gridlock creates patronage jobs to hand out and spurs campaign contributions to flow in. It's always easier to respond to a crisis by adding regulations than by paring them away. Even the post–9/11 rebuilding of the World Trade Center site in downtown Manhattan has been slowed by gridlock. New York State, the city, Port Authority, leaseholders, insurance companies, and other players each protects its own interest, but collectively, they delay the planned reconstruction.

I discussed regulatory streamlining with Richard Riordan back when he was mayor of Los Angeles. He told me that fixing BANANA republics was a "NIMTOO." A NIMTOO, he explained, "is a worthy legislative reform, but 'not in my term of office.'"[81] To his credit, Riordan did improve matters in Los Angeles, but building there remains a challenge.

Even if city-level reforms fall short, all is not lost. State legislatures can step in and roll back BANANA regulations by amending the local government's zoning authority. But NIMTOO incentives often apply at the state level as well. States add their own inconsistent layers of well-intentioned regulation.

No one should be surprised when politicians force private owners to waste scarce resources. Bad decisions do not bankrupt regulators; good ones do not make them rich. Eventually, though, markets punish cities (and countries) that allow themselves to become BANANA republics.

Block parties, share choppers, and BANANA republics can all be avoided. The first step is to notice the problem; the second is to be creative and persistent about solutions. There is nothing magical here. But it takes individual initiative and political guts.

six

EMPTY MOSCOW STOREFRONTS

*The news of Berlioz's death spread through the build-
ing with supernatural speed and from seven o'clock on
Thursday morning, Bosoi started to get telephone calls.
After that people began calling in person with written
pleas of their urgent need of vacant housing space.
Within the space of two hours Nikanor Ivanovich had
collected thirty-two such statements. They contained
entreaties, threats, intrigue, denunciations, promises to
redecorate the flat, remarks about overcrowding and
the impossibility of sharing a flat with bandits. Among
them was a description, shattering in its literary
power, of the theft of some meat-balls from someone's
jacket pocket in flat No. 31, two threats of suicide and
one confession of secret pregnancy.*

—MIKHAIL BULGAKOV, *The Master and Margarita*

Nowhere has gridlock been more costly than in countries that banished markets. The Soviet Union had a rich endowment of natural resources and human abilities, but an inside-out economy. In

late 1991, as the USSR was crumbling, I traveled to Moscow as part of a World Bank team. Boris Yeltsin's new government wanted to know what it would take to create a market economy in a country with no living memory of capitalism.

I was impressed at how socialism got things backward. In the Moscow winter, my friends left their windows open so apartments wouldn't overheat.[1] Why? Energy was not priced, so there were no thermostats. Everyone commuted long distances to work. Why? Land and transport were not priced, so Moscow had cottages close to the city center and towering apartment buildings in the distant suburbs.[2] Millions were stuck in obsolete housing blocks, but there was no way to redevelop close-in land. These costs became visible as soon as the Russians started pricing land, energy, and other resources at the world market value. Transition was wrenching.

Even so, Russia's housing privatization was a relative success. In the early 1990s, more than one hundred million people suddenly became home owners, able to buy, sell, rent and, most important, move. At the start of the transition, one of my Russian colleagues, a leading Soviet economist, still lived with her ex-husband, a violent KGB officer, and their son in a four hundred–square-foot apartment.[3] Their situation was not unusual: divorced couples often lived together because they were not allowed to move and there was no place to go, except perhaps back to their parents. Following housing privatization, vibrant real estate markets appeared almost overnight, even in outer Siberia. This was before the Russians had drafted laws on condominiums, tenant protections, zoning, historic preservation, mortgage finance, property taxes, foreclosure and eviction, or any of the other elements of modern real estate ownership and management.[4]

Russia's success with housing privatization has been overshadowed by its corporate privatization fiascos.[5] In the early 1990s, control of large Soviet state-owned enterprises passed to an elite few; Russia's natural resources were taken wholesale by the "oligarchs" we heard about in the news. Commercial real estate privatization fell somewhere between housing success and enterprise debacles. That middle ground is where I first discovered the tragedy of the anticommons.[6]

DISCOVERING THE ANTICOMMONS

In 1992, Russia's deputy prime minister, Igor Gaider, asked my team to figure out why the sidewalks were full of metal kiosks selling everything, while privatized storefronts still remained empty. The contrast was striking: bustling commerce on the streets across from dimly lit, bare storefront shelves. Although there were many partial explanations, an overlooked key was Russia's new property rights system. Talking with Moscow merchants, I learned that it was easy to set up a kiosk, but a nightmare to open a store.[7] In time, for me, the image of empty but private stores crystallized into the "tragedy of the anticommons" concept—any setting in which too many owners block each other and waste a scarce resource through underuse.

In an ordinary market economy, the usual way to privatize is to transfer coherent bundles of property rights in ordinary spaces. For example, you would sell the state-owned bakery to new owner Alexa, the collective bookstore to new owner Boris, the corner grocery to new owner Catarina, and so on. That's what England did when Margaret Thatcher's government privatized public housing to the sitting tenants; it's what Italy is doing today in shedding state-owned enterprises and assets.[8]

Russia's reformist leaders, however, were in a rush because they feared imminent restoration of Soviet rule. On one visit, I saw the White House, Russia's parliament building, still smoldering after being shelled during a coup attempt.[9] Another time, one of my counterparts, the deputy minister for housing reforms, was late for our morning meeting because he had spent the night ordering ministry dump trucks to block key avenues in case tank columns pressed into Moscow. Everyone was edgy. Locking in reform quickly was the overriding goal.

With commercial real estate privatization, the government decided to give old Soviet functionaries, the apparatchiks, an immediate, personal economic stake in reform. So the reformers relabeled preexisting socialist legal interests as "private property" and then privatized each interest.[10] For the bakery, apparatchik Alexa received the socialist law "right to sell," Boris received the "right to lease," Catarina received the "right to manage," and so on. The bookstore and corner grocer were privatized in the same odd way— former socialist managers and institutions were given new, overlapping

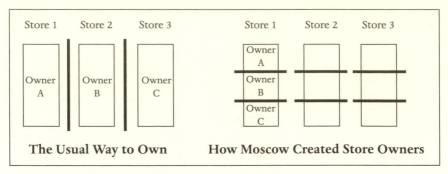

FIGURE 6.1: *Contrasting private and anticommons ownership.*[11]

"private property" rights in the same space. The new rights were fragments of private property, not standard bundles of ownership (fig. 6.1).

Alexa, Boris, and Catarina could compete with each other to get rich instead of joining together to restore socialism. But the complex privatization scheme had dire and unanticipated consequences. To feel secure investing in the bakery, aspiring merchant Dmitri would have needed to acquire all the fragments of property rights owned by Alexa, Boris, Catarina, and others. The new owners were not keen to cooperate, however, because each felt entitled to most of the rental or sales price. Thus, many stores remained empty. Leasing was slow and brutal. Some conflicts were settled by hand grenades and drive-by shootings. For Dmitri, our fledgling entrepreneur, kiosks were a safer bet.

Kiosks became icons of capitalist transition. Their disappearance was a visual index of progress from anticommons to private property. In Poland, kiosks appeared briefly in the early 1990s but receded with the quick emergence of viable private-property rights in commercial storefronts. According to my kiosk index, Poland's commercial real estate gridlock lasted less than one year. But in Russia, kiosks still dominated many sidewalks years after the collapse of Soviet communism.[12]

HUMPTY DUMPTY GRIDLOCK

Before you criticize Russia's reformers (or their World Bank advisers) too harshly, notice how closely the empty storefronts parallel the story of the missing Compound X. In both cases, well-intentioned reformers did not consider how overly exuberant privatization might inadvertently create grid-lock. The government followed a standard neoclassical economic recipe: create clear property rights, step back, and let owners trade those entitlements. In theory, the invisible hand of the market would rearrange these rights into coherent property bundles and move resources to their highest valued uses.

But bundles are not always easy to put together; initial entitlements stick, but not necessarily to each other. The Russian storefront experience taught me a fundamental lesson about ownership: the *content* of property rights can matter as much as the *clarity* of ownership.

Empty Moscow storefronts are a stark example of Humpty Dumpty gridlock. Regulators inadvertently fragment ownership into so many unco-ordinated rights that it becomes impossible to reassemble the ownership egg, even for the state. In Russia, as in the United States, once something is labeled "private property," legal protections kick in that prevent the state from taking the property without paying "just compensation." Russian law is reasonably tough in this regard. I know because the deputy minister and I sat together one night and talked through an early draft of what became Russia's equivalent to the U.S. Constitution's "takings" clause.

"Maybe they didn't try hard enough."

FIGURE 6.2: *The assembly dilemma.*[13]

Notice how the BANANA republics I discussed in Chapter 5 differ from Russia's real estate gridlock. In complex, layered regulatory systems, people accept that rights shift, up to a point. Unlocking that grid isn't so hard if there's political will. By contrast, Humpty Dumpty gridlock is more difficult to fix: condemnation costs governments cash and upsets owners (fig. 6.2). Gridlock based on ownership should be prevented up front if possible. When you see governments creating ownership from scratch, pay attention. That's where the most dangerous gridlock will likely arise.

Postsocialist reforms make useful examples because they are so stark. Russia may seem far away, but wholesale economic transition teaches powerful lessons.[14] In advanced market economies, mistakes may be less visible, but even more costly. Whenever legal systems adapt to govern some new resource, we run the risk that wealth will disappear into a tragedy of the anticommons. Don't forget that governments are creating property rights every day, right here, all along the innovation frontier. Corporate law, mergers and acquisitions, subprime mortgage regulations, bankruptcy law, Internet regulation—they can each create invisible tragedies of the anticommons.

FROM SOVIET OWNERSHIP TO STOREFRONT ANTICOMMONS

Real estate matters a lot to any economy. In market economies, the value of commercial real estate may exceed that of industrial plant and equipment. Housing is an even larger share of an economy, accounting for up to one-third of reproducible national wealth.[15] In combination, commercial and residential real estate made up a valuable asset base in Russia. But the country began the transition to a market economy with indistinct property-rights boundaries and overlapping ownership. To understand what happened, you need the briefest background in Soviet law. Here, in a nutshell, are the four key elements.[16]

1. *No Real Estate.* First, the Soviets rejected the concept of "real estate," the idea that land and a building can be owned together as a distinct economic asset.[17] A core tenet of Soviet socialism was that the state owned all the land

indivisibly and without boundaries. Second, all productive assets in principle belonged to "the people as a whole," so there was no reason to be precise about the line dividing two parcels. The Soviets rejected land registries and other tools that would legally distinguish one plot from another. The state also owned all buildings but for administrative reasons tracked them through a system unrelated to the land. They handed out opaque "use rights" in buildings to state organizations. In short, property boundaries were strange. In the early 1990s, I was struck when residents and public officials could not begin to answer, "Who decides how the land on which we stand will be used?"

2. *Expediency and Hierarchy.* In addition to unclear boundaries, "state property" was governed by principles of expediency and hierarchy. Conflicts between owners were resolved to maximize socialist political goals rather than through market transactions or through appeal to abstract legal principles. Judges sometimes decided cases according to "telephone law": party officials called them up and told them how to rule. In addition, socialist law was more concerned with the identity of the owner than with the type of property or scope of rights. Property owned by the state received more protection than cooperative property; in a conflict between the two, state interests would likely prevail. Personal property held by individuals received the least regard of all.

3. *Breakdown.* To create tradable private property, Russian reformers first had to break down the socialist legal regime. This task generally involved eliminating the hierarchy of property owners, making property legally divisible and tradable, and putting private ownership on an equal footing with state ownership. Transition reformers also began to redefine owners and objects in terms analogous to those in market economies. In short, they needed to rebundle land and buildings as discrete units of "real estate." The Russian legal system had no up-to-date language for basic terms such as *real estate, mortgage,* or *foreclosure.* As a first step, my ministry counterparts had to decide on new property words and write their legal definitions into state decrees.[18] As we've seen, creating the right lexicon can be the first step to resolving ownership conflicts.

4. The Inverse Gradient of Protection and Performance. While in Russia, I noticed an odd pattern. The higher a resource was in the socialist legal hierarchy, the more likely that, during the transition, it would become stuck in
gridlock.[19] Conversely, resources that began the transition with the least socialist legal protection were most easily transferred into well-functioning
private property. Thus, storefronts (highly protected within the socialist legal order) were slower to emerge than were kiosks (which were disfa-
vored). Markets in communal apartments (medium protection) emerged
more painfully than did markets in single-family apartments (low protection). And state-owned enterprises, which began the transition with the
most fragmented ownership and highest socialist legal protection of all,
had the roughest time making the leap to a market economy (fig. 6.3).

In the early stages of privatization, control over real estate passed from
the central government to local and regional government agencies, enterprises, and individuals. Four categories of competing rights holders
emerged: "owners," "users," "balance-sheet holders," and "regulators."[21]
"Owners" began the transition with weaker rights than those that owners
enjoy in market economies. For example, Russia's federal government re-
tained rights to specify the sale or lease process and to define the range of
possible prices. "Users" were often the workers' collectives of the defunct
state enterprise previously assigned to the space. Their rights, like those of
owners, were ambiguous, grounded in strong occupancy expectations from
seventy years of socialist law and practice. No one knew if workers would
become like ordinary tenants and, if so, on what terms. "Balance-sheet holders" were based in an archaic Soviet form of property ownership analogous

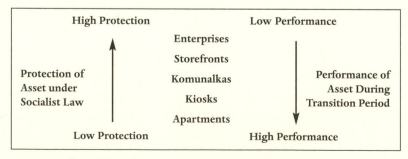

FIGURE 6.3: *The gradient of property in transition.*[20]

to a "trust" relationship in the West. Conversion of balance-sheet rights into marketable property rights was uneven. Stronger balance-sheet holders could emerge as co-lessors, weaker ones as something less. Finally, there was a large range of new "regulators" able to block sale or transfer.

None of these rights holders had sole authority to open a store, but each could block the others from doing so. Figure 6.4 (see next page) shows a typical blend of state enterprises, research institutes, maintenance organizations, and local, regional, and federal governmental bodies that might have had interests in a given storefront and the ability to exclude others' use. This figure suggests further complexities. First, multiple parties might have shared rights. They had to agree among themselves how to exercise their interest, such as the "right to lease." Second, government agencies were distinguished from the actual bureaucrats who controlled the property. Because the difference between official rents and market rents was significant, lease rights could be a source of revenue for local officials in their private capacities. Put more colloquially, officials might take bribes to make leases at below-market rents.

Almost any use of a storefront required agreement from multiple parties. Any party that opposed the use could block others from exercising their rights. The Moscow storefront thus met, and indeed gave rise to, my definition of anticommons property. The tragedy of the storefront anticommons was that the potential value of the property was lost when owners failed to agree. Empty stores resulted in lost jobs and forgone economic opportunity. Through the first years of transition, about 95 percent of commercial real estate in Russia remained in some form of divided local ownership; much of it went unused.

FROM ANTICOMMONS TO PRIVATE MOSCOW STOREFRONTS

Moving a storefront from anticommons waste to well-functioning private ownership required unifying fragmented rights. In other words, creating private property meant moving from too many owners, each able to exclude others, to a sole decision maker controlling a conventional bundle of rights, including rights to sell or lease the property, receive the revenue

Property Right	"Owner"
Right to sell	Local administration Property committee Committee for Architecture and Historical Preservation Budget organization State enterprise or institute (as balance-sheet holder) Relevant council
Right to receive sale revenue	Federal government Regional administration Local administration Property committee Committee for Architecture and Historical Preservation
Right to lease	Property committee State enterprise or institute Maintenance organization
Right to receive lease revenue	Relevant administration Property committee Committee for Architecture and Historical Preservation State enterprise or institute Maintenance organization
Right to determine use	Planning committee Property committee Balance-sheet holder
Right to occupy	Workers' collective

FIGURE 6.4: *"Owners" of Moscow storefront rights, 1992.*[22]

from the sale or lease, occupy the premises, and determine how a lessee could use the property.

Market Transactions and Government Bundling

After Russia's transition government accidentally created anticommons property, how did new owners bundle the fragmented rights? There were two main routes: market transactions and government interventions.

In market transactions, entrepreneurial property bundlers could assemble control over stores by negotiating, legally or illegally, with all the holders of fragmented rights. In legal transactions, property bundlers could buy each right from its holder using formal, enforceable contracts. But with storefronts, bundlers more often employed corrupt back-channel negotiations with public officials. There was too much money to be made. This routine corruption was not cost-free. Bribery imposes its own hard-to-measure drag on economic development, particularly from forgone long-term investments.[23] Over time, store by store, individual transactions helped overcome the storefront anticommons. By the late 1990s, one no longer saw streets eerily lined with well-lit but empty stores.

Governments can also help overcome gridlock when they intervene to redefine or reallocate property rights—for instance, they may use eminent domain for land assembly, forced patent pooling for aircraft manufacturing, or compulsory licensing of music copyrights for radio play. In Russia, the federal government could have abolished fragmented storefront rights and eliminated control rights held by subordinate government agencies. Or local governments could have consolidated in a single public decision maker the rights held by competing local agencies. Neither of these reforms happened. Every department clung tenaciously to rights that were potentially its sole means of bureaucratic survival in a rapidly evolving environment.

Revoking privately held anticommons rights without compensation would have presented a big risk for Russia's government. Investors in Russia might have been even more discouraged from entering the market than they otherwise were. But paying compensation was impossible for the nearly bankrupt treasury. So the Russian government muddled through—markets emerged fitfully through contracts, bribery, violence, and regulatory tinkering. This may have been all the government could do, given the initial conditions of reform. But it has meant that ordinary Russians have suffered the violence and corruption needed to overcome the gridlock created during those first tense days of postsocialist transition.

Is Corruption the Answer?

What explains the contrast between the storefront anticommons and the vibrant kiosk market?[24] During the early years of transition, kiosk merchants were also faced with an anticommons: a property regime in which many parties could block access to street-vending locations. But early in the 1990s, merchants figured out how to acquire informal (that is, illegal) rights on the streets to set up commercial outlets. Kiosk merchants negotiated around the anticommons regime by bribing local government rights holders and paying protection money to local mafia. One reporter noted at the time that mafia groups "have become increasingly important to kiosk owners. Unlike government officials, they act like industrious owners. For example, while the state imposes a 50 percent or more tax on profits, [mafia] are satisfied with a 5 percent to 10 percent cut. [Mafia] also protect traders from rival gangsters."[25]

Kiosks provided a partial solution to the problem of establishing commercial outlets in a country desperately short of retail services. Indeed, the markets for kiosks and storefront real estate are linked. The success of kiosks may have reduced pressure initially to overcome the missing market in stores. Kiosk merchants faced a "limited exclusion" anticommons in which they had to pay off only a few municipal officials and an easily identifiable criminal organization. According to Andrei, a kiosk owner, to set up shop "[I had to] bribe tax inspectors, pay protection money to mafia toughs and fork over 'gifts' to officials whose approval is needed for a business license. . . . When a date was set for delivery of the kiosk, [I] took care of a key business matter: making peace with the 'protection' racketeers who have carved Moscow up into fiefdoms and punish those who resist."[26] By creating routine paths for corruption, entrepreneurs quickly reduced the costs of assembling bundles of illegal access rights in kiosk locations. Another kiosk owner, Karlamov, told a reporter:

> Regular payments must be made to local officials and a powerful mafia. . . .
>
> You have to pay bribes to get financing. You have to pay bribes to get permission to put your kiosk up on a promising site. And even after things are all set up, you have to pay bribes to make sure they don't close you down.
>
> The mafia is the easiest of all to deal with. They don't charge too much, they tell you exactly what they want up front, and when an agreement is made, they live up to it. They don't come back later asking for more. . . .

> The hardest part was finding out who was the right person to
> bribe. . . . At first, we had no idea who could do what, so we began
> visiting the local prefect's office almost every day. We gave candy and
> other presents to people we met there, and eventually they directed us
> to people who could help.[27]

Commercial space obtained through bribery and protection money can
be reasonably stable if procedures become routine and entrepreneurs can
rely on official forbearance. Still, a kiosk system does not generate the levels of economic activity achievable by a well-functioning retail sector. One
problem: kiosks are easy to steal. A rival might come at night, winch a
kiosk up onto a flatbed, drive it away, and open up the following morning
somewhere across town with a fully stocked store. Also, kiosks offered in-
ferior service and less diversity of goods than could be provided in a secure
storefront.

Hernando de Soto, a leading theorist on law and economic development, argues that a vibrant underground economy should be viewed as an
important contribution to overall economic performance, rather than a
drain.[28] Kiosk merchants are net social contributors, not crooks. But he
contends that we should not mistake a vibrant scene for an optimal one.
People create an underground economy because the law drives them to it.
Kiosk merchants could contribute much more if the regulatory system
made it possible for them to work legally.

For de Soto, "third world underdevelopment" arises from a combination
of badly specified legal property rights and their rearrangement through illegal means.[29] As he argues (and as I saw working in Latin American shantytowns during the 1980s), the underground economy represents a
"second-best solution." It is the triumph of poor people's ingenuity in the
face of bad law. De Soto argues that a better solution for poor people would
be to create the "good law" that characterizes successful economies: property registries, land titles, and provisions for reliable enforcement of long-
term contracts.[30]

The proliferation of kiosks in Russia suggests that one way to overcome gridlock in commercial real estate may be to tolerate informal corruption; after all, it's better than nothing. But de Soto's work suggests that

the resulting property rights will operate less efficiently than will well-bundled legal property rights. With illegal property, the incentives for upgrading and expanding are blunted. As one kiosk owner told me, "It's easy to bribe the prefect officials, but it's hard to keep them bribed." More important, you can't borrow against your illegal kiosk to finance another location, get a building permit to expand, or contract for electrical or water service to attract a more upscale clientele. Illegal capital can't be easily leveraged to create new wealth. The difference between the economic multiplier generated by legal stores and the flat line of service afforded by kiosks is a hidden cost of storefront gridlock.

The kiosk example shows how property regimes are connected: the resolution of the gridlock on the streets and the persistence of underuse in stores reinforce each other. Bribery overcame the kiosk anticommons, but one cost of this path was to entrench third world market structures. According to one observer writing in 1995, "Economists have said that ideally, kiosks should have died out of their own accord, as owners moved into more stable premises. In Moscow, they said, that isn't taking place. 'There is the huge challenge of business premises, which are so horrendously expensive,' said Semyon Bekker, head of the city's Department for the Development of Small Business. 'In some sense kiosks should regulate themselves, since stores will eventually take their place. That hasn't happened yet.'"[31]

THRIVING MARKETS IN APARTMENTS

In stark opposition to storefronts stands Russia's thriving private market in apartments.[32] Apartments provide a useful counterpoint, in part because the space is often identical to storefronts. In a typical urban Russian apartment building, the ground floor may be commercial while the matching units directly above are residential. Thus, the difference in performance can be attributed more to the legal and cultural milieu than to the physical environment.

Location, Location—and Clear Title

In socialist regimes, rights in apartments were divided between private and public actors—anticommons tragedy was certainly possible for apartments just as for storefronts. Under Soviet law, after a local government or enterprise assigned a family to an apartment, the family had lifelong tenancy rights. This form of property included strong rights to occupy and some rights to pass the unit on to children. Various government departments held the balance of the rights, but no one could sell or lease the apartment.

Residential privatization laws offered current tenants, either for free or very cheaply, the balance of rights previously held by state institutions and enterprises. Rights to sell and receive sale revenue, lease and receive lease revenue, occupy, and mortgage all went to households, with little competition from other potential claimants such as local governments or state enterprises. Governments reserved only the limited regulatory rights typical in advanced market economies, such as rights to zone and eminent domain. Combined with preexisting lifelong tenancy, privatization gave apartment dwellers control of a property-rights bundle that would be familiar to any Western condominium owner.[33]

New housing markets were remarkably successful across the former socialist world, not only in terms of raw numbers of units that changed hands but also, and more important, in the private-property relations that were nurtured. This is not to say that these markets worked perfectly. Many countries struggled to create the basic framework for private property in housing: cities needed to create real estate taxation and land registries, draw boundaries, resolve ownership disputes, and establish condominium and other rules. They had to create the entire apparatus of modern property regulation. And they lacked the prerequisites for mortgage finance systems, including foreclosure and eviction systems. Cash-only sales crimp real estate markets.

Despite this lack of legal infrastructure, Russia in the early 1990s created vibrant apartment markets almost overnight. I traveled to Barnaul, the capital of the Altai High Republic, far out in Siberia, and met fledgling real estate brokers. In the earliest moments of post-Soviet opening, many time zones away from Moscow, new brokers already had a sophisticated understanding of what makes real estate markets work. Their mantra: location, location—and clear title.

The Fairness Trade-off?

But there were trade-offs. In achieving well-functioning bundles, governments ignored other fairness goals. Many people were given apartments with almost no market value because their units were so poorly maintained, had such high energy costs, or were badly located out on the urban fringe. Worse still, millions who had been queued up for years waiting for homes, particularly young families stuck in their parents' tiny apartments, simply lost out on getting new homes. By contrast, under Soviet rule, a small number of well-connected government officials had received well-maintained apartments in city centers. During privatization, these appa-ratchiks (and their elderly neighbors who had received their units decades earlier) kept a tight hold on the most valuable apartments.

Though privatization of housing was not fair in terms of ruble values conveyed, it had a political benefit for the reform government. Apparatchiks with valuable apartments got an immediate stake in the new regime. Also, simply turning renters into owners was administratively manageable for a weak new government. From the gridlock perspective, housing privatiza-tion was a coherent process. Apartments were conveyed with near-stan-dard private-property bundles, unlike storefronts in which many parties gained partial rights.

Not surprisingly, some Western academics tried to persuade govern-ments to make a different trade-off between jump-starting the market and treating individuals fairly. For example, one proposal called for local gov-ernments to retain a lien on all privatized apartments so they could cap-ture capital appreciation when the units were resold.[34] These ideas were not well received, even by tenants who were net losers in privatization. They resisted proposals that kept government involved in their lives.

While working in Hungary in 1992, I met with the two dozen reformist district mayors of Budapest to discuss a World Bank proposal to finance re-habilitation and renovation of grand old apartment buildings. The project would have recycled its profits to subsidize the mortgages of elderly and low-income residents. We wanted to show Budapest that people could pay to fix up housing without necessarily displacing poorer tenants. But the loan's proposed subsidies prompted one of the mayors to stand up and de-clare, "You World Bankers are communists!" That was an odd moment. Local officials in Hungary, like tenants in Russia, rejected projects that might have fragmented rights in apartments.

When ownership is first created, there can be a trade-off between avoid-ing a tragedy of the anticommons and achieving fairness. By granting near-standard bundles of rights, governments can jump-start markets even before they create basic real estate laws or functioning courts. Achieving an equitable distribution is more difficult. For those left out, the toll was often high—recall the housing situation of my colleague stuck in a small apartment with a violent ex-spouse.

THE DRAMA OF COMMUNAL APARTMENTS

Communal apartments, known as *komunalkas* in Russia, are a nice parallel to gridlock in storefronts.[35] Many komunalkas were large prerevolutionary apartments, well situated in downtown apartment buildings. At some points in Soviet history, several dozen people might have been forced to share a komunalka, with three generations of a family assigned to just one room. Kitchens and bathrooms were shared.[36]

These arrangements engendered a special loathing throughout the Soviet Union. Residents said that communal apartments were "often home to at least one alcoholic along with children of all ages, [and the komunalkas] slowly drive those who live there crazy from lack of privacy."[37] Even in the Soviet Union's heady early days, life in communal apartments was a struggle. Satirist Mikhail Zoshchenko wrote in his 1925 short story "Nervous People," "Not long ago, a fight took place in our communal apartment. Not just a fight, but an out-and-out battle. . . . The main reason is—folks are very nervous. They get upset over mere trifles. They get all hot and bothered. And because of that they fight crudely, as if they were in a fog."[38]

With privatization, communal tenants received some ownership rights in their separate rooms. Thus, each indirectly gained the right to block any move to restore the whole apartment to single-family use. Every room owner could keep the others from selling the whole apartment in its most valuable form.

Even fifteen years after socialism ended, gridlock in communal apartments still exists. In 2006, St. Petersburg alone had over 120,000 communal apartments housing about 700,000 people.[39] About $30 billion in value is locked up in St. Petersburg's communal spaces, despite the city's long-standing policy of resettling residents out of these apartments.

Spatial versus Legal Anticommons

The division of rights in communal apartments helps distinguish the concept of *spatial* from *legal* anticommons regimes. Communal apartments were more like big inches than phantom tollbooths. Both types lead to gridlock, but they do so through different mechanisms and with different consequences. In a spatial anticommons, an owner may have a relatively standard bundle of rights but too little space for ordinary use. In a legal anticommons, substandard bundles of legal rights are allocated to competing owners in a normal amount of space.

With komunalka ownership, selling the apartment is impossible so long as any room owner vetoes the deal; only if all the owners agree can the apartment be marketed as a single piece of real estate. Russian entrepreneurs quickly discovered that well-situated komunalkas could be converted to ordinary private property by exchanging the room owners' rights for small complete apartments on the city outskirts.[40] According to one account, "The trend is particularly noticeable in the centre of [Moscow], where competition for prestigious addresses among members of Russia's emerging business class and well-heeled foreigners has sent prices soaring. The area has many former mansions that the Bolsheviks converted into barracks-like communal apartments after the 1917 revolution. And for enterprising developers there is only one obstacle to reconverting those once-elegant buildings to high-quality private housing: the current tenants."[41]

In the case of some old komunalkas in central Moscow, the market value of the entire apartment might have been $500,000 by the mid-1990s. (Now the numbers are much higher.) Komunalka owners could be tracked down through *propiskas,* the old internal passports that the Soviets used to control movement and identify each individual in every residence. Such records assured bundling entrepreneurs that once all the listed people were bought off or killed, additional claimants would not appear.

Assume a hypothetical komunalka with four registered tenants, each occupying one room. Because of the discomforts and irritations of communal living, each room might have a market value of only $25,000, so that the whole apartment would have an apparent fair market value of

$100,000. The same space unified in a sole owner might be worth $500,000. So, converting the komunalka from anticommons to private property offered a $400,000 gain—reminiscent of the *New York Times*'s calculus when it converted Orbach's corner of Times Square.

Most komunalka owners wanted a place of their own, not just a room with a view.[42] After an apartment was put in play and conversion seemed possible, tenants would not sell out for $25,000 each, but would typically demand a substitute apartment instead. Adequate apartments could usually be found on the city outskirts for perhaps $75,000 each. Removing the four room owners might thus cost an entrepreneur $300,000. In my simplified example, the four tenants capture half of the available profits. In addition to paying off the room owners, entrepreneurs would incur the costs of bundling. These costs involved finding and negotiating with komunalka owners, locating and buying alternative apartments, renovating and finding buyers for the empty apartment, enforcing the deals, and incurring various carrying costs and market risks. Assume those costs total $50,000. Thus, in this example, overcoming the anticommons might leave the entrepreneur a net profit of $150,000.

In this multiparty bargain, each tenant is a monopolist with incentives to engage in strategic behaviors, such as holding out for the bundling surplus. Also, to this day, "simmering resentments among residents often complicate the deals." Entrepreneurs often managed to keep their costs down by coercing komunalka owners. Some property bundlers intimidated or murdered recalcitrant tenants. People got "bopped on the head" when deals went bad, according to Lisa Kreutz, a St. Petersburg real estate agent, who is now a "practiced hand at the delicate deal-making that untangles communal apartments."[43] Remember also that all this is happening in a country with no mortgage system. Apartment buyouts are all-cash deals (involving briefcases of cash), with multiple moves happening at once. Whether such deals take place depends on the entrepreneur's ability to keep conversion costs low, get the tenants out fast, sell high, and not get killed.

An unintended consequence of creating anticommons property during the privatization of communal housing has been the exposure of komunalka tenants to predatory property bundlers. In this spatial anticommons, each apartment has only a small number of often elderly room owners. Estimates are that thousands have been killed.

Overcoming a Humpty Dumpty Anticommons

The best way to deal with a Humpty Dumpty anticommons is to avoid creating it. But if regulators have already cracked the egg, then what? What allowed Russians to overcome some forms of gridlock, however brutally, while Moscow stores remained empty? Here are five factors to consider.[44] Not all forms of gridlock are created equal.

1. *Are the Owners Public or Private?* Negotiating with private owners is often cheaper than dealing with state and corporate parties. Komunalka owners were private individuals, not well positioned to resist concerted pressure by aggressive entrepreneurs. Bundling entrepreneurs could avoid holdouts by sharing the gains and by engaging in intimidation. By contrast, storefronts began mostly with corporate, quasi-state, and state owners. Storefront owners had more access to power and protection and were less easily strong-armed by property bundlers. They had to be bribed or persuaded instead. It may be difficult to identify whom to bribe, and then to keep them bribed.

2. *Are There Many Owners with Divergent Interests?* Komunalka tenants were fewer and had more convergent interests than rights holders in stores. With a few anticommons owners, familiar bargaining problems could surface, but they are manageable. So transaction costs are lower for bundling komunalkas, and intimidation is more effective. By contrast, there were a larger number of corporate and state owners of storefront rights, with interests that ranged from current income to long-term bureaucratic survival. Bribes to one bureaucratic owner may not bind others even within the same organization, at least until such bribery channels become routine.

3. *Are New Boundaries Intuitive?* Each komunalka could be easily bounded as private property. People knew where the four walls of the apartment were located, even if ownership of the rest of the building was unclear. Who controls the land, shared walls, facade, hallways, elevators, lobbies, and at-

tics? Who's responsible for leaking plumbing, roofs, and basements? People generally understood that the living area of each apartment was the core object of value. By contrast, store boundaries were less transparent. For example, a workers' cooperative might claim that the single bakery they occupied was theirs. Another type of "owner," such as a defunct state bread-making enterprise, might claim that an entire chain of several dozen enterprise bakery outlets was a single indivisible corporate asset. A district administration might claim that all local storefronts belonged to it and were subject to privatization through auction. What were the boundaries of commercial property?

4. *Are There Spatial or Legal Property Fragments?* Overcoming spatial gridlock, such as a privatized komunalka, may be less difficult than overcoming a legal one in which rights are difficult to understand and exchange. In a storefront, the problem is not that the space was overly subdivided but that legal rights were handed out to too many owners. These dispersed rights are more difficult to delineate and trade than tangible physical control over discrete spaces such as rooms in a komunalka.

5. *Are the Initial Conditions Bizarre?* Komunalka tenants began the transition to markets holding more of the familiar property-rights bundle than did owners of storefronts. When komunalkas were privatized, local governments gave up their socialist control rights, so tenants received relatively standard legal bundles. The tenants got most of what people expect from ownership, including physical possession of the room, the right to keep others out, and the right to sell. By contrast, stores often entered the reform era as part of the holdings of a maze of bankrupt state enterprises and political organizations.[45]

Whenever governments create property, and they do so every day, they may unknowingly create a tragedy of the anticommons. Politicians may be responding to pressure by lobbying groups, addressing other short-term policy concerns, or generally trying to solve too many problems at once.

Rather than assigning a usable bundle of rights in a well-scaled resource to a sole owner—or to a group property regime like a condominium, BID, or LAD—governments may fragment rights or objects. Regulators may believe that we (or they) are better off if many people can get a piece of each pie. They overlook the problem that fragmenting ownership too much has a hidden cost, the cost of gridlock.

In Russia, privatization faced pressure from all sides. Federal control passed to local actors and created competing power centers. Public officials held on to plausible ownership rights as a tool for self-preservation and sometimes as a source of bribes. Reformers parceled out rights broadly to avoid declaring winners who received entire property bundles, and losers who got nothing and fought back. The resulting empty storefronts were a stark emblem of a tragedy of the anticommons.

Although Russia's transition from Marx to markets may seem exotic and far away, the dynamics of ownership are similar to real estate development (and intellectual property creation) in the United States and other established market economies. Interest-group politics works more or less the same everywhere. Once initial rights are set, resources can be put to use in a well-functioning market or wasted in a gridlock economy.

seven

THE WORLD IS MINE
OYSTER

Get it today! Hell with tamar!
Leave it to tamar, somebody else'll get it.
—CHESAPEAKE BAY OYSTERMEN FOLK SAYING

Overharvesting destroys oyster beds, and when the beds are destroyed, the oysters do not come back. But folks on the water will tell you, "If a waterman caught the last oyster in the Chesapeake Bay, he'd sell it." Oysters should be extinct, but they aren't. Why not?[1]

In previous chapters, I've shown you the myriad hidden costs of a gridlock economy and suggested some solutions. Here I want to make a more general point about how to fix gridlock. Oysters' improbable survival illustrates almost every approach humans have taken throughout history to avoiding the tragedy of the commons. Much of what we now call law, morals, and even good manners rests on the calcified remains of such struggles. The oyster you enjoy today is the survivor of these battles—its expense is itself part of the subtle palette of solutions that respond to commons tragedy. Because tragedies of the commons and anticommons often mirror each other, so should their solutions. Oyster lore can point us to gridlock fixes.

WHY AREN'T OYSTERS EXTINCT?

Oysters are a seductive locus for understanding commons tragedy because they are among the earliest and most fought-over resources in human commerce. Parking lots, highways, antibiotics, and ozone are all well and good, but we have been shucking and eating oysters since before recorded history. The archaeological record is full of great oyster "middens," yards-deep heaps of shells that attest to exuberant prehistoric oyster orgies. Given their long intercourse with human society—as bar snacks for the poor and the wealthy alike; as aphrodisiac, medicine, industrial compound, and jewelry; as currency and item of trade—it's curious that every last oyster has not been consumed.

The problem for oysters is that they give of their virtues too readily.[2] They prefer shallow and accessible coastal waters where freshwater mixes with saltwater. Since before history, people have been drawn to just these places for ports, trade, and fishing. Oysters were a bonus: cheap and easy to harvest with a high nutritional payoff.

Although impressively fecund and resilient, oysters have been vulnerable to human population growth and to harvesting technologies that stress oyster beds. Except for a few days as free-floating spawn, or "spat," oysters can neither run nor hide. If they are to survive, spat must attach themselves to "cultch," the gravel and old shells on the ocean's bottom. Dredging for oysters breaks up cultch. Unless people return old shells to the sea and replenish the cultch, oyster beds turn to "ouse" (an early variant of "ooze"—oystering has a rich vocabulary) and the "spatfall" is wasted.

So oysters' tragic equation is simple. Yields drop when people remove more oysters than they allow to reproduce. For oysters to thrive, any society must limit the harvest and motivate people to repair damaged beds. But oyster beds cannot easily be protected with padlocks or barbed wire. Every oyster catcher with a well-tended bed has known that any other may drift in at night and scoop up the prize. This knowledge has driven each oysterman to the same conclusion: better to haul in a certain catch today, even if none is left for tomorrow. An oyster bed can be destroyed in a single season. So how have oysters survived?

OPEN-ACCESS OYSTERS

When people first encounter any new resource, it often seems inexhaustible. But superabundance can soon turn to near-extinction depending on the ownership rules we impose. These rules depend in part on the resource's location, structure, biology, history, and social milieu. The resulting ownership is never simply private, commons, state, or anticommons. Rather, as the oyster story will show, a conservation regime always involves a subtle and intricate amalgam of ownership techniques, including conquest and its analogues, market solutions such as trade and privatization, formal and informal customary norms, direct state regulations such as minimum catch sizes, and indirect regulations such as state-sanctioned monopolies.

Throughout early American history, oysters were cheap and plentiful, thanks to the Chesapeake Bay. Native Americans consumed what they could of bay oysters, leaving behind their enormous middens of empty shells. Colonists found the bay so stocked with oysters, such great mountains of oysters, that no amount of dredging seemed able to diminish their bounty: "Oysters were so plentiful in the Bay [around 1600] that occasionally ships would run aground on oyster beds."[3] Bay oysters were an open-access form of a commons: anyone could take, and no one invested for tomorrow. In this early stage, there was no tragedy because human consumption did not outpace natural reproduction.

By the mid-1800s, though, there began to be signs of trouble (fig. 7.1). Harvesting technology was changing from the ancient, low-tech method of tonging to the modern, high-capacity method of dredging. Tongs are like scissors—two rakes at the end of long wooden poles. The image shown in figure 7.2 depicts tongers at work. The small capacity of their boats and the reach of their tongs limited the damage they could do to oyster beds.[5] Tongers could work in water up to about twenty feet deep, just the level of the most prolific oyster beds.

FIGURE 7.1: *Maryland oyster ad from the 1870s.*[4]

FIGURE 7.2: *Tongers on the Chesapeake Bay.*[6]

As an aside, note that the tongers shown are African Americans—oyster harvesting, shucking, and pirating crossed color lines. Black oystermen found a sort of freedom and equality when tonging on the bay, being paid the same for a bushel as were their white counterparts. Thousands of freed slaves made their living as oystermen on the bay and as shuckers in the packing plants.[7]

By contrast with the tongers, dredgers developed larger "skipjacks," sailboats that could work at any depth. "Drudgers" pull a toothed scoop with a chain sack along the seabed, bringing up everything in its path. After dredgers have "licked" an oyster bed, it may be broken up and ruined. Figure 7.3 shows skipjacks at work.

When dredgers proliferated, oysters started becoming scarce. With scarcity, open access creates a vicious downward spiral: harvesting today earns a high and certain price; leaving oysters to reproduce seems a folly. Open access is the enemy of conservation, just as pirates are the antithesis of orderly markets. The tools to solve overuse tragedy all work by limiting access.

OYSTER WARS ON THE CHESAPEAKE

Few remember the Oyster Wars today, but the conflicts bitterly split the Chesapeake for nearly a hundred years, until a truce was brokered in 1962.[9] Skipjacks were sunk, sailors were gunned down, and bodies floated ashore. Quaint Maryland tourist towns such as Cambridge and St. Michaels were, until recently, military garrisons. Oysters were like gold or oil—worth killing over.

The battle over access to the bay reaches back to 1632, when England's King Charles I first drew the water boundary between Maryland and Virginia.[10] He split the bay not where the current flowed fastest (the usual approach), but at the high-water mark on the Virginia side, thus putting all

the oyster beds in Maryland waters. This initial "inequity" trig-
gered more than three centuries
of dispute. In 1785, at his Mount
Vernon   plantation,   General
George Washington brokered a
deal between Maryland and Virginia representatives.[11] The "1785
Compact" redivided the bay waters, but the line satisfied neither
side, and oyster plundering continued. (On a happier note, the

FIGURE 7.3: *Oyster pirates dredging at night.*[8]

oyster negotiations also helped prompt George Washington, James Madison, and George Mason to conceive of a more ambitious and enduring
gathering of the states—a constitutional convention.)[12]

As late as the mid-1800s, the Maryland and Virginia legislatures were
still able to act cooperatively: they jointly expelled "foreign" oystermen
from New Jersey, New York, and elsewhere along the eastern seaboard
who had wiped out their natural beds.[13] These New Englanders had been
sailing down to the bay to collect seed oysters that they could plant or bed
back at home. Although Maryland and Virginia reserved the bay solely for
their own citizens, their attempt to close access was ineffectual. Neither
state was willing to limit its own oystermen. No one took seriously the
idea that the bay's natural beds could be depleted. Looking back from the
vantage point of 1891, William Brooks, the foremost oyster biologist of
the day, lamented in his celebrated book *The Oyster* that "the residents supposed that their natural beds were inexhaustible until they suddenly found
that they were exhausted."[14]

During this time, almost a thousand dredge boats were operating on the
bay and in adjoining rivers. In a flash, skipjack fleets could drift into bay in-
lets, strip-mine oysters, wreck the beds, and leave no oyster behind. Even
though northerners had been excluded, Marylanders and Virginians were
still scrambling to make a living. They began pushing against each other.
As competition for oysters intensified, each state passed an elaborate body

of oyster conservation measures to regulate oyster harvesting and to protect their domestic industry.[15]

The 1860s was the fateful transition decade. In 1862, *overuse* first entered English as a noun—"The oyster beds are becoming impoverished, partly by over-use."[16] Oyster production on the bay peaked and began declining. In a controversial move, Maryland began leasing oyster beds in its waters solely to Maryland oystermen. The idea was that privatization would spur private investment and cultivation where there were no natural beds. But Virginia oystermen rejected the conservation move: many watermen were "fanatical in [their] belief that the oyster, as a product of nature, is not amenable to such laws as apply to other kinds of food or property," according to a study from the period.[17] Marylanders called the Virginians "pirates." Fair enough. One state's pirate is another state's defender of the ancient principle of equal and open access to a commons. (I hear echoes here of academic biotech researchers' disregard of gene patents.)

Conflicts intensified. All sides armed themselves. Violence became more frequent. The Maryland legislature took notice, and in 1868 it commissioned Commodore Hunter Davidson to create and captain the Maryland Oyster Navy. At the start of his campaign, Commodore Davidson wrote that the dredgers were "a class of sailors, who, from the free and roving habits of their lives, removed from the restraints of society, and even of the law (until the Police Force was appointed), have grown to think themselves masters of the Oyster situation."[18] With mandate in hand, the commodore bought the armored side-wheel steamer *Leila,* his flagship, and acquired a respectable fleet of gunboats with howitzers and repeating rifles.

Virginia, too, had cause for concern from Maryland pirates. Charles I and George Washington had demarcated boundaries, but not well enough. Alongside battles on the water, there were onshore fights in the courts. For example, in 1877, the U.S. Supreme Court redivided the bay waters so as to award the most valuable oyster beds to Virginia. The "Line of '77" became a rallying cry for Maryland's Smith Islanders. They refused to accept the Court's award because it cut them off from their livelihood.[19] Smith Island pirates led Virginia to enlarge its own Oyster Navy.

Probably the most notorious oyster pirate on the bay was Virginian Gus Rice, described by a contemporary observer as "a dilapidated specimen in foul-weather clothing and a battered waterproof hat." Early on a January morning in 1871, he led his henchmen out from St. Michaels, Maryland, in a small skiff toward the *Leila* lying at port.[20] The pirates' goal was to assassinate Maryland's Commodore Davidson. The pirates boarded Davidson's flagship, knocked out the man on duty, and headed for the commodore's cabin. As they were breaking down his door, Davidson awoke, grabbed his Colt revolver, fired two shots, and drove the pirates back to their skiff. With the crew alerted, they hoisted rifles and shot at the pirates, who surrendered and were brought back on board in shackles. Davidson later told a state fisheries inspector that when he went to sea he never dreamed anyone would try to kill him over an oyster. After the attack, Davidson upped his pursuit of the pirate fleets. But the Maryland Oyster Navy was always a step behind, underfunded, outgunned, and outrun. Although some pirates would flee when challenged, other well-armed and armored fleets would charge straight at the navy ships (fig. 7.4).

Gus Rice continued pirating oysters for almost twenty years. In 1887, his fleet, with crews recruited from Baltimore docks and jails, plundered Maryland's rich Chester River oyster beds. The pirates would work on moonlit nights with a sentinel ship hoisting a globe light to warn of anyone's approach. In early 1888, Chester River oystermen grew so desperate that they mounted a pair of cannons onshore to drive away Rice's dredgers. Rice ignored the cannon shot for months, but eventually he organized a landing party, captured the cannons, stripped the watchman and sent him running, naked and terrified, as a warning to the neighboring communities.

Later in 1888, Rice made a public relations mistake. He fired on what he thought was an Oyster Navy steamer, but it turned out to be the *Corsica,* a passenger steamboat ferrying women and children. This incident riled the Baltimore and Annapolis newspapers, which in turn pushed the governor to order Rice stopped. The navy's new flagship, the *Governor McLane,* was quickly fitted

FIGURE 7.4: *Pirates attack the police schooner* Julia Hamilton.[21]

FIGURE 7.5: *The capture of a pirate ship.*[22]

with a twelve-pound howitzer, extra crew, and rifles. In December 1888, the navy spotted Rice's fleet dredging the Chester and quietly captured some outlying dredgers (fig. 7.5).

But Rice was ready. He had prepared a giant raft from a dozen dredge boats lashed together and fitted with armored plates. As he charged the navy ships, he shouted, "Join me boys in victory or in Hell!"[23] The navy crew fired their howitzer, but the pirates were too close and their fleet too well armored. The *Governor McLane* was caught in a cross fire, and the mate at the howitzer was severely wounded. The navy crew fought back and sank several pirate boats, drowning an unknown number of shanghaied crewmen who had been left chained in their boats' forepeaks. (Many crew were newly arrived Irish, Italian, and German immigrants who had been forcibly impressed to cruel service.) The wily Rice escaped again.

The Chesapeake Bay is a big place, and Rice was not the only pirate captain. While the *Governor McLane* took control of the Chester River, battles on the Little Choptank River went the other way. Pirate schooners surrounded the police sloop *Eliza Howard* and drove it off. On January 12, 1889, the navy's *E. B. Groome* ran out of ammunition after a long battle against another pirate fleet. The ship was captured, stripped of its rigging, and left adrift. The *Groome's* first mate wrote that the pirates had been eager to fight, "seeing how utterly powerless we were to cope with so many boats, each of which appeared to be better armed than our own vessel."[24] The captured navy sailors were put to hard labor on a pirate ship for some days before being allowed to row home in a skiff.

That same year, Cambridge, Maryland, organized a militia to protect local oyster beds, but pirates fired on the town and threatened to burn it to the ground if challenged. The sheriff wrote that the "dredgers seem more determined to carry their point this winter than ever before. The oysters are scarce in the bay and they seemed determined to get the oysters from the rivers at any risk."[25] The pirate fleet looted the Choptank of its last large oyster cache and sailed away. By then, the flagship *Governor McLane* was busy elsewhere, protecting Maryland dredgers against Virginia's territorial claims backed by the Virginia Oyster Navy. War, it turns out, can be one tool to close access and limit overuse tragedy, though brute force has other countervailing costs.

THE ONSHORE STRUGGLE TO CLOSE ACCESS

Military campaigns dovetailed with regulatory skirmishes. As he sailed off to wage oyster war, Commodore Davidson implored the Maryland legislature to create a legal environment worth fighting for. He advocated for laws "restraining and regulating the present thoughtless and improvident industry that takes every Oyster wherever found, regardless of season, size, or condition."[26] Davidson believed that ending overuse would require widespread leasing of public beds to private oystermen and enforceable catch limits.

Like Commodore Davidson, scientist and regulator William Brooks blamed the decline of Maryland's oyster fishery on "improvidence and mismanagement and blind confidence." Brooks tried to persuade his contemporaries that the bay's deterioration was no different from what had happened "in France, in Germany, in England, in Canada, and in all northern coast states" before those jurisdictions moved aggressively to shift control of oyster beds away from open access and toward private management. The main reason that bay oysters had not yet been wiped out, Brooks insisted, was only that "the immense area covered by our own beds has enabled them to withstand the attacks of the oystermen for a much longer time."[27]

Brooks too argued for leasing out bay oyster beds: "Oyster-planting can be carried out only on private grounds, and it cannot flourish in a community which does not respect the right of the private owner to the oysters which he has planted." But he recognized that "the most serious obstacle" with leasing, a problem that continued for more than a century on the bay, was the oystermen's "absence of all respect for private property in oysters." Respect could not be legislated or created even by Davidson's gunboats; rather, it required the "formation of a public sentiment in favor of private cultivation."[28] Self-policing usually comes before external policing.

Virginia had gained control of scarce beds through the Supreme Court's award of the "Line of '77." The Court extended this control in 1894 when it allowed Virginia to exclude Maryland oystermen altogether from key oystering waters.[29] The Court said the water was Virginia's common property to manage as it pleased (a "limited-access commons").

Virginia kept beating Maryland in court, but both sides lost in practice. Virginia refused to allow transfer of seed oysters to Maryland waters; Maryland retaliated by refusing to allow export of cultch to revitalize Virginia beds—each side blocked the other in a small-scale tragedy of the anticommons.[30] Warfare continued with all sides using artillery, rifles, grappling hooks, and other weapons. Fortunately, as *Harpers Weekly* noted in an 1894 story on the oyster battles, "They have fired abundantly, but not accurately, and enough lead has been wasted to supply sinkers for all the fishing lines along the Atlantic Coast."[31] On the bay, there was too much at stake for anyone to give up. Baymen fought against New Englanders, Marylanders against Virginians, tongers against dredgers, and leaseholders against commoners. Each side struggled to keep intact its own oystering lifestyle.

As the 1800s drew to a close, observers continued to offer warning after warning. None were heeded. Oyster biologist Brooks cautioned, "All who are familiar with the subject have long been aware that our present system can have only one result—extermination."[32] Even after decades of Oyster Wars and steep declines in annual harvests, oysters were still "the chief fishery product in the United States." They were "more valuable than any other single product of the fisheries, and . . . an important factor in the food-supply." Oysters were a commonplace, "one of the cheapest articles of diet in the United States" (see fig 7.6).[33] Laws limited how frequently employers could feed oysters to their servants. Well into the twentieth century, when guests entered a proper home, they would be offered a few oysters to settle their stomachs and pique their appetites for the coming meal.

Soon after 1900, however, the long-feared decline in oyster production accelerated. Prices rose. Oysters became a luxury good in America, to be downed with champagne. Did the shift in consumption reflect a move from open access to private property? No. At all times, oystermen roamed widely across the bay. Policing was always difficult. Imagine you were a farsighted, clearheaded, quick-witted "oyster catcher" concerned with overuse. Would you throw some oysters back? No. Even into the 1940s, battles were fought and people were shot for oysters on the bay.

At lunch recently, I told this pirate tale to a colleague. He replied that early in his career, he had witnessed perhaps the last round of the Oyster Wars. In 1960, when he was a law clerk for U.S. Supreme Court Justice Stanley Reed, the justice called up the governors of Maryland and Virginia and pressed them to work out a deal on dividing

FIGURE 7.6: *Eating oyster soup, 1887.*[34]

bay oysters. In 1962, President John Kennedy signed that deal into law: the Potomac Fisheries Bill brought the Oysters Wars to a close—more than three hundred years after the bay was first divided, nearly two hundred years after George Washington thought he had put the dispute to rest, and almost one hundred years after the first Supreme Court decision in the case. The states' oyster navies, renamed "fish and game police," still exist today.

THE JIGSAW PUZZLE OF OYSTER CONSERVATION

During the 1800s, bay oysters were a resource located at the intersection of many crosscutting divides: tongers and dredgers, bay oystermen and New Englanders, Marylanders and Virginians, seamen and packers, pirates and licensed captains. But the biggest divide was between those treating the resource as open access and those committed to all other competing forms of resource management—conquest, trade, custom, privatization, regulation, and monopoly.

The Oyster Wars teach that open access and open warfare are not a great combination for wise resource management. Gunboats alone do not preserve oysters, but neither does law. Law is not powerful enough by itself to switch a resource from open access to private property. Instead, oysters' diminished survival depends on a constantly shifting matrix of strategies—simultaneously public and private, individual and community—and on their constant renegotiation. Despite decades of naval and legal battles, the bay did not resolve itself into a system that looked to be recognizably private property or its alternatives.

This is an important and general point about property: when you look closely at any resource, you will see a jigsaw puzzle of commons, private, and state ownership, along with elements of anticommons ownership. What's tricky is fitting the pieces together so the resource is reasonably well managed from a social perspective. We need an array of finely honed tools to conserve a single depleting resource or to assemble rights in a newly emerging one. The challenge is most acute when values and technologies are shifting. We don't necessarily require optimal use (not an easy goal because there are genuinely competing conceptions of the term). Instead, the best we may be able to achieve is tolerably good use—avoiding extremes of overuse in a tragedy of the commons and underuse in a tragedy of the anticommons.

The oyster you eat today is not nature, raw on a half-shell; rather, it is the fussed-over survivor of ancient strategies to ensure the mollusk's continued existence. The same strategies at work on the bay would have been familiar to the ancient Romans, to oystermen in Shakespeare's England, and to people overusing resources today. We have always mixed and matched a small handful of conservation tools: trade and conquest, privatization and cultivation, custom and regulation. As it turns out, none of these approaches was unique to the Chesapeake Bay in the 1800s. The Oyster Wars just recapitulate in miniature the larger cycles of oyster lore. The following pages put the bay solutions in context, show a few surprising modern analogues, and explain how these overuse fixes might help address gridlock today.

GREED AND AVARICE IN ANCIENT ROME

Maryland and Virginia were not the first states to notice that trade and conquest are important tools to relieve pressure on overstressed local beds. When overharvesting made oysters scarce in ancient Rome, the Romans began trading for them across and outside the empire. As the Romans conquered new territories, they acquired untapped sources of oysters. For example, soon after Julius Caesar's forces landed in Britain in 55 BC, Sallust, a Roman commentator, noted dryly that "the poor Britons, there is some good in them after all, they produce an oyster."[35] But Britain's conquest produced only temporary windfalls, which Roman demand soon exceeded. One emperor allegedly ate a thousand of them at a single—presumably lengthy—sitting.[36]

Roman entrepreneurs developed multiple strategies to ensure private domestic production. Tasty young varieties of oysters were gathered, packed in straw and ice, transported long distances across the empire, bedded close to home in privately controlled waters, and then allowed to mature for several years before being gathered and brought to market. This was the same approach that New England oystermen were pursuing before Virginia and Maryland joined together to close the bay to outsiders. Trade in seed oysters is nothing new.

Neither is privatization of oyster beds. Pliny the Elder details cultivation methods that survive into the present: "The first person who formed artificial oyster-beds was Sergius Orata. . . . This was done by him, not for the gratification of gluttony, but of avarice, as he contrived to make a large income by this exercise of his ingenuity. . . . [To improve the oysters' flavor], a plan has been more recently hit upon, of feeding [them in Orata's lake], famished as they must naturally be after so long a journey."[37]

Although private control may cause rebellion and piracy, as we saw on the bay, it can also spur investment. Sergius Orata seeded oyster beds for his personal profit, but his actions indirectly ensured oysters' conservation for everyone else. As the Roman literature attests, oysters went through cycles of scarcity and plenty. Naturally occurring sites were discovered and depleted; cultivation methods were tested and improved; entrepreneurs bred new varieties and raised them in private lakes. Ancient Romans used conquest, trade, privatization, and cultivation as tools to mitigate open access overuse.

OYSTERING FROM SHAKESPEARE TO DICKENS

Jump forward a millennium and a half from the Roman oyster orgies. The standard references credit Shakespeare with coining the phrase, "The world is mine oyster."[38] But why did Shakespeare compare the world to an oyster rather than to a clam or mussel? The playwright was not the first oyster maven. Rather, he was most likely repeating a much older folk locution. Ancient Babylonian, Egyptian, and even Hebrew cosmologies likened the earth to an oyster, a craggy firmament with fathomless waters below, the heavens floating above, and great riches within.[39]

As in ancient Rome, oysters in Shakespeare's England cycled between bar snacks for the poor and the stuff of aristocratic high jinks. In the shellfish taverns of Shakespeare's day, oysters were given "free"—only wine and such was paid for. For example, in 1630, poet John Taylor praised oysters and "their meat / which freely, friendly scot-free all do eat."[40] (By the way, a "scot" was slang for a bar tab, unrelated semantically to any Scot.)

A few decades later we have a rich account of how oysters played a role in seduction. The underappreciated memoirs of the Chevalier du Grammont tell a lively tale.[41] Banished from France in 1662 for bedding a favorite mistress of the king, Grammont relocated to the libertine court of the Merry Monarch, Charles II (son of Charles I, who had divided the bay between Maryland and Virginia). In England, Grammont seduced one Miss Warmestre, of whom it was said that she "had no shape at all, and still less air; but . . . it very plainly appeared that her consent went along with her eyes to the last degree of indiscretion."

Lord Taaffe, Grammont's rival, was similarly intent on seducing Warmestre. Although Taaffe required "free egress and regress to her at all hours of the day or night: this appeared difficult to be obtained." His obstacle was the Lady Sanderson, the famously incorruptible governess of the queen's maids of honor. Yet Sanderson consented that Taaffe and Warmestre "should sup as often as they pleased in Miss Warmestre's apartments, provided their intentions were honourable, and she one of the company. The good old lady was particularly fond of green oysters, and had no aversion to Spanish wine: she was certain of finding at every one of these suppers two barrels of oysters; one to be eaten with the party, and the other for her to carry away: as soon, therefore, as she had taken her dose of wine, she took her leave of the company."

As so often happens in these stories, things did not go well for the lively Miss Warmestre, who was soon with child. Called to account by the queen, the governess Sanderson defended herself with an (abridged) version of

Taaffe's courtship. Taaffe, the cad, "neither acknowledged Miss Warmestre nor her child, and . . . he wondered why she should rather father it upon him than any other."[42] Warmestre soon quit the court and married a modestly endowed country lord whom she had once brutally spurned. Oysters were her downfall or, if you enjoy rural life, her salvation.

Though oysters were scarce and dear in Grammont's day, by the early 1800s in England the cycle had turned again, and they were food for the poor. The wealthy would no longer touch them for either seduction or gluttony. In *The Pickwick Papers,* Charles Dickens writes:

> "It's a wery remarkable circumstance, Sir," said Sam, "that poverty and oysters always seem to go together."
>
> "I don't understand you, Sam," said Mr. Pickwick.
>
> "What I mean, Sir," said Sam, "is, that the poorer a place is, the greater the call there seems to be for oysters. . . . Blessed if I don't think that ven a man's wery poor, he rushes out of his lodgings, and eats oysters in reg'lar desperation."[43]

But by the latter part of the nineteenth century, oysters in England had again become "so rare as to disappear as an article of trade, and only to be found on the tables of the rich."[44] The cycle of conservation and overuse kept turning. In addition to the ancient Romans' strategies, Elizabethan English practice highlights a few more familiar solutions to overuse tragedy.

Custom is one. The familiar advice to eat oysters only in months with an *r* (all but May, June, July, and August) is not primarily a health warning, as many people believe today. Rather, it reflects an old custom designed to protect summertime spatfall.[45] British oystermen also created elaborate rituals for sharing and preserving oyster beds. Accounts of seventeenth-century gangs located in particular harbors, such as the records kept by Faversham "oyster catchers," would seem equally contemporary to ancient Romans and to today's Chesapeake oystermen.

Custom, in turn, often became the basis for state regulation. The summer closing period became a widespread law in Elizabethan England and later in the American colonies and on the bay. During this period, the British Crown also developed an elaborate set of regulations specifying the minimum size of oysters that could be legally taken, maximum catches, how oysters could be caught, and who could catch them. Local oystering rules were aggregated into the national legislation and later into international treaties and agreements. When oysters became scarce, exports to France were banned, aggressively policed, and heavily sanctioned. Later, when oysters were plentiful again, export trade was encouraged. It was the same with imports: bans during times of plenty, encouragement when supplies were low.[46]

State sanction of private monopolies was another regulatory tool to limit overuse. Royal charters empowered fishermen from ports such as Faversham to harvest oysters exclusively and to exclude all others from a defined territory. Monopoly power can have costs, but it can also provide a significant benefit. Royal charters gave port gangs the incentive to manage local oysters effectively. Armed with a charter, oystermen had a structure for internal cooperation, a reason to invest securely, and a legal basis for excluding outsiders—much like the conservation incentives noted in Chapter 2 that Australian lobstermen have today.[47]

MODERN ANALOGUES TO CONQUEST

In each cycle of oyster conservation, the same tools recur: conquest and trade, privatization and cultivation, custom and regulation. These strategies were all in play on the Chesapeake; all are still in use today. Oystermen today are involved with trade in seed oysters and cultch, leasing of beds and development of new oyster varieties, reputation management through gossip in bay harbors, and extensive oyster regulations enforced by fish and game police. Today, however, we rarely see sovereigns taking

FIGURE 7.7: *A panoramic view of oil derricks at Signal Hill, Los Angeles, 1923.*[52]

control of territory from each other, whether by purchase, court decision, or outright conquest.

Conquest is now prohibited in international law. Every now and then a country will try it, sometimes to solve an overuse dilemma. One important motivation for Saddam Hussein's invasion of Kuwait in 1990 was to gain sole control of the massive Rumaila oil field that underlies both countries.[48] Each country had an incentive to race to drill because whoever got the oil out first owned it; the slowpoke got nothing. But when too many people poke holes in a field and extract oil too fast, then the pressure drops and much of the oil becomes trapped underground. Oil fields and oyster beds are equally vulnerable to overuse tragedy. Both Iraq and Kuwait thought the other was overdrilling. One solution is to have a single decision maker manage the field. Conquest can get you there, but nowadays we have created a few less violent approaches, at least within a single state.

In some countries and many U.S. states, voluntary or compulsory "unitization" of all landowners overlying an oil pool stops the racing dilemma—this is a hybrid public-private solution.[49] Without unitization, each landowner could sink a well, as parcel owners did in Signal Hill, Los Angeles, after oil was discovered there in 1923 (fig. 7.7).[50] Three hundred wells rapidly depleted the LA field, which for a time in the 1920s was said to produce about one-quarter of the world's oil. After a field is unitized, landowners get a share of the field's revenue but lose the right to sink their own wells. To optimize oil production, a single professional manager decides well placement and extraction rates.[51] Unitization exemplifies a successful cooperative property institution "retrofitted" over too fragmented resources (like the "business improvement districts" for street amenities noted in Chapter 5).

Unitization can work well when there's a single sovereign, like California, able to coerce cooperation, but not so well when oil fields sit beneath two countries (or when oysters lie between two warring states).

A second modern substitute to conquest is the "exclusive economic zone." At one time, countries exercised jurisdiction in coastal waters up to the international law limit of three nautical miles—more or less the distance a cannonball could be fired from the shore. Under that regime, offshore resources, such as fisheries, more than three miles out were open access, and could be rapidly destroyed. So countries claimed twelve miles and then more and more. In 1982, the United Nations Convention on the Law of the Sea recognized claims that some countries were asserting to an "exclusive economic zone" up to two hundred miles out (or farther for resources on or under a continental shelf). Instead of using naval occupation, coastal countries negotiated treaty law that validated their self-serving national claims. A massive swath of the world's oceans was transferred straight from the global commons into national control. An upside of this "conquest," however, has been that a single sovereign can mitigate overuse tragedies within its zone. For example, scarce fish stocks can be privatized through quotas, quotas can be traded and policed, catches can be limited, and commercial fisheries can be conserved. Open access to the oceans has been partly domesticated.[53]

OYSTERS AND THE ANTICOMMONS

What can we take from oysters that will help in solving gridlock? As I mentioned earlier, commons and anticommons tragedies mirror each other, so solutions for one may inform the other.

Conquest and trade have analogues as gridlock fixes. For example, global treaty organizations can mitigate underuse in a world with multiple countries. Fragmented sovereignty means that many anticommons tragedies will be intrinsically hard to solve; it also means we should be alert to gridlock at the international level. The robber baron story that opens this book is the paradigmatic example. Adam Smith in *The Wealth of Nations* noticed just this type of cross-border gridlock: "The navigation of the Danube is of very little use to the different states of Bavaria, Austria and

Hungary, in comparison of what it would be if any of them possessed the whole of its course till it falls into the Black sea."[54]

When you think about solving gridlock, it pays to be a citizen of the world. International law and institutions are often our modern substitute for conquest. At the end of World War II, world leaders resolved to create a "three-legged stool" of global governance aimed at preventing war by managing global overuse and underuse tragedies. One leg is the United Nations, designed to address underprovision of global security. The second leg includes the International Monetary Fund and the World Bank, institutions charged with avoiding competitive currency devaluations (a commons tragedy), promoting global development, and ensuring fiscal and monetary stability. The third leg was intended to overcome gridlock in goods and services, but it proved the most controversial. For decades, there were interim agreements (called the GATT). The World Trade Organization (WTO) came into being only in 1995, fifty years late.

One way to appreciate the contribution of the WTO is to see it as a tool for distinct economies to get goods and services flowing. National tariffs can operate like toll booths on the Rhine. Free trade was supposed to expand economic opportunity, link markets together, and prevent war. Through the WTO and its predecessor agreements, every member country agreed simultaneously to stop blocking everyone else—up to a point. Indeed, global wealth has grown immensely through lowered tariffs. The WTO has become the prime engine to avoid global economic gridlock. There are still many challenges: minimum environmental and labor standards are not enforced, hidden "nontariff barriers" still block trade, and some tariffs could still be negotiated away. You can think of the WTO as a global version of oil unitization, patent pooling, or LAD creation. It's an alternative to conquest that knits fragmented economies together and overcomes gridlock.

Although we've made progress on trade, we have not created all the international institutions our planet probably needs. The Kyoto Protocols were a partial (failed) attempt to solve global gridlock on global warming. Every country can block every other from reaping conservation gains. Americans ask why they should suffer the economic costs of stopping pollution if China will just build more coal-fired plants. The Chinese reasonably ask why they should limit their economic growth when the United States is the biggest polluter today and has gained the most from pollution historically. Everyone blocks everyone else, and in time, we may cook our planet. Crafting the right international institutions to solve global environmental gridlock is one of the great challenges of our lifetimes.

Custom is also a powerful tool to fix gridlock. Self-policing is the key. If everyone stood by their rights all the time, society would grind to a halt. But drivers obey many informal rules of the road, like stopping short of a crowded intersection. When they don't, we see the kind of traffic congestion for which the word *gridlock* was originally coined. We often avoid gridlock because people are well socialized to cooperate automatically. Across an innumerable array of social settings, deviants are few. Don't assume you always need regulation or conquest (or its analogues) to solve gridlock—people are primed to get along in creative and subtle ways even if the law does not reach their behavior. Look for these habits of cooperation. Law, when it is effective, often builds on and reinforces existing custom and norms. It's much easier to direct people where they already want to go.

When custom is not enough, we can fix gridlock by adapting the other approaches from the tool kit of solutions to commons tragedy. For example, regulators may sometimes strategically create monopolies to overcome gridlock just as they can use them to help solve overuse. Monopolies are not always a bad thing, at least to the extent they can help cure the tragedy of privatization gone too far.

In the United States, market competition is usually ensured through a specialized area of law called *antitrust*. Antitrust law often works to ensure that we have multiple suppliers of substitute goods. The idea is to keep one widget maker from controlling all the others, creating a "trust" or monopoly, charging too high a price, and harming the economy. In response, governments may fragment monopolies—for example, AT&T's court-ordered breakup in 1982 or Microsoft's antitrust litigation settlement in 2001.

Trust busting may make sense when substitutes are scarce, but fragmentation is not necessarily good policy for complementary goods. (Recall from Chapter 2 the distinction between "substitutes" and "complements.") If property fragments are complements, if ownership starts out in an anticommons, then gridlock is a danger and monopoly can be the solution. Government policy should focus on pushing these owners together, not keeping them apart.

To cure underuse in an anticommons, the correct social policy should be *protrust*, to coin a term. Protrust should be a legitimate English word like antitrust. Patent pools and copyright collectives are protrust. The U.S. Department of Justice should have a protrust division just as it now has one for antitrust. Protrust policy and antitrust enforcement together should constitute national "competition law," to use the European Union's umbrella category for this regulatory arena.

In sum, from conquest to monopoly, every solution to oyster overuse offers a useful anticommons analogue.

We have always loved oysters (fig 7.8). As one Maryland commentator noted in the 1870s, "Nobody tires of oysters. Raw, roasted, scalded, stewed, fried, broiled, escalloped, in pâtés, in fritters, in soup, oysters are found on every table, sometimes at every meal, and yet no entertainment is complete without them."[55]

FIGURE 7.8: *Oyster stands at Fulton Market, New York, 1867.*[56]

Was it inevitable that oysters would move from being "one of the cheapest articles of diet in the United States" to a luxury? No. Oysters could be as common as water itself or extinct. There is no single story or magic cure to overuse. Virginian and Marylander oystering families feuded and intermarried. Deviant nephews went off on midnight raids. A cousin engineered a better windlass (the winch that lifts oyster dredges). At times, the bay may have looked more private or more like open access. Along the way, cultural norms and off-the-books practices emerged that discouraged outsiders and helped with conservation. Communities shamed those who stole away at night to dredge oysters by jailing them or sinking their boats. There were legal mechanisms, such as closing times for beds, maximum catch amounts, and prohibitions on summer catches. People threw back cultch. Governments leased oyster beds.

While the Oyster Wars were particular to the bay, all the conservation methods used by Commodore Davidson were as familiar to Pliny the Elder and Shakespeare as they are to oystermen today. Every successful society assembles its own version of the solution tool kit particular to the resource, culture, and technology of the time. When these strategies work in concert, the effect is to move a scarce resource out of an open-access setting—where tragedy is hard to avoid—and into a setting in which people have reason to conserve. Over millennia, we have watched oysters grow scarce, yet we have ensured their survival to this day. Solving overuse remains a challenge, even after thousands of years of experimentation.

Avoiding underuse in a tragedy of the anticommons is harder because we are just now discovering its pervasive reach and hidden costs. If we have one advantage for fixing gridlock, it's the head start gained from our hard-earned experience with oysters and their kin.

eight

A SOLUTIONS TOOL KIT

Tragedies of the anticommons are harder to spot and therefore more difficult to overcome than the mirror-image commons dilemmas. Fixing gridlock takes practice. For each type of underuse in this book, I have proposed a solution. This chapter gathers these solutions into a comprehensive kit whose tools can be deployed singly or in combination. After learning to spot gridlock, you should feel confident tackling it in your roles as citizen, voter, advocate, and entrepreneur.

STEP 1: SPOT AND NAME GRIDLOCK

I cannot stress enough that the first, crucial, and most important step to solving gridlock is to see it. Gridlock is a major source of waste and loss in every society, yet underuse is mostly hidden from view. When lifesaving drugs are missing, we sigh and make excuses: medical discovery is serendipitous; God works in mysterious ways. When wireless is slow, housing expensive, or Native American land idle, we may never give it a second thought. The losses seem abstract, inevitable, or remote.

They are not. Gridlock is a human creation that does not follow from any immutable laws of nature. It is not intrinsic to an economy or culture. Instead, underuse results from mistakes and gaps in economic, legal, and social organization. It is an artifact of ownership gone awry.

I have described a few large examples of gridlocked markets. For each, I illustrated the diverse paths through which underuse has taken hold and may be solved. But I have just scratched the surface of the anticommons literature: people are uncovering new examples all the time. Anywhere you look—from software to shopping malls—there are entrepreneurial opportunities to make a profit while helping society overcome gridlock.

Language Up the Problem

To spot gridlock, you need the right language. Add *underuse* to the familiar concept of overuse. Add *anticommons* to your everyday awareness. If you're into fairy tales, this book is about the "Humpty Dumpty" problem of property and the "Goldilocks Quest" for optimal design of ownership. If you like aphorisms, this is a "too many cooks spoil the broth" story. If you prefer economic lingo, mine is a riff on "Cournot complements." Whatever works. The notion of underuse in a tragedy of the anticommons should be squiggly no more.

At core, I am showing what happens when people own small chunks of things that can best be used in larger bundles. The chunks can be spatial like the big inches or legal like the empty storefronts, concurrent like the gene fragments or sequential like the Rhine tollbooths. Gridlock can arise in many ways—when ownership is first created or later on, when property is regulated by governments or managed by private individuals and corporations. Value is wasted if we fragment ownership too much.

Look for the Cutting Edge

Emerging markets can be killed in the moment of their birth. The greatest risk of gridlock arises when governments define property rights for the first time. They do this at the cutting edge of technology, culture, art, and science. Regulators don't have a strong passion to get rights right. They want to please competing constituencies—everyone should get something—and they fail to realize that privatization can go too far. Unfortunately, new markets are potentially emerging all the time. Because anticommons property is often invisible, people rarely recognize the hidden dynamics of underuse.

No one speaks up. But you can. This is not some distant mystery that happens in Washington, D.C., Moscow, Tokyo, London, or Paris. Wher-

ever you live, there is a cutting edge of property rights where you may discover a gridlock economy.

Some years ago, I wrote an article called "The Cutting Edge of Poster
Law" about students hanging posters on the walls at the University of
Michigan Law School, where I then taught.[1] A student in class had challenged me to give a close-to-home example of gridlock in the making. Just
outside the classroom door was the answer, a poster asking, "Where is the
keg party tonite?" Staircase walls were congested with flyers right next to
bulletin boards that were oddly underused—a poster commons and anticommons. Students had a rich array of made-up rules: there were "no
overpostering" norms and escalating retaliations against deviant posterers.
This all went on in the shadow of the law, in the form of an associate dean
who took a dim view of disordered hallways. "This is not a high school,"
she would remind me. The serious point of my tongue-in-cheek article
was that "poster law" is law even if it is written down nowhere and passed
on from student to student. Too much ownership or too little can waste resources even in everyday life.

Ask Why the Grass Is Greener

Parents teach their kids not to think the grass is greener over there ("Don't
covet"). But often the grass over there really is greener. The over-there
people water their lawn and you don't. One good way to spot gridlock is to
pay attention to these differences. For example, in 1880, a British investiga-
tor noticed:

> The lamentable state of our oyster fisheries, as we now find them,
> furnishes a curious and instructive contrast with those in neighboring
> countries. In France, Holland, Spain, Portugal, Russia, and America,
> the fisheries of those countries yield abundant supplies. In point of
> quality, of course, the oysters we import are not to be compared with
> our own products. Many of the [French and other imports] in flavor,
> as is well known, are little, if anything, superior to mussels; yet [they
> are cheap and in high demand]. . . .
>
> The secret of their prosperity is well-known to be entirely due to the
> maintenance of large parent stocks, protection during the close season,
> and artificial breeding. On the other hand, the deterioration of our once

famous beds is attributable to the stupid policy we have been pursuing: that policy being in every respect the *reverse* of what we see producing such beneficial results to other nations. . . . The cause is obvious; the remedy simple; therefore all the more difficult to accomplish.[2]

Jump from oysters in 1880 to cell phones today. In Japan, high-speed wireless broadband is woven into the fabric of everyday life much more than in the United States.[3] This is not intrinsic to Japanese culture. Speedy telecom happens because Japan avoided gridlock in assigning rights to spectrum and overcame patent thickets in telephony.

Housing works in reverse: on average, Americans today live in better, bigger spaces than the Japanese. This is not because the Japanese prefer tiny apartments. It's not part of Japanese culture or history. It's not because Japan is an island or land is scarce. Before World War II, Japanese on average had larger living spaces than Americans. The reverse is recent and accidental. It stems from policies that unintentionally created gridlock. Following the war, the Occupation Government transferred the American planning model into Japanese law. This was a well-intentioned move, but the transfer came at a low point in planning theory. America exported to Japan the rigid BANANA-republic regulations that were then making Berkeley and New York City such expensive places to live. Just try building anything in Tokyo.[4]

The point is: notice variation. If a market is working better next door, or one town over, or across the globe, that is often a clue that there may be hidden gridlock at home.

Be Nostalgic about the Good Old Days

Much about the good old days wasn't so good. Some things, however, worked better. Pay attention to those items and ask why. Tragedies of the anticommons often arise because property rights that made sense in the past have perverse consequences in a later era.

Copyright collectives emerged when paying artists for radio play was a major concern. But these collectives did not keep up with the changing locus of value in media production. Today, the cutting edge is multimedia assemblies, mash-ups, repackaging, rebundling, mix-this and multi-that.

Perhaps it's time to rethink ASCAP and BMI. African American farms and Native American land also worked better under sole ownership. The subtle intersection of land law, culture, and time led to fragmented ownership, gridlock, and wasted assets. Why not tweak the law, as some German states have done, so those who want to keep a farm in the family can do so more easily, and those who want to sell can get a fair price?

It's easy to spot tragedies of the commons: we choke on polluted air; we catch fewer oysters. With practice, hidden gridlock can be made just as visible. Making a problem visible doesn't solve it, but it's a necessary first step.

Step 2: Unlock the Grid

Once you've spotted gridlock, fixing it is not always easy. Mathematically, tragedies of underuse and overuse are symmetrical, but our lived experience tells us otherwise. Cognitive psychologists and experimental economists have shown that people don't have the knack for overcoming anticommons dilemmas as smoothly as the equivalent commons tragedies.[5] Partly, this is a matter of familiarity and experience. It may have something to do with how our brains are wired. Regardless, with greater challenge comes more reward.

Throughout this book, I've applied an implicit medical model in structuring solutions. First and best is prevention: don't let gridlock become entrenched. Second is treatment: look to fix gridlock after it is created. Finally, there's alternative medicine. Custom and norms often keep commons resources humming along. The same happens in most anticommons settings. More generally, analogize from solutions to commons tragedy— there lie the most fruitful clues for fixing gridlock. Who knew that oysters could help in discovering drugs and speeding up wireless broadband?

The balance of this chapter sets out a ten-part tool kit of solutions. The first three deal with prevention, the middle four with treatment, and the last are alternative medicine.

Monitoring

Just as regular checkups may detect disease, so forethought and vigilant advocacy may deter people from creating gridlock in the first instance. Not always, though: backroom deals get cut; someone may benefit from, and have an interest in, promoting tragedy; greed, racism, indifference, and ordinary politicking can intervene. Nevertheless, sometimes the problem is just missing information, and monitoring and advocacy are the solutions.

Recall that *underuse* is not yet a recognized word in many dictionaries. Lawmakers often do not know that they may be pushing resources into the gridlock economy. Once informed (and pressured by citizens and media), they might consider less destructive reforms. After the Patent and Trademark Office realized the dangers to innovation from gene-fragment patents, it raised the standards for patentability. After the National Institutes of Health learned how licensing of federally funded discoveries might be blocking new noncommercial research, it modified the licensing guidelines. Public outrage may be spurring belated attention to the plight of Native American allotment owners and African American heir property farmers.

Vaccination

Currently, governments create gridlock without suffering much direct consequence. They have little reason to avoid confusion, error, and lack of coordination. With BANANA republics, private developers go bankrupt awaiting permits, but regulators pay little price. Regulators do not even know the average delay they impose, nor do they know how their city permitting process compares with those in other cities. Collecting data can be a first step toward finding out which cities are most punishing for new development. Some real estate investors are already on top of this. Vornado Realty Trust makes its profits finding and arbitraging BANANA republics.

The next step may be for states, which authorize and control local governments, to mandate "one-stop shops" or "deemed approved" remedies for permits. These procedural reforms could act like a vaccine for the worst offenders. Even if the city keeps adding environmental and safety hurdles, a vaccinated city may not develop into a BANANA republic.

Isolate Outbreaks Early

Quick isolation of gridlock can reduce the harm it imposes while giving legislators time to craft other solutions. Turning back the ratchet of property rights is hard to do, but governments can stop the wheel from spinning more resources into the anticommons side of the property spectrum.

One step is simply to put people on notice about how the law may be changing, so further fragmentation will not give rise to legally protected "vested rights." For example, as soon as murder rates of store owners in Moscow spiked and people knew something was amiss, regulators could have frozen the initial misguided form of privatization, contained it, and then started experimenting with smarter approaches. Another approach is based in comparative study: pay attention to differences across time and geography; ask why markets work better there than here. Advocate to keep market-killing reforms from spreading.

Tune Up Existing Laws

Prevention does not always work. Sometimes it is more costly than a cure. Treatment rather than prevention is especially important in block-party or BANANA-republic settings. Be warned, though. These solutions represent a form of social surgery. The side effects may be serious.

The simplest way to change the behavior of people stuck in gridlock is to tune up laws so that potential market makers have a reasonable opportunity to prevail. The German farm-preservation tweak, for example, allows family members to escape an all-or-nothing dilemma. While such a tune-up may be too late for many African Americans, versions of it could ease conflict among the growing numbers of siblings who are inheriting farms, summer homes, and other real estate from aged parents.

The intense activity around biotech patent policy is mostly about tweaking the law. Fine-tuning isn't always easy, but adding the anticommons perspective pushes debate in the right direction. In the drug-development context, we need solutions that will preserve the drive to innovate, while easing access to research inputs. And that means getting the existing market participants on board. Otherwise, they block reforms and we stay gridlocked. Let's make some deals.

Create Assembly Tools

If you want people to unlock grids, make it easier to put rights together. Empowering market makers with new assembly tools is not as difficult as it may seem. Oil-field unitization is an Anglo-American legal innovation that is spreading around the world. Condominiums came in the opposite direction, hopping from European civil law to Puerto Rico and then to the rest of the United States. Since the 1960s, America went from no condo owners to fifty million. Thailand imported the condo form more recently, and suddenly developers started building up instead of out. Canada developed business improvement districts in the 1970s, and now thousands of BIDs provide benches, landscaping, and security patrols. Center-city shops can finally compete with suburban malls. Similarly, LADs may be able to solve the block-party dilemma.

Off-the-rack assembly tools give entrepreneurial private market makers the law they need to overcome gridlock, while protecting individual owners from abuse. Not everyone needs to invent a new legal form, but we all can advocate for those that exist and can propose new arenas where they might be useful: New forms of timeshares? Fractional ownership of vacation homes? BID-like structures to fix sidewalks and plant trees in aging residential areas? More prudent financial instruments for dividing and repackaging mortgage risk?

Get the Labels Right

Twenty-five years ago, doctors realized that patients feared the *nuclear* in "nuclear magnetic resonance" (NMR) testing, even though the procedure involved no radiation. So they relabeled NMR "magnetic resonance imaging" (MRI). MRIs are now part of routine medical practice, no more frightening-sounding than a cuddly CAT scan.

Similarly, regulation of mergers and monopolies in the United States has been labeled "antitrust" policy, a term that misleads regulators and harms consumers. When fragmented ownership is the underlying problem, mergers and monopolies may improve social welfare. For example, commercial aviation got off the ground and transistors revolutionized the economy in part because competitors were forced into "patent pools." America should adopt the European label and rename "antitrust" as "competition" policy. A simple label change might help legislators recognize that achieving the ultimate regulatory goal—healthy market competition—requires both antitrust and "protrust" approaches. Once you know the anticommons lexicon, you can be creative in naming the particular forms of gridlock you encounter.

Pick-Up Sticks

As much as possible, you should be free to use your property without collective coercion. To protect liberty and autonomy, governments should first try to solve gridlock with the less coercive prevention and treatment solutions I've mentioned above, and the alternative approaches I discuss below.

But if these softer solutions fail, and if gridlock is imposing an intolerable cost in resource underuse, then the state is sometimes justified in wiping out existing rights and starting over. In real estate, this is called *eminent domain*. In drug patenting, it is the *march-in right* (for U.S. patents partially based on federally funded research). For co-owned land, it is *partition*. Even bankruptcy law has a "pick-up sticks" rule that lets a bankruptcy trustee sell a "wasting asset"—such as a partly built house where the general contractor has defaulted—free and clear of competing liens.[6] Pick-up sticks tools pervade the law. They can all be seen as examples of last-ditch solutions to overcoming a tragedy of the anticommons.

This solution ensures that gridlock cannot cause unreasonable harm. It gets around minority tyranny, the costs imposed on us all when individuals veto use. Pick-up sticks can avoid what happened in Russia, when owners used hand grenades and hired killers to bundle fragmented ownership. Faced with intractable gridlock, we should be able to condemn rights, pay just compensation, assemble the resource, and move it to the higher-valued use.

Gossip, Shame, and Reputation

Alternative and nontraditional approaches make up the final group of solutions. These solutions are hard to measure, so they are often overlooked. Yet they are often the most effective, especially when used as complements to tools like legal tweaking. You should see if these approaches are already at work when you spot gridlock.

Like the lobster gangs in Maine, close-knit communities often work out successful ways to resolve conflict without reliance on state intervention. Instead of needing the state to privatize or regulate a misused resource, people can talk to each other about their neighbors' activities. Gossip, shame, and reputation are powerful levers for managing potential grid-lock—often more powerful than direct legal sanctions or market incentives. These solutions tend to work best in communities in which people have multiple links to one another, meet for repeat dealings, and control low-value uses. Shaming a deviant can be a powerful tool.

A branch of modern economics, called *game theory*, studies such interactions. Tragedies of the commons and anticommons can be seen as forms of "prisoner's dilemmas" and "chicken games" in which individual rational choices add up to collective misery. Game theorists noticed that people learn to cooperate when they play against each other repeatedly. Even without law, players punish defectors and reward cooperators using a playground strategy called "tit-for-tat." Reputation is decisive. But gossip, shame, and reputation work less well with large, diverse, or anonymous groups who are in onetime transactions.

Voluntary Agreement

Sometimes people succeed in overcoming gridlock through voluntary agreement. Patent pools can be such a solution. Early ones were forced by the government, but the DVD and digital imaging pools were voluntary. On the copyright side, Hollywood and Broadway songwriters formed AS-CAP and singer-songwriters formed BMI to license copyrighted music for public performances. These copyright collectives managed to get exemptions from antitrust regulators, but they negotiated only a limited reach: for example, ASCAP does not solve the problem of compiling DVDs or creating other new media. "Standard-setting organizations" (SSOs) offer a similar approach. For example, every manufacturer uses the same technical standards for wireless routers. With SSOs, each player knows that individual investments will be complementary with the products made by others.

Sometimes neighbors come together to assemble their land for higher-valued uses. But not often. The problem for land assembly, as for voluntary agreement generally, is that it becomes costly to negotiate and police as numbers increase. Holdouts and free riders can torpedo consensus. Everyone wants the benefit of agreement; few want to incur the costs of getting there. On the intellectual property side, we've seen the "open source" movement and Creative Commons help people voluntarily assemble computer software and related intellectual property. These regimes are not anarchic. They are complex legal and institutional forms with a simple goal: to help dispersed individuals overcome gridlock without government coercion.

Philanthropy

More and more philanthropic and nonprofit organizations are dealing with gridlock. The Golden Rice Project brought together dozens of competing patent holders to create a lifesaving new food. Similarly, the Bill and Melinda Gates Foundation has been trying to catalyze creation of a malaria vaccine. The foundation has been assembling patent rights held by competing vaccine developers and making them widely available, overcoming a patent thicket and gridlock. By guaranteeing bulk purchases of a successful vaccine, the Gates Foundation is giving entrepreneurial market makers a powerful incentive for invention.

To give a final example, environmentalist Patrick Noonan used his MacArthur Foundation "genius grant" to set up a nonprofit Conservation Fund, which brings together business and conservation groups locked in block parties and BANANA republics over timber. As *Forbes* noted:

> The Conservation Fund has made itself the middleman in a fractious relationship between rival rights owners. The result, writ large, could unlock new value in myriad timber investments. . . . Some 7 million acres of woods, worth $4 billion in total, are idle and up for sale. . . . But often a simple sale is all but impossible because of the cobweb of rights for land, trees, and the minerals beneath, which are owned by separate companies that rarely agree on much of anything. Adding to the strain is the pressure from state officials and green activists pushing to set aside ever more undeveloped lands.[7]

By now, this type of gridlock should be familiar. When private negotiations failed, the Conservation Fund stepped in. One recent beneficiary of this market-maker philanthropy, International Paper, owned seventy-five thousand acres of prime Tennessee timberland that was tied up in a "foot-deep thicket of deeds, buyback rights, and other legal paper."[8] Sound familiar? International Paper owned the land and timber rights; Tennessee Mining Company claimed the coal, oil, and gas reserves underneath. Neither could agree on how to proceed without interfering with the other.

In time and at great expense, the two companies might have untangled the legal mess and returned the land to use, or the state and its environmentalist allies might have bankrupted the firms. Instead of pointless delays and all-or-nothing solutions, Noonan's Conservation Fund structured a deal in which all the parties got most of what they wanted. And it earned a fee that covered its expenses. This is an elegant way to overcome gridlock. The fund took on "the mountain of paperwork required to divvy up rights into neat and sellable strata. . . . They also stripped the tract of its development rights and stipulated that much of the land must stay open for recreation and that wetlands and wildlife must be protected."[9]

According to the fund's chief executive, Lawrence Selzer, "As a result of this project we now have a bold new model for forestland conservation in America."[10] And it's an attractive one for timber and coal companies. The bottom line is that fixing gridlock can be profitable and ecologically sound—a win-win solution that replaces the losing anticommons game.

We create gridlock all the time, but tragedy is not our fate. Just as the European powers removed robber barons from the Rhine after 1815, we too can dismantle phantom tollbooths in the economy today. With practice, we can spot and avert potential tragedies of the anticommons. If ownership become too fragmented, we can creatively use politics, law, finance, and plain neighborliness to reassemble resources.

Fixing our gridlock economy is a worthy and noble goal. By doing so, we can jump-start innovation, save millions of lives, and unleash trillions of dollars in lost productivity. Let's unlock the grid.

Acknowledgments

I've gotten so much help on this book from so many people that it seems churlish to thank just a few. That said, first mention must go to my co-authors Hanoch Dagan, Becky Eisenberg, Merritt Fox, Rick Hills, and Jim Krier. The articles we wrote together are the pillars on which this book is built.

Thanks to the growing band of scholars who write on the anticommons—they have taught me a great deal; they made this book possible. To single out a few, I want to acknowledge James Buchanan, Ben Depoorter, Lee Anne Fennell, Fiona Murray, Francesco Parisi, Norbert Schulz, Scott Stern, Yong Yoon, and Rosemarie Ham Ziedonis. Thanks also to the late Mancur Olson, who encouraged me as I was starting out.

I've presented the gridlock idea in so many academic forums that a simple list of people who have given me truly useful feedback would run on for pages. Nevertheless, I would be remiss not to thank at least Bob Ellickson, Richard Epstein, Mark Kelman, Mark Lemley, Larry Lessig, Frank Michelman, Rick Pildes, and Carol Rose. On telecom, thanks especially to Tom Hazlett, Reed Hundt, and John Thorne—each combed through the chapter and made it stronger; on post-socialist transition, Alain Bertaud, Bob Buckley, Bertrand Renaud, Ray Struyk, and the late Steve Mayo; on LADs, Henry Hansmann, Louis Kaplow, Mitch Polinsky, Eric Posner, and Steve Shavell.

I began writing this book during the 2004–05 academic year as a fellow at the Center for Advanced Study in the Behavioral Sciences, Stanford,

California. If you want to endow a national treasure, give them a lot of money. I hope *The Gridlock Economy* will be a worthy addition to the center's intimidating and inspiring library—every book on the shelves was conceived or written there. I am grateful to center staff Cynthia Brandt and Kathleen Much. Susan Shirk organized a group of fellows writing for audiences beyond academia. Our group launched my project. Many fellows engaged with my work, including Susan Athey, Jon Bendor, Steve Feierman, Brad Inwood, Mary and Peter Katzenstein, Bob and Nan Keohane, David Konstan, Nolan McCarty, Eric Mueggler, Ed Muir, Josh Ober, Sam Popkin, Julio Rotemberg, and especially Gregory Ward.

Columbia Law School has been the perfect home for writing this book. Dean David Schizer has supported this project in every conceivable way. I owe him more than I can say. Thanks also to my amazing colleagues, including Jeff Gordon, Avery Katz, Clarissa Long, Tom Merrill, Elizabeth Scott, and especially Scott Hemphill and Tim Wu, who provided invaluable comments. My assistant Tricia Philip offered indefatigable support. She overcame gridlock in copyright clearances for the book. The law library provided superb research support. Jessica Berch, Jesse Dungan, Kim Jaimez, Lisa Sandoval, and Peter Schwingler expertly checked every citation in the manuscript. My greatest thanks go to my incredible research assistant Seth Davis, who ran the citation checking campaign, edited every line of the book, and redrafted many. I'm lucky that Seth is still a student; he'll be a colleague soon enough.

During 2006–07, I spent a wonderful year at UCLA Law School teaching and writing this book. Thanks to Dean Mike Schill, who gave me fantastic feedback and the time I needed to draft a big chunk of the manuscript. Stuart Banner showed me the colorful examples from early air travel. Ann Carlson, Susan French, Russell Korobkin, Gia Lee, Stephen Munzer, Kal Raustiala, Seana Shiffrin, Eugene Volokh, and many others at UCLA made this a better book. My assistant Christine Chung helped at every turn. The law library was always wonderfully resourceful. Alice Ko and Keri Livingston were excellent research assistants. Thanks also to the USC Law School, Dean Bob Rasmussen, and especially Gregory Keating, Dan Klerman, George Lefcoe, and Ed McCaffrey, for hosting a week in 2007 of intense and productive discussions on the book. My enduring gratitude to the University of Michigan Law School where I spent eight wonderful years, learned to be a scholar, and developed many of the ideas that evolved into this book.

Finally, thanks to my students at Columbia, Michigan, NYU, UCLA, and Yale Law Schools—they've challenged and refined every idea I've had. Everything from the story of declining African American farm ownership to the law of postering came from them.

At Basic Books, I had the privilege of working with a top-notch and enthusiastic team, including John Sherer, Michele Jacob, Sandra Beris, Annette Wenda, Timm Bryson, Alix Sleight, and most of all, my editor, Bill Frucht. Bill has stood behind this book from the first day the proposal crossed his desk, and at every step since. Every line in the book has benefited from his keen intelligence.

Angela Hayes and Lynn Goldberg at Goldberg McDuffie Communications have been creative advocates for this book as they've guided the publicity effort. Thanks also to Erin Kelly and Jim O'Neil at Columbia Law School for helping to get the book out to a wide audience.

My deepest thanks go to my agent, Tina Bennett. I still can't believe she took me on. When I was searching for an agent, I looked in the books I admired most, and one after the other, the authors thanked her. It's no accident. Tina is a passionate advocate for ideas that matter. She guides writers to their best work. There's no one I'd rather have at my side in the idea business.

A handful of friends and family have stood by this project for years. Solly Angel taught me how to write a book and first inspired me to embark on this one. Adam Cohen, Annie Murphy Paul, and Alissa Quart helped me navigate the book publishing world. Daniel Rothenberg read every line and improved many. Mary Goldenson made sure the book actually got written. Thanks also to Peter and Paula Noah, Karen Parker, Tamar Schapiro, John Schmitt, Miki and Brad Shelton, and Josh Singer for all their support. My cousin Aram Sinnreich has taught me a lot about, among other subjects, copyright policy. I am fortunate to have a wonderful, supportive family: Dan, Kathy, and niece Joelle; Rafael, Michal, and nephews Eitan and Gilad; and parents Jack and Naomi, who provided not only encouragement but also careful proofreading.

More or less every day for many years, I've relied on Virginia Rutter for guidance on all things. Among her many gifts, she's a remarkable translator of academic ideas for wider audiences. She believed in this book long before I did and has been its most constant cheerleader.

At the head of this bounteous table of thanksgiving sit Debora and Ellie, the loves of my life. Many authors thank spouse and kid for patience and support during the dark years of book writing. Debora certainly kept the family running, but that's the least of her contributions. She's the best writer I know. At every important juncture in the book—page 1 for example—I simply turned my clunky draft over to Debora, left the room, and came back to a far, far better thing. This is her book as much as mine.

Notes

*All Web addresses were verified as of May 1, 2008. For updated information,
see the book's Web site, www.gridlockeconomy.com.*

Chapter 1

1. John E. Kelly, senior vice president at IBM, quoted in Steve Lohr, "Sharing the Wealth at I.B.M.," *New York Times*, April 11, 2005, Business section, 1, 4. Kelly continues, "It seemed to us the pendulum has swung way too far in the direction of companies blindly chasing patents, and blindly chasing the enforcement of patents. . . . We don't know quite where this is headed."

2. Dennis Gilbert, chief science officer at Celera Genomics, quoted in Andrew Pollack, "Celera to Quit Selling Genome Information," *New York Times*, April 27, 2005, Business section, 2.

3. Peter Ringrose, chief scientific officer at Bristol-Myers Squibb, quoted in Andrew Pollack, "Bristol-Myers and Athersys Make a Deal on Gene Patents," *New York Times*, January 8, 2001, Business section, 2.

4. Estate-planning lawyer Beth Kaufman, quoted in John Leland, "Breaking the Silence," *New York Times*, March 18, 2008, Business section, 1, 5.

5. Hanoch Dagan and Michael A. Heller, "The Liberal Commons," *Yale Law Journal* 110 (2001): 549–623, at 614. According to *The American Law of Property*, "If the cotenants cannot agree neither law nor equity can settle such differences; nor can they specifically settle how the property shall be used and enjoyed" (A. James Casner, ed., *The American Law of Property* [Boston: Little, Brown, 1952], vol. 2, sec. 6.18, p. 78). European civil code systems would reach the same outcome on these facts: each owner can block the others (Dagan and Heller, "The Liberal Commons," 615n.254).

6. J. P. Chamberlain, *The Regime of the International Rivers: Danube and Rhine* (New York: Columbia University Press, 1923), 147–57.

7. See generally Roy Gardner, Noel Gaston, and Robert T. Masson, "Tolling the Rhine in 1254: Complementary Monopoly Revisited" (unpublished manuscript, August 2002, www.indiana.edu/~workshop/papers/gardner_102802.pdf). By 1780, there were still nine toll stations on the fifty-mile stretch between Mainz and Koblenz and another sixteen from there to the Dutch border (Frederic M. Scherer, "The Economics of Gene Patents," pt. 2, *Academic Medicine* 77 [2002]: 1348–67, at 1363). According to Scherer, "The multiplication of tolls suppressed most of the traffic that otherwise would have traversed that artery—absent tolls, the least costly means of travel in an era of hopelessly bad roads—and thereby impeded German economic development. Not until 1831 were treaties concluded that allowed essentially free navigation and hence full development of the waterway's potential" (ibid.).

8. See also the map designed by Ludwig Schäfer-Grohe in Walther Ottendorf-Simrock, *Castles on the Rhine* (Chicago: Argonaut, 1967), title page.

9. Anthony Ramirez, "Mapping Out the Wireless-Phone Future," *New York Times*, November 12, 1992, National Desk, 1.

10. Dennis Roberson quoted in Scott Woolley, "Dead Air," *Forbes*, November 25, 2002, 139–50, 141 (Roberson), 140 (Woolley).

11. Thomas Hazlett popularized this term to describe anticommons tragedy in the telecom sector ("Tragedies of the Tele-commons," FT.com, April 18, 2003, http://search.ft.com/nonFtArticle?id=030418005136). An earlier use is J. Gregory Sidak and Daniel F. Spulber, "The Tragedy of the Telecommons: Government Pricing of Unbundled Network Elements under the Telecommunications Act of 1996," *Columbia Law Review* 97 (1997): 1081–1161.

12. See Michael A. Heller and Rebecca S. Eisenberg, "Can Patents Deter Innovation? The Anticommons in Biomedical Research," *Science* 280 (May 1, 1998): 698–701.

13. The term *patent thicket* was coined by Carl Shapiro, a leading patent and innovation economist, in "Navigating the Patent Thicket: Cross Licenses, Patent Pools, and Standard-Setting," *Innovation Policy and the Economy* 1 (2001): 119–50. On drugmaker secrecy, see John S. James, "Medical Innovation and Patent Gridlock," *AIDS Treatment News*, May 27, 2005, www.aidsnews.org/2005/06/patent-gridlock.html. "This problem tends to remain invisible, because those involved are usually pledged to secrecy, and are also trying to work something out so that their projects can proceed at all, however unsatisfactorily" (ibid.).

14. See Heller and Eisenberg, "Can Patents Deter Innovation?" 699–700 (distinguishing concurrent fragments from license stacking). See also Francesco Parisi,

Norbert Schulz, and Ben Depoorter, "Simultaneous and Sequential Anticommons," *European Journal of Law and Economics* 17 (2004): 175–90, at 185.

15. On big inches, see generally Michael A. Heller, "The Tragedy of the Anticommons: Property in the Transition from Marx to Markets," *Harvard Law Review* 111 (1998): 621–88, at 682–84. The big-inch scheme spawned copycats, then scams. According to one story, "There's a strong suspicion that the poor Chinese customers are being had. Some of them seem to believe that owning even a tiny slice of America increases one's chances of winning U.S. citizenship or at least a visa" (Nina Munk, "A Cheap Ticket to the Promised Land?" *Forbes,* February 1, 1993, 90).

16. Reprinted with permission of the Quaker Oats Company.

17. I argue that such rules constitute a "boundary principle" buried in American law that limits people's rights to subdivide property into useless fragments (Michael A. Heller, "The Boundaries of Private Property," *Yale Law Journal* 108 [1999]: 1163–1223, at 1173–74). Scholars have reformulated this theory into a testable hypothesis, according to which "courts and legislators, consciously or unconsciously, already account for the asymmetric effects of property fragmentation when considering the optimal choice of rules and the optimal structure of remedies" (Parisi, Schulz, and Depoorter, "Simultaneous and Sequential Anticommons," 185).

18. Heller, "Tragedy of the Anticommons," 682.

19. The most famous and tragic saga of airport parochialism involves Japan's construction of Narita Airport. Since the mid-1960s, farmers holding tiny plots have blocked construction and caused billions in damage to Japan's economy. See "Narita Fiasco: Never Again," *Japan Times*, July 26, 2005, editorial, http://search.japantimes.co.jp/cgi-bin/ed20050726a1.html. To avoid gridlock, the four most expensive new airports in the world—Hong Kong, Osaka, Nagoya, and Seoul—have been built offshore on land reclaimed from the sea.

20. Gridlock continues even as the O'Hare expansion project is finally under way. Chicago has bought 549 residential and commercial properties in Bensenville; of these, 522 are vacant, but the village is using environmental review as a delay tactic to keep the empty houses from being demolished for a new runway (Sarah Schulte, "O'Hare Expansion Moves into New Phase," abc7chicago.com, February 25, 2008, http://abclocal.go.com/wls/story?section=news/local&id=5979987). Donald W. Tuegel, "Airport Expansions: The Need for a Greater Federal Role," *Washington University Journal of Urban and Contemporary Law* 54 (1998): 291–319, at 299–300 (summarizing the controversies); Dick Swauger, technology coordinator, Air Traffic Controllers Association, testimony before the House Committee on Transportation

and Infrastructure, Subcommittee on Aviation, April 26, 2001, 24, http://commdocs
.house.gov/committees/Trans/hpw107-14.000/hpw107-14_0.htm.

21. Michael Idov, "Gridlock at 30,000 Feet: What Went So Catastrophically Wrong," *New York Magazine*, November 5, 2007, www.nymag.com/news/features/2007/airports/40314/.

22. Alexandra Marks, "Gridlock over How to End Flight Gridlock," *Christian Science Monitor*, October 29, 2007, USA section, 3.

23. Details on *Eyes on the Prize* are available on the film's Web site, www.pbs.org/wgbh/amex/eyesontheprize.

24. Katie Dean, "Eyes on the Prize Hits P2P," *Wired*, January 27, 2005, www.wired.com/entertainment/music/news/2005/01/66410.

25. Katie Dean, "Cash Rescues Eyes on the Prize," *Wired*, August 30, 2005, www.wired.com/entertainment/music/news/2005/08/68664. See also Nancy Ramsey, "The Hidden Cost of Documentaries," *New York Times*, October 16, 2005, Arts and Leisure section, 13, 23.

26. Photograph by Marion S. Trikosko of Dr. King at a press conference, March 26, 1964. Image courtesy of the Library of Congress, Prints and Photographs Division, U.S. News & World Report Magazine Photograph Collection, LC-U9-11696-9A.

27. Marcia Biederman, "They Right the Songs," *New York Times*, March 14, 1999, New York and Region section, 4.

28. Rena Kosersky, quoted in Dean, "Eyes on the Prize Hits P2P."

29. James Surowiecki, "Righting Copywrongs," *New Yorker*, January 21, 2002, 27.

30. Katie Dean, "Bleary Days for Eyes on the Prize," *Wired*, December 22, 2002, www.wired.com/culture/lifestyle/news/2004/12/66106. The 2004 study was titled "Untold Stories: Creative Consequences of the Rights Clearance Culture for Documentary Filmmakers."

31. Dean, "Bleary Days for Eyes on the Prize."

32. See Ramsey, "Hidden Cost of Documentaries," 13.

33. Amy Sewell quoted in ibid.

34. See generally Barry Williams and Chris Kreski, *Growing Up Brady* (New York: HarperCollins, 1992), 142. In this vein, one federal judge asked, "Can Paramount cast Shelley Long in *The Brady Bunch Movie* without creating a triable issue of fact as to whether it is treading on Florence Henderson's right of publicity?" (*Wendt v. Host Int'l, Inc.*, 197 F.3d 1284, 1286 [9th Cir. 1999] [Kozinski, J., dissenting]).

35. For a synopsis, see HBO, "*Curb Your Enthusiasm*—Episode 6, Season 1," www.hbo.com/larrydavid/episode/season1/episode06.html.

36. Chris Anderson writes that "rights are a total hairball." *WKRP in Cincinnati,* he continues, "is considered one of the hardest popular TV shows of all to clear; it's the lead standard against which all other clearance challenges are considered" (*The Long Tail: Why the Future of Business Is Selling Less of More* [New York: Hyperion, 2006], 196).

37. Katie Dean, "Copyrights Keep TV Shows Off DVD," *Wired,* March 1, 2005, www.wired.com/entertainment/music/news/2005/03/66696.

38. David Lambert, cited in Dean, "Cash Rescues Eyes on the Prize."

39. See Bryan Reesman, "The Song Doesn't Remain the Same," *Hollywood Reporter,* November 15, 2005, S10, S55.

40. Public Enemy, "Caught, Can We Get a Witness?" *It Takes a Nation of Millions to Hold Us Back* (lyrics from compact disc liner, Def Jam/PolyGram Records, 1988).

41. Kembrew McLeod, "How Copyright Law Changed Hip Hop," *StayFree Magazine,* Fall 2002, www.stayfreemagazine.org/archives/20/public_enemy.html. According to Chuck D, "Putting a hundred small fragments into a song meant that you had a hundred different people to answer to. It's easier to sample a groove than it is to create a whole new collage. . . . That entire collage element is out the window" (ibid.).

42. Nicholas Reville, cofounder of Downhill Battle (a nonprofit music activism group), quoted in Katie Dean, "Remixing to Protest Sample Ruling," *Wired,* September 22, 2004, www.wired.com/entertainment/music/news/2004/09/65037.

43. Kalefa Sanneh, "With Arrest of DJ Drama, the Law Takes Aim at Mixtapes," *New York Times,* January 18, 2007, Arts section, 1, 7.

44. A federal appeals court held that the hip-hop group NWA infringed the band Funkadelic's copyright in a one-and-a-half-second clip—just three notes (*Bridgeport Music, Inc. v. Dimension Films,* 410 F.3d 792 [6th Cir. 2005]). To read the court's decision and hear the songs involved in every music copyright infringement case that has generated a published judicial opinion, see "Columbia Law School and UCLA Law Copyright Infringement Project," http://cip.law.ucla.edu/caselist.html. See also Dean, "Remixing to Protest Sample Ruling."

45. Daniel Fisher, "Name That Note," *Forbes,* October 18, 2004, 54.

46. Gridlock increases not only when fair use shrinks but also when copyright terms lengthen. Whenever the Mickey Mouse copyright is about to expire, the Walt Disney Company lobbies Congress for more retroactive protection. The Copyright Term Extension Act of 1998, also known as the Mickey Mouse Protection Act, gave Disney (and other corporate authors) twenty more years—a corporate subsidy from the public domain that further entrenches gridlock.

47. For an argument that anticommons theory justifies fair-use doctrine even if technology were to make it costless for copyright holders to collect fees, see Ben

Depoorter and Francesco Parisi, "Fair Use and Copyright Protection: A Price Theory Explanation," *International Review of Law and Economics* 21 (2002): 453–73. See also Neil Weinstock Netanel, *Copyright's Paradox* (New York: Oxford University Press, 2008), 143.

48. In New York, where I teach, the controlling case is *Basic Books, Inc. v. Kinko's Graphics Corp.*, 758 F. Supp. 1522 (S.D.N.Y. 1991), which determined that a commercial copy shop went too far in making and selling educational course readers. A federal appeals court in the Midwest came to a similar conclusion (*Princeton University Press v. Michigan Document Services, Inc.*, 99 F.3d 1381 [6th Cir. 1996] [en banc]).

49. Aristotle, *The Politics and The Constitution of Athens*, edited by Stephen Everson, translated by Benjamin Jowett (Cambridge: Cambridge University Press, 1996), 33. Before Aristotle, Thucydides noted that people "devote a very small fraction of time to the consideration of any public object, most of it to the prosecution of their own objects. Meanwhile each fancies that no harm will come to his neglect, that it is the business of somebody else to look after this or that for him; and so, by the same notion being entertained by all separately, the common cause imperceptibly decays" (*History of the Peloponnesian War*, translated by Richard Crawley [New York: E. P. Dutton, 1910], bk. 1, sec. 141).

50. Jared Diamond, "Easter's End," *Discover*, August 1995, 62–69, at 68.

51. Garrett Hardin, "The Tragedy of the Commons," *Science* 162 (1968): 1243–48, at 1244.

52. See examples in "The Digital Library of the Commons," http://dlc .dlib.indiana.edu.

53. See Heller, "Tragedy of the Anticommons," 624. For prior definitions of *anticommons* and my reworking, see ibid., 667–69.

54. Lee Anne Fennell, "Common Interest Tragedies," *Northwestern University Law Review* 98 (2004): 907–90, at 936–37.

55. John Tagliabue, "A Debate in Europe over Air Traffic Control," *New York Times*, August 25, 2002, Travel section, 3.

56. Robert Gramlich, policy director for the American Wind Energy Association, quoted in Clifford Krauss, "Move Over, Oil, There's Money in Texas Wind," *New York Times*, February 23, 2008, Business section, 1.

57. I discuss the dilemma of "share choppers" in Chapter 5.

58. See Gardner, Gaston, and Masson, "Tolling the Rhine," 4–5. Around the same time that the European powers overcame gridlock on the Rhine, internal French political reforms overcame gridlock in domestic irrigation canal construction. See Jean-Laurent Rosenthal, "The Development of Irrigation in Provence,

1700–1860: The French Revolution and Economic Growth," *Journal of Economic History* 50 (1990): 615–38.

59. Chamberlain, *Regime of the International Rivers,* 148.

60. There is a large and growing literature arguing that if patents are too easy to win, then innovation will be stifled. For example, see Adam B. Jaffe and Josh Lerner, *Innovation and Its Discontents: How Our Broken Patent System Is Endangering Innovation and Progress, and What to Do about It* (Princeton: Princeton University Press, 2004), 170–71. See also James Bessen and Michael J. Meurer, *Patent Failure: How Judges, Bureaucrats, and Lawyers Put Innovators at Risk* (Princeton: Princeton University Press, 2008), 39–42; and Lawrence Lessig, *The Future of Ideas: The Fate of the Commons in a Connected World* (New York: Random House, 2001).

61. James Buchanan and Yong J. Yoon, "Symmetric Tragedies: Commons and Anticommons," *Journal of Law and Economics* 43 (2000): 1–13, at 2. Others have extended the formal economic model. For example, see Norbert Schulz, Francesco Parisi, and Ben Depoorter, "Fragmentation in Property: Towards a General Model," *Journal of Institutional and Theoretical Economics* 158 (2002): 594–613; and Francesco Parisi, Norbert Schulz, and Ben Depoorter, "Duality in Property: Commons and Anticommons," *International Review of Law and Economics* 25 (2005): 578–91.

62. Sven Vanneste et al., "From 'Tragedy' to 'Disaster': Welfare Effects of Commons and Anticommons Dilemmas," *International Review of Law and Economics* 26 (2006): 104–22; Ben Depoorter and Sven Vanneste, "Putting Humpty Dumpty Back Together: Pricing in Anticommons Property Arrangements," *Journal of Law, Economics, and Policy* 3 (2006): 1–23.

63. For examples of anticommons research conducted in a business school setting, see Fiona Murray and Scott Stern, "Do Formal Intellectual Property Rights Hinder the Free Flow of Scientific Knowledge? An Empirical Test of the Anti-Commons Hypothesis," *Journal of Economic Behavior and Organization* 63 (2007): 648–87; and Rosemarie Ham Ziedonis, "Don't Fence Me In: Fragmented Markets for Technology and the Patent Acquisition Strategies of Firms," *Management Science* 50 (2004): 804–20.

Chapter 2

1. The spell-checkers in Microsoft Word and Corel WordPerfect reject *underuse,* but, oddly, the dictionary tool in WordPerfect accepts it. *Merriam-Webster's Dictionary* dings the word; the *Oxford English Dictionary* and *American Heritage Dictionary* endorse it. For casual Scrabble players, *underuse* went from being a risky bluff to a legitimate word in June 2005 on publication of the fourth edition of the *Official Scrabble Players Dictionary* (www.scrabble-assoc.com/boards/dictionary/ospd4-changes.html). For

serious players, however, *underuse* was still squiggly until adoption in March 2006 of the revised *OWL*, the *Official Tournament and Club Word List*. (*Squiggly* is a word, by the way, in all these sources.)

2. See generally www.iascp.org.

3. In 1999, the "Anticybersquatting Consumer Protection Act" amended federal law on property in domain names. Now, the winner of the race to the registrar's office loses in certain circumstances. The law aims to keep people from registering famous names and then holding them hostage. For example, the first owners of www.vw.com were forced to hand over the site to Volkswagen, the "VW" trademark owner (*Virtual Works v. Volkswagen of America,* 238 F.3d 264 [4th Cir. 2001]).

4. See Harold Demsetz, "Toward a Theory of Property Rights," *American Economic Review* 57 (1967): 347–59, at 354–59. On philosophical foundations, see generally Jeremy Waldron, *The Right to Private Property* (New York: Oxford University Press, 1991); and Stephen R. Munzer, *A Theory of Property* (New York: Cambridge University Press, 1990).

5. See generally Elinor Ostrom, *Governing the Commons: The Evolution of Institutions for Collective Action* (Cambridge: Cambridge University Press, 1990); and Ostrom, "Coping with Tragedies of the Commons," *Annual Review of Political Science* 2 (1999): 493–535.

6. Lawyers refer to this up-and-down ownership as the "ad coelum" doctrine. For a lively historical account, see Stuart Banner, *Who Owns the Sky? The Struggle to Control Airspace from the Wright Brothers On* (Cambridge: Harvard University Press, forthcoming, 2008). See also Thomas W. Merrill and Henry E. Smith, *Property: Principles and Policies* (New York: Foundation Press, 2007), 13–15.

7. Reproduced with permission of Curtis Brown Group Ltd., London, on behalf of the Estate of William Empson. Copyright © William Empson 1928. Quoted in John Haffenden, *William Empson: Among the Mandarins* (Oxford: Oxford University Press, 2005), 1:47.

8. Some cities have active markets in air rights. See William Neuman, "Selling the Air Above," *New York Times,* March 5, 2006, Real Estate section, 1, 8. According to Neuman, air rights in New York City can sell for 50 to 60 percent of the underlying land price, in some cases reaching more than four hundred dollars a square foot.

9. For an array of plausible legal solutions, see Merrill and Smith, *Property*, 14–15.

10. See Victor Appleton, *Tom Swift and His Airship* (New York: Grosset and Dunlap, 1910), www.books.google.com/books?id=8GsCAAAAYAAJ.

11. Victor Appleton, *Tom Swift and His Great Searchlight* (New York: Grosset and Dunlap, 1912), 127, www.gutenberg.org/etext/4635, chap. 14.

12. *Hinman v. Pacific Air Transport,* 84 F.2d 755, 758 (9th Cir. 1936) (Haney, J.).

13. *United States v. Causby,* 328 U.S. 256, 261 (1946). As an aside, the farmer won on the merits because the overflights rendered his land uninhabitable and (literally) scared his chickens to death when they flew into walls of their coop: warplanes crossed his farm only eighty-three feet up, an altitude that fell below Congress's definition of "navigable air space" (263–64).

14. Lawrence Lessig, *Free Culture: The Nature and Future of Creativity* (New York: Penguin Press, 2004), 1–3.

15. "Authors Guild Sues Google, Citing 'Massive Copyright Infringement,'" Authors Guild press release, September 20, 2005, www.authorsguild.org/news/sues_google_citing.htm.

16. See Lawrence Lessig, www.lessig.org/blog/archives/003202.shtml and www.lessig.org/blog/2005/09/google_sued.html. See also Lessig, "Let a Thousand Googles Bloom," *Los Angeles Times,* January 12, 2005, Metro section, 11. For a summary of the debate, see Merrill and Smith, *Property,* 15.

17. *Manufacturers Aircraft Association v. United States,* 77 Ct. Cl. 481, 483–84 (1933).

18. Image from U.S. Patent 821,393, issued to the Wright brothers in May 1906, www.google.com/patents?vid=USPAT821393&id=h5NWAAAAEBAJ&dq=821,393.

19. See George Bittlingmayer, "Property Rights, Progress, and the Aircraft Patent Agreement," *Journal of Law and Economics* 31 (1988): 227–48, at 230–32; Herbert A. Johnson, "The Wright Patent Wars and Early American Aviation," *Journal of Air Law and Commerce* 69 (2004): 21–63, at 57.

20. Bittlingmayer, "Property Rights," 234.

21. On patent holdouts in the early development of computer memory, see Charles J. Bashe et al., *IBM's Early Computers* (Cambridge: MIT Press, 1986), 267–71.

22. *Oxford English Dictionary,* "overuse, *v.*," http://ed2.oed.com/cgi/entry/00168291.

23. This was the earliest example of *overuse* as a noun in the 1989 second edition of the *Oxford English Dictionary* (http://ed2.oed.com/cgi/entry/00168290). The draft 2004 revision uncovers an earlier use (http://dictionary.oed.com/cgi/entry/00338190).

24. On the property trilogy, see Michael A. Heller "The Dynamic Analytics of Property Law," *Theoretical Inquiries in Law* 2 (2001): 79–95, at 82–92. Most property regimes are best described as mixtures of these basic categories. See, for example, Henry E. Smith, "Semicommon Property Rights and Scattering in the Open Fields," *Journal of Legal Studies* 29 (2000): 131–69.

25. William Blackstone, *Commentaries on the Laws of England: In Four Books*, bk. 2, *2.

26. On open-access versus group-access property, see Thráinn Eggertsson, "Open Access versus Common Property," in *Property Rights: Cooperation, Conflict, and Law*, edited by Terry Anderson and Fred McChesney (Princeton: Princeton University Press, 2003), 74–85. See also Carol M. Rose, "Left Brain, Right Brain, and History in the New Law and Economics of Property," *Oregon Law Review* 79 (2000): 479–92, at 479–88. I advocate that we use the term *liberal commons* to describe many forms of legally sanctioned group ownership. See generally Dagan and Heller, "The Liberal Commons" (see chap. 1, n. 5).

27. Yoram Barzel, *Economic Analysis of Property Rights* (Cambridge: Cambridge University Press, 1989), 71.

28. *Oxford English Dictionary*, "under-use, *n.*," http://dictionary.oed.com/cgi/entry/50265168.

29. Ibid., "under-use, *v.*"

30. See, e.g., Allan Gaw, "The Care Gap: Underuse of Statin Therapy in the Elderly," *International Journal of Clinical Practice* 58 (2004): 777–85.

31. See generally James Acheson, *Lobster Gangs of Maine* (Hanover, N.H.: University Press of New England, 1988).

32. John Tierney, "A Tale of Two Fisheries," *New York Times*, August 27, 2000, Magazine section, 40.

33. Acheson, *The Lobster Gangs of Maine*, 75, 48–52. See also Robert C. Ellickson, Carol M. Rose, and Bruce A. Ackerman, eds., *Perspectives on Property Law*, 3d ed. (New York: Aspen Law and Business, 2002), 134–35.

34. Robert C. Ellickson, *Order without Law: How Neighbors Settle Disputes* (Cambridge: Harvard University Press, 1991).

35. Quoted in Jim Rutenberg, "Grand Central Terminal, in the Curl," *New York Times*, August 14, 2005, Week in Review section, 4.

36. See Tierney, "Tale of Two Fisheries," 41–42.

37. See ibid., 42–43.

38. See Carol M. Rose, "Expanding the Choices for the Global Commons: Comparing Newfangled Tradable Allowance Schemes to Old-Fashioned Common Property Regimes," *Duke Environmental Law and Policy Forum* 10 (1999): 45–72, at 47–52. For an evaluation of the New Zealand fishing-quota system, which is similar to Australia's, see Richard G. Newell, James N. Sanchirico, and Suzi Kerr, "Fishing Quota Markets," *Journal of Environmental Economics and Management* 49 (2005): 437–62.

39. For example, see Depoorter and Vanneste, "Putting Humpty Dumpty Back Together" (see chap. 1, n. 62). Used by permission.

40. Dagan and Heller, "The Liberal Commons," 552–54. See also Hanoch Dagan and Carolyn J. Frantz, "Properties of Marriage," *Columbia Law Review* 104 (2004): 75–133.

41. I develop an early version of this spectrum in Heller, "Boundaries of Private Property," 1194–98 (see chap. 1, n. 17).

42. From Buchanan and Yoon, "Symmetric Tragedies," 8, fig. (see chap. 1, n. 61). Used by permission.

43. Ibid., 12.

44. One group of scholars concludes that "it is easier to fragment than to reconvene fragmented property. In the realm of nonconforming property arrangements, this generates one-directional stickiness in the transfer of legal entitlements" (Parisi, Schulz, and Depoorter, "Simultaneous and Sequential Anticommons," 186 [see chap. 1, n. 14]). See also Parisi, Schulz, and Depoorter, "Duality in Property," 578–91 (see chap. 1, n. 62). Game theory, a branch of economics, is also useful for parsing anticommons dynamics using colorful terms such as *prisoner's dilemma* and the *chicken game*. For an example, see Lee Anne Fennell, "Common Interest Tragedies," *Northwestern University Law Review* 98 (2004): 907–90.

45. On the current usefulness of Cournot's insights, see Hal R. Varian, "In Europe, G.E. and Honeywell Ran Afoul of 19th-Century Thinking," *New York Times,* June 28, 2001, Business section, 2. Cournot noticed that copper and zinc were both necessary inputs to making brass. He showed that if there was a single supplier of each input, then we might have less brass produced at higher prices than if the copper and zinc suppliers were merged into a single monopoly. In this example, the two inputs are "complements" (ibid.). In 1839, Charles Ellet Jr. appears to have independently come upon the same idea as Cournot. Ellet showed that divided ownership of segments of a railway may produce less profit for the railways and higher prices for consumers (*An Essay on the Laws of Trade in Reference to the Works of Internal Improvement in the United States* [Richmond: P. D. Bernard, 1839]). See also Yossi Feinberg and Morton I. Kamien, "Highway Robbery: Complementary Monopoly and the Hold-Up Problem," *International Journal of Industrial Organization,* 19 (2001): 1603–21. Today, "Cournot complementarity" usually describes the multiproduct problem; when one input producer and a downstream manufacturer both have market power, economists may call it "double marginalization." In either case, merger or vertical integration is a standard solution.

46. On the problem of complements in an information economy, see Hal R. Varian, Carl Shapiro, and Joseph V. Farrell, *The Economics of Information Technology: An Introduction* (Cambridge: Cambridge University Press, 2004), 43–45. On the interaction of substitutes and complements in the anticommons context, see

Giuseppe Dari-Mattiacci and Francesco Parisi, "Substituting Complements," *Journal of Competition Law and Economics* 2 (2006): 333–47.

47. Carl Shapiro, "Navigating the Patent Thicket" (see chap. 1, n. 13).

48. Vanneste et al., "From 'Tragedy' to 'Disaster,'" 116–17 (see chap. 1, n. 62). Follow-up studies looked at why negotiations fail when presented in anticommons form. They found more failure as the number and complementarity of fragment owners increase. Also, as uncertainty increases, losses become even more pronounced (Depoorter and Vanneste, "Putting Humpty Dumpty Back Together," 21–23).

49. Steven Stewart and David J. Bjornstad, "An Experimental Investigation of Predictions and Symmetries in the Tragedies of the Commons and Anticommons," Joint Institute for Energy and Environment Report, No. JIEE 2002–07 (August 2002), 17.

50. On the costs of "excessive anarchy" in the oil industry, see Gary D. Libecap and James L. Smith, "The Economic Evolution of Petroleum Property Rights in the United States," *Journal of Legal Studies* 31 (2002): S589–S608. The same tragedy affects excessive pumping of groundwater. See Barton H. Thompson Jr., "Tragically Difficult: The Obstacles to Governing the Commons," *Environmental Lawyer* 30 (2000): 241–78, at 250.

51. Gary D. Libecap and Steven N. Wiggins, "Contractual Responses to the Common Pool: Prorationing of Crude Oil Production," *American Economic Review* 74 (1984): 87–98, at 89–90.

52. Depoorter and Vanneste, "Putting Humpty Dumpty Back Together," 20–23.

53. These points are developed in Heller, "Tragedy of the Anticommons," 676 (see chap. 1, n. 15).

54. Just as an anticommons theoretically may lead to overuse, it is possible for a commons to be associated with underuse. See ibid. For a real-world example, see William W. Buzbee, "The Regulatory Fragmentation Continuum, Westway, and the Challenges of Regional Growth," *Journal of Law and Politics* 21 (2005): 323–63. See also Fennell, "Common Interest Tragedies," 934–37, for an argument that commons and anticommons, overuse and underuse, are different facets of a single underlying tragedy.

55. Carol Rose, "The Comedy of the Commons: Custom, Commerce, and Inherently Public Property," *University of Chicago Law Review* 53 (1986): 711–81. See also Robert C. Ellickson, "Property in Land," *Yale Law Journal* 102 (1993): 1315–1400, at 1336–38.

56. On the potential use of an anticommons to preserve Central Park, see Abraham Bell and Gideon Parchomovsky, "Of Property and Antiproperty," *Michigan Law Review* 102 (2003): 1–70, at 3–4, 31–36, 60–61.

57. See Julia D. Mahoney, "Perpetual Restrictions on Land and the Problem of the Future," *Virginia Law Review* 88 (2002): 739–87, at 785.

58. On the role of multiple vetoes in producing political stability, see Josephine T. Andrews and Gabriella R. Montinola, "Veto Players and the Rule of Law in Emerging Democracies," *Comparative Political Studies* 37 (2004): 55–87; and George Tsebelis and Eric C. C. Chang, "Veto Players and the Structure of Budgets in Advanced Industrialized Countries," *European Journal of Political Research* 43 (2004): 449–76.

59. John Davidson quoted in Alexandra Twin, "Gearing Up for Gridlock," CNNMoney.com, November 2, 2006, http://money.cnn.com/2006/11/01/markets/markets_election/index.htm?postversion=2006110210. See also Associated Press, "Stocks Rise on Election Results," FOXNews.com, November 8, 2006, www.foxnews.com/story/0,2933,228159,00.html.

Chapter 3

1. On September 7, 2007, the House of Representatives passed the Patent Reform Act of 2007, a bill that would, among other reforms, limit the remedies available to owners whose patents are infringed (H.R. 1908 [2007]: http://frwebgate.access.gpo.gov/cgi-bin/getdoc.cgi?dbname=110_cong_bills&docid=f:h1908eh.txt.pdf). Also note that the Genomic Research and Accessibility Act of 2007, introduced in the House, would bar new gene patents (H.R. 977 [2007]: www.govtrack.us/congress/bill.xpd?bill=h110-977). Michael Crichton, author of this chapter's epigraph, supports such a measure ("Patenting Life," *New York Times*, February 13, 2007, Op-ed section, 23; and "This Essay Breaks the Law," *New York Times,* March 19, 2006, Op-ed section, 13). Crichton's views are often controversial, but he does know how to turn a phrase.

2. BIO, a biotechnology industry association, argues that the anticommons threat is overstated. See Ted Buckley, "The Myth of the Anticommons," Report for BIO, May 31, 2007, 12–13, www.bio.org/ip/domestic/TheMythoftheAnticommons.pdf. See also Ann Mills and Patti Tereskerz, "Proposed Patent Reform Legislation: Limitations of Empirical Data Used to Inform the Public Policy Debate," Consultants' Report for BIO, January 28, 2008, 19–20, www.bio.org/ip/domestic/UVA_Limitations_of_Empirical_Data.pdf. Most firms in biotech are relatively small. For example, BIO represents 1,473 organizational members, of which 314 are publicly traded companies with most employing fewer than 50 people. See Ann Mills and Patti Tereskerz, "'Junk' Patents and Biotechnology: An Illusion or a Real Threat to Innovation?" *Biotechnology Law Report* 26 (2007): 226–30, at 226.

3. For a nonpartisan consideration of the issues, see Wendy H. Schacht, "Gene Patents: A Brief Overview of Intellectual Property Issues," Congressional Research Service Report RS22516, October 3, 2006, 2–6, www.ipmall.info/hosted_resources/crs/RS22516_061003.pdf.

4. "Inventing a New System," *Los Angeles Times,* March 23, 2006, editorial, 10.

5. Heller and Eisenberg, "Can Patents Deter Innovation?" 698 (see chap. 1, n. 12).

6. See Lori Pressman et al., "The Licensing of DNA Patents by U.S. Academic Institutions: An Empirical Survey," *Nature Biotechnology* 24 (2006): 31–39, at 33, 35. See also Timothy Caulfield et al., "Evidence and Anecdotes: An Analysis of Human Gene Patenting Controversies," *Nature Biotechnology* 24 (2006): 1091–94, at 1092.

7. Stephen M. Maurer recounts the failed efforts between 1999 and 2001 to create a self-supporting database for discoveries relating to human genetic variations ("Inside the Anticommons: Academic Scientists Struggle to Build a Commercially Self-Supporting Human Mutations Database, 1999–2001," *Research Policy* 35 [2006]: 839–53, at 848–50).

8. See generally David E. Adelman and Kathryn L. DeAngelis, "Patent Metrics: The Mismeasure of Innovation in the Biotech Patent Debate," *Texas Law Review* 85 (2007): 1677–1744, at 1692–93.

9. From Kyle Jensen and Fiona Murray, "Intellectual Property Landscape of the Human Genome," *Science* 310 (2005): 239–40, at 239, fig., www.sciencemag.org/cgi/content/full/310/5746/239/F1. Reprinted with permission from AAAS.

10. W. Wayt Gibbs, "Patently Inefficient: A New Industry Is Thrashed by Waves of Litigation," *Scientific American,* February 2001, 34.

11. From Gibbs, "Patently Inefficient," 34. Copyright © 2001 by Scientific American, Inc. All rights reserved.

12. National Academy of Sciences, Committee on Intellectual Property Rights in the Knowledge-Based Economy, *A Patent System for the 21st Century* (Washington, D.C.: National Academies Press, 2004), 48–59, www.nap.edu/catalog.php?record_id=10976. For an opposing view, see Mills and Tereskerz, "Proposed Patent Reform Legislation," 12–14.

13. Mark A. Lemley and Carl Shapiro, "Probabilistic Patents," *Journal of Economic Perspectives* 19 (2005): 75–98, at 95.

14. Mark A. Lemley and Carl Shapiro, "Patent Holdup and Royalty Stacking," *Texas Law Review* 85 (2007): 1991–2049, at 2019 and n. 71. Litigated patents are atypical: very strong, weak, or commercially worthless patents won't likely be litigated. The PTO's error rate over the total universe of patents is probably at most a few percent (National Academy of Sciences, *Patent System for the 21st Century,* 49). The problem for innovators is that they don't know which ones are bad unless they litigate. The PTO may worry that spending more initially to weed out bad applications and fix gridlock will introduce other new costs such as deterring applications for good patents.

15. National Research Council, *Intellectual Property Rights and Research Tools in Molecular Biology: Summary of a Workshop Held at the National Academy of Sciences,*

February 15–16, 1996 (Washington, D.C.: National Academies Press, 1997), 48–49, www.nap.edu/catalog/5758.html.

16. On SARS and patents, see generally Matthew Rimmer, "The Race to Patent the SARS Virus: The TRIPS Agreement and Access to Essential Medicines," *Melbourne Journal of International Law* 5 (2004): 335–74. See also Peter K. Yu, "SARS and the Patent Race: What Can We Learn from the HIV/AIDS Crisis?" *FindLaw,* May 29, 2003, http://writ.news.findlaw.com/commentary/20030529_yu.html.

17. James H. M. Simon et al., "Managing Severe Acute Respiratory Syndrome (SARS) Intellectual Property Rights: The Possible Role of Patent Pooling," *Bulletin of the World Health Organization* 83 (2005): 707–10, at 708, www.who.int/bulletin/volumes/83/9/707.pdf.

18. World Health Organization, *Patent Applications for SARS Virus and Genes* (2003), www.who.int/ethics/topics/sars_patents/en.

19. Rimmer, "Race to Patent," 374 and n. 233.

20. See Pete Moore, *The New Killer Germs: What You Need to Know about Deadly Diseases in the Twenty-First Century* (London: Carlton Press, 2006).

21. See World Health Organization, "Micronutrient Deficiencies," www.who.int/nutrition/topics/vad/en/. See also Golden Rice Humanitarian Board, "Golden Rice–FAQ," www.goldenrice.org/Content3-Why/why3_FAQ.html.

22. See citations noted in David E. Adelman, "A Fallacy of the Commons in Biotech Patent Policy," *Berkeley Technology Law Journal* 20 (2005): 985–1030, at 997 and nn. 65–67. See also Sara Boettiger and Alan B. Bennett, "Bayh-Dole: If We Knew Then What We Know Now," *Nature Biotechnology* 24 (2006): 320–23, at 322.

23. Andrew Pollack, "The Green Revolution Yields to the Bottom Line," *New York Times*, May 15, 2001, Science section, 1, 2.

24. Ingo Potrykus, "The Golden Rice 'Tale,'" *In Vitro Cellular and Developmental Biology Plant* 37 (2001): 93–100, 97; and www.goldenrice.org/PDFs/The_GR_Tale.pdf. A "material transfer agreement" is a contract that governs the transfer of tangible materials between two organizations, where one plans to use the materials for research purposes. For a discussion of MTAs, see "A Quick Guide to Material Transfer Agreements at U.C. Berkeley," www.spo.berkeley.edu/guide/mtaquick.html.

25. Golden Rice Humanitarian Board, "Golden Rice–FAQ."

26. On the land-grant system, see, for example, Cornell University, College of Agriculture and Life Sciences, "The Land-Grant Colleges," www.cals.cornell.edu/cals/about/overview/land-grant.cfm.

27. Pollack, "Green Revolution Yields," 1–2.

28. Ibid.

29. Gregory Graff and David Zilberman, "An Intellectual Property Clearing-house for Agricultural Biotechnology," *Nature Biotechnology* 19 *(2001): 1179–80*, at 1179.

30. Arti Kaur Rai, "Regulating Scientific Research: Intellectual Property Rights and the Norms of Science," *Northwestern University Law Review* 94 (1999): 77–152, at 94.

31. Ziedonis, "Don't Fence Me In," 804 (see chap. 1, n. 63).

32. National Research Council, *Intellectual Property Rights,* 49.

33. For evidence that MAD strategy can work, see John R. Allison et al., "Valu-able Patents," *Georgetown Law Journal* 92 (2004): 435–79, at 474, which notes that semiconductor patents are litigated only one-third as often as other patents and ar-gues that the symmetry of competitors explains the difference. On the rise of de-fensive patenting, consider this blog entry from Microsoft's manager for Word software Chris Pratley: "At Microsoft, we used to pay little attention to patents—we would just make new things, and that would be it. Then we started getting worried—other big competitors (much bigger than we were at the time) had been patenting their inventions for some years, and it made us vulnerable. One of these big companies could dig through their patent portfolio, find something close to what we had done, then sue us, and we would have to go through an elaborate de-fense and possibly lose. So Microsoft did what most big companies do, which is start to build what is called a 'defensive' patent portfolio. So if a big company tried to sue us, we could find something in our portfolio they were afoul of, and counter-sue. In the cold war days, this strategy was called 'mutual assured destruc-tion,' and since it was intolerable for all parties to engage, it resulted in a state called 'détente,' or 'standoff.' This is what you see today for the most part in lots of industries" (OneNote Blog, May 1, 2004, http://blogs.msdn.com/ Chris_Pratley/archive/2004/05/01/124586.aspx).

34. The term was coined in 2001 by Peter Detkin, then a lawyer at Intel, to de-scribe companies that "try to make a lot of money off a patent that they are not practicing and have no intention of practicing and in most cases never practiced" (Alan Murray, "War on 'Patent Trolls' May Be Wrong Battle," *Wall Street Journal,* March 22, 2006, A2). Now Detkin works with Intellectual Ventures, a firm that buys up and licenses large numbers of patents. Is Detkin a troll? See Sarah Lai Stir-land, "Will Congress Stop High-Tech Trolls?" *National Journal,* February 26, 2005, www.nationaljournal.com/about/njweekly/stories/2005/0225nj2.htm#. How about universities that don't practice their inventions? See Mark A. Lemley, "Are Universities Patent Trolls?" Stanford Public Law Working Paper No. 980776 (2007), 8. Lemley answers "no," but the story is complex. How about big drug companies? Are they trolls if they leverage their patents against generic drugmak-

ers? See Jeremiah S. Helm, "Why Pharmaceutical Firms Support Patent Trolls: The Disparate Impact of *eBay v. MercExchange* on Innovation," *Michigan Telecommunications and Technology Law Review* 13 (2006): 331–43, at 338, www.mttlr.org/volthirteen/helm.pdf.

35. Lemley and Shapiro, "Patent Holdup," 2009–10. Lemley argues, "We will solve the troll problem not by hunting down and eliminating trolls, but by hunting down and eliminating the many legal rules that facilitate the capture by patent owners of a disproportionate share of an irreversible investment" ("Are Universities Patent Trolls?" 19).

36. Iain M. Cockburn, "The Changing Structure of the Pharmaceutical Industry," *Health Affairs* 23 (2004): 10–22, at 10.

37. See also James, "Medical Innovation and Patent Gridlock" (see chap. 1, n. 13). "The 'golden age' of drug development about 50 years ago may have been a legacy of the previous environment before gridlock set in—a small taste of what could have been possible with modern science, if it had not been choked off by a new golden age of overgrowth of patent rights and litigation" (ibid.). For an opposing view, see Buckley, "Myth of the Anticommons," 2, which argues that the data show that drug discoveries under the current patent regime are going up, not down.

38. From Cockburn, "Changing Structure," 11. Copyright © 2004 by Project Hope/Health Affairs Journal. Reproduced with permission of Project Hope/Health Affairs Journal.

39. See Heller and Eisenberg, "Can Patents Deter Innovation?" 700–701, which distinguishes concurrent fragments from license stacking. See also Parisi, Schulz, and Depoorter, "Simultaneous and Sequential Anticommons," 185 (see chap. 1, n. 14).

40. This section expands on Heller and Eisenberg, "Can Patents Deter Innovation?" 698–99.

41. Gary Stix, "Owning the Stuff of Life," *Scientific American,* February 2006, 76–83, at 81.

42. See Robert P. Merges, "A New Dynamism in the Public Domain," *University of Chicago Law Review* 71 (2004): 183–203, at 188–89.

43. U.S. Patent and Trademark Office, "Utility Examination Guidelines," *Federal Register* 66 (January 5, 2001): 1092–99. See also Michael M. Hopkins et al., "DNA Patenting: The End of an Era?" *Nature Biotechnology* 25 (2007): 185–87, at 186.

44. *In re Fisher,* 421 F.3d 1365 (Fed. Cir. 2005); Hopkins et al., "DNA Patenting," 187.

45. According to one evaluation, "Despite the countless number of patent applications, experts believe that most of these patent applications will never be

granted. . . . Gene databases like the Merck, the Institute for Genomic Research, and the Human Genome Project will further reduce the number of granted genomic patents by placing genomic information in the public domain" (Bradley J. Levang, "Evaluating the Use of Patent Pools for Biotechnology: A Refutation to the USPTO White Paper Concerning Biotechnology Patent Pools," *Santa Clara Computer and High Technology Law Journal* 19 [2002]: 229–51, at 241).

46. This section is drawn from Heller and Eisenberg, "Can Patents Deter Innovation?" 699–700. See also Lemley and Shapiro, "Patent Holdup," 2025–29, which examines and provides examples of royalty stacking.

47. Organization for Economic Co-operation and Development, *Genetic Inventions, Intellectual Property Rights, and Licensing Practices: Evidence and Policies* (Paris: Organization for Economic Co-operation and Development, 2002), 62, which notes that stacked royalties may amount to such a high percentage of eventual sales that commercialization of a proposed drug is no longer viable.

48. National Institutes of Health, "Principles and Guidelines for Recipients of NIH Research Grants and Contracts on Obtaining and Disseminating Biomedical Research Resources," *Federal Register* 64 (December 23, 1999): 72090–96, at 72091. For a discussion of these guidelines, see Pressman et al., "Licensing of DNA Patents," 32; and Boettiger and Bennett, "Bayh-Dole," 321.

49. Boettiger and Bennett, "Bayh-Dole," 321.

50. Organization for Economic Co-operation and Development, *Genetic Inventions*, 62.

51. National Research Council, *Intellectual Property Rights*, 48.

52. See Heller and Eisenberg, "Can Patents Deter Innovation?" 700–701.

53. Pressman et al., "Licensing of DNA Patents," 35.

54. A good overview of this research and analysis of the relevant studies is Charles R. McManis and Sucheol Noh, "The Impact of the Bayh-Dole Act on Genetic Research and Development: Evaluating the Arguments and Empirical Evidence to Date," in *Perspectives on Commercializing Innovation*, F. Scott Kieff and Troy A. Paredes, eds. (New York: Cambridge University Press, forthcoming, 2009) and law.wustl.edu/CRIE/publications/mcmaniscommercializinginnovationpaper.pdf.

55. See, for example, the pending Patent Reform Act of 2007.

56. John Markoff, "Two Views of Innovation, Colliding in Washington," *New York Times*, January 13, 2008, Business section, 3. See also Ephraim Schwartz, "Patent Reform Favors High Tech over Biotech," *Infoworld*, September 7, 2007, http://weblog.infoworld.com/realitycheck/archives/2007/09/patent_reform_f .html; and "Patent Reform Acts Ugly," *Nature Biotechnology* 25 (2007): 1187 (editorial opposing proposed patent reforms as harmful to biotech-firm incentives to innovate).

57. See Federal Trade Commission, *To Promote Innovation: The Proper Balance of Competition and Patent Law and Policy* (2003), www.ftc.gov/os/2003/10/innovationrpt .pdf; National Academy of Sciences, Committee on Intellectual Property Rights in the Knowledge-Based Economy, *Patent System for the 21st Century*, www.nap.edu/ catalog.php?record_id=10976; and National Research Council of the National Academy of Sciences, Committee on Intellectual Property Rights in Genomic and Protein Research and Innovation, *Reaping the Benefits of Genomic and Proteomic Research: Intellectual Property Rights, Innovation, and Public Health* (Washington, D.C.: National Academies Press, 2006), www.nap.edu/catalog.php?record_id=11487. See also an older NIH study that found "rising frustration" among research scientists with the difficulties and delays in licensing ("Report of the National Institutes of Health [NIH] Working Group on Research Tools" [presented to the Advisory Committee to the Director, June 4, 1998], www.nih.gov/news/researchtools/ index.htm).

58. For a summary of the three reports from the biotechnology industry perspective, see Mills and Tereskerz, "Proposed Patent Reform Legislation," 4.

59. Federal Trade Commission, *To Promote Innovation,* chap. 6, 29 (quote), 18–20.

60. On patent quality, see National Academy of Sciences, *Patent System for the 21st Century,* 47–59. For conclusions, see 81–83.

61. On raising the bar for obviousness, see *KSR International Co. v. Teleflex, Inc.,* 127 S.Ct. 1727 (2007). On limitations to the automatic grant of injunctions for patent infringement, see *eBay, Inc. v. MercExchange, LLC,* 547 U.S. 388 (2006). See generally Steve Seidenberg, "Reinventing Patent Law: The Pendulum Is Swinging for a System that Has Long Favored the Rights of Patent Holders," *ABA Journal* (February 2008), 58–63.

62. John P. Walsh, Ashish Arora, and Wesley M. Cohen, "Effects of Research Tool Patents and Licensing on Biomedical Innovation," in *Patents in the Knowledge-Based Economy,* edited by Wesley M. Cohen and Stephen A. Merrill (Washington, D.C.: National Academies Press, 2003), 285–340, at 324, www.nap.edu/catalog.php?record_id=10770. See also Caulfield et al., "Evidence and Anecdotes," 1092–93 (noting increasing secrecy).

63. Walsh, Arora, and Cohen, "Effects of Research Tool Patents," 324–25.

64. The Iowa study is mentioned in Boettiger and Bennett, "Bayh-Dole," 321.

65. Kara Moorcroft, "Scofflaw Science: Avoiding the Anticommons through Ignorance," *Tulane Journal of Technology and Intellectual Property* 7 (2005): 71–93, at 80–85.

66. On delays in publication associated with patenting, see Fiona Murray and Scott Stern, "Do Formal Intellectual Property Rights Hinder the Free Flow of Scientific Knowledge?" 683 (see chap. 1, n. 63).

67. National Research Council, *Reaping the Benefits*, 2.

68. John P. Walsh, Charlene Cho, and Wesley M. Cohen, "View from the Bench: Patents and Material Transfers," *Science* 309 (2005): 2002–03, at 2003.

69. Walsh, Arora, and Cohen, "Effects of Research Tool Patents," 289.

70. Caulfield et al., "Evidence and Anecdotes," 1093.

71. Paul David, "The Economic Logic of 'Open Science' and the Balance between Private Property Rights and the Public Domain in Scientific Data and Information: A Primer," in *The Role of Scientific and Technical Data and Information in the Public Domain: Proceedings of a Symposium,* edited by Julie M. Esanu and Paul F. Uhlir (Washington, D.C.: National Academies Press, 2003), 19–34, at 31–32. See also Michael S. Mireles, "An Examination of Patents, Licensing, Research Tools, and the Tragedy of the Anticommons in Biotechnology Innovation," *University of Michigan Journal of Law Reform* 38 (2004): 141–235, at 188nn.355–59.

72. David, "Economic Logic," 31–32.

73. There is a debate on this point. For an argument that there are likely to be plenty of research targets and therefore little anticommons threat, see Adelman, "Fallacy of the Commons."

74. *Madey v. Duke University,* 307 F.3d 1371 (Fed. Cir. 2002).

75. National Research Council, *Reaping the Benefits,* 3.

76. Stix, "Owning the Stuff of Life," 82.

77. See Marilyn Chase, "Gates Won't Fund AIDs Researchers Unless They Pool Data," *Wall Street Journal,* July 21, 2006, B1; Boettiger and Bennett, "Bayh-Dole," 322.

78. On the use of patents to block subsequent improvements, see Robert P. Merges and Richard R. Nelson, "On the Complex Economics of Patent Scope," *Columbia Law Review* 90 (1990): 839–916, at 865. On trolls, see notes 34 and 35. See also Tim Wu, "Weapons of Business Destruction," Slate.com, February 6, 2006, www.slate.com/id/2135559.

79. In this vein, Richard A. Epstein and Bruce N. Kuhlik write, "We think Heller and Eisenberg have overstated the case against patent protection at both the theoretical and empirical levels. The number of patents filed in recent years has continued to move sharply upward across the board. We see no reason to believe that the sole or dominant purpose for individual patentees is to block innovations by others" ("Is There a Biomedical Anticommons?" *Regulation* 27 [2004]: 54–58, at 54). For a more extended argument on drug innovation and law, see Richard A. Ep-

stein, *Overdose: How Excessive Government Regulation Stifles Pharmaceutical Innovation* (New Haven: Yale University Press, 2006).

80. For example, see Anatole Krattiger et al., "Intellectual Property Management Strategies to Accelerate the Development and Access of Vaccines and Diagnostics: Case Studies of Pandemic Influenza, Malaria, and SARS," *Innovation Strategy Today* 2 (2006): 67–134, at 67, www.biodevelopments.org/innovation/ist5.pdf.

81. Lemley offers useful suggestions for innovation-promoting licensing practices and for prodding better behavior by recalcitrant universities ("Are Universities Patent Trolls?" 14–17).

82. Merges, "New Dynamism," 185–86.

83. Ibid., 189–92.

84. Adelman, "Fallacy of the Commons," 1001 and n. 87; Walsh, Arora, and Cohen, "Effects of Research Tool Patents," 329.

85. Hopkins et al., "DNA Patenting," 187.

86. For an empirical analysis of royalty stacking in the patent-pool context, see Lemley and Shapiro, "Patent Holdup," 2025–29.

87. Patrick Gaulé, "Towards Patent Pools in Biotechnology?" *Innovation Strategy Today* 2 (2006): 123–34, at 128, www.biodevelopments.org/innovation/ist5.pdf.

88. Rochelle Seide, Michelle LeCointe, and Alex Granovsky, "Patent Pooling in the Biotechnology Industry," *Licensing Journal* 27 (October 2001): 28–29.

89. Gaulé, "Towards Patent Pools in Biotechnology," 124–25. On the role of patent pools and standard-setting organizations, see Hajime Yamada, "Patent Exploitation in the Information and Communication Sector: Using Licensing to Lead the Market," *Quarterly Review* (Japan) 19 (April 2006): 11–21, at 13–16.

90. Joshua A. Newberg, "Antitrust, Patent Pools, and the Management of Uncertainty," *Atlantic Law Journal* 3 (2000): 1–30, at 24–29.

91. Gavin Clarkson, "Objective Identification of Patent Thickets: A Network Analytic Approach for Measuring the Density of Patent Space" (Ph.D. thesis, Harvard University, 2004).

92. Federal Trade Commission, *To Promote Innovation*, chap. 3, 28n174.

93. For a concurring view, see Organization for Economic Co-operation and Development, *Genetic Inventions*, 67.

94. See generally Gavin Clarkson and David DeKorte, "The Problem of Patent Thickets in Convergent Technologies," *Annals of the New York Academy of Sciences* 1093 (2006): 180–200, at 191.

95. Iain M. Cockburn, "Blurred Boundaries: Tensions between Open Scientific Resources and Commercial Exploitation of Knowledge in Biomedical Research,"

in *Advancing Knowledge and the Knowledge Economy*, edited by Brian Kahin and Dominque Foray (Cambridge: MIT Press, 2006), 351–68.

96. On peer production, see Yochai Benkler, *The Wealth of Networks: How Social Production Transforms Markets and Freedom* (New Haven: Yale University Press, 2006), 59–90. On the Creative Commons, see www.creativecommons.org. The Creative Commons is a nonprofit organization founded by Lawrence Lessig to increase the amount of shared creative materials. The organization provides new types of copyright licenses that make it easy for authors to contribute some of their intellectual property rights to the commons.

97. See www.pipra.org.

98. See www.bios.net; and Boettiger and Bennett, "Bayh-Dole," 322.

99. Organization for Economic Co-operation and Development, *Genetic Inventions,* 31.

100. See Rochelle Cooper Dreyfuss, "Varying the Course in Patenting Genetic Material: A Counter-proposal to Richard Epstein's Steady Course," *Advances in Genetics* 50 (2003): 195–208, at 204–8; Richard R. Nelson, "The Market Economy and the Scientific Commons," *Research Policy* 33 (2004): 455–71, at 465–67.

101. A recent study on the "end of an era" in DNA patenting states, "National and international guidelines along with developments in case law, and prior art, have raised the bar on patentability. . . . Patent offices have responded to criticism by raising thresholds that make it much less attractive for applicants to file speculative, broad claims in the hope of obtaining what many would view as undue rewards" (Hopkins et al., "DNA Patenting," 187).

102. Such rules cover "demonstrating utility (industrial applicability), novelty, nonobviousness (inventive step), full written description (sufficiency), and unity of invention (that is, that the parts of the invention as described are intrinsically linked)" (ibid., 186). See also Dan L. Burk and Mark A. Lemley, "Policy Levers in Patent Law," *Virginia Law Review* 89 (2003): 1575–1696, at 1578–79, 1676–83.

103. March-in rights are codified at 35 U.S.C. sec. 203 (2002). More closely analogous to eminent domain is the government right, codified at 28 U.S.C. sec. 1498(a) (2002), to use any invention, even those developed without government funding, provided the government pays money damages. Outside the drug context, there are a number of narrow statutory provisions for mandatory patent licensing. See Jerome H. Reichman and Catherine Hasenzahl, "Non-voluntary Licensing of Patented Inventions: Historical Perspective, Legal Framework under TRIPS, and an Overview of the Practice in Canada and the USA" (UNC-TAD/ICTSD Capacity Building Project on Intellectual Property Rights and Sustainable Development, Issue Paper No. 5, 2003), 21.

104. For example, see David Malakoff, "NIH Declines to March in on Pricing AIDS Drug," *Science* 305 (2004): 926.

105. See Arti K. Rai and Rebecca S. Eisenberg, "Bayh-Dole Reform and the Progress of Biomedicine," *Law and Contemporary Problems* 66 (2003): 289–314, at 310–13. See also Arti K. Rai, "Engaging Facts and Policy: A Multi-institutional Approach to Patent System Reform," *Columbia Law Review* 103 (2003): 1035–1135, at 1041.

106. See Caulfield et al., "Evidence and Anecdotes," 1091. Along with Myriad's licensing practices, the alarm has sounded over a few other high-profile patents aggressively managed by their owners. Families affected by Canavan disease—a gene-linked, neurological birth disorder—organized themselves to find a cure. They donated the crucial biological materials, funded much of the research, and then were stunned when the resulting genetic test was patented. Outrage ensued when Miami Children's Hospital, owner of the gene-test patent, began selling testing services back to suffering families. See Arthur Allen, "Who Owns Your DNA?" Salon.com, March 7, 2000, http://archive.salon.com/health/feature/2000/03/07/genetic_test/index.html; and Debra L. Greenfield, "*Greenberg v. Miami Children's Hospital:* Unjust Enrichment and the Patenting of Human Genetic Material," *Annals of Health Law* 15 (2006): 213–49. In addition, people have been concerned about high costs and limited access to Athena's Alzheimer's "ApoE" test (Organization for Economic Co-operation and Development, *Genetic Inventions,* 16–17).

107. Stix, "Owning the Stuff of Life," 83.

108. Organization for Economic Co-operation and Development, *Genetic Inventions,* 17. In Canada, most provinces have been ignoring Myriad's injunctions to stop offering breast cancer genetic testing. In England, in 2002, the influential Nuffield Council on Bioethics recommended strengthening the "research exemption" and increasing "compulsory licensing" (Caulfield et al., "Evidence and Anecdotes," 1091). European countries have rejected most of Myriad's patents, so testing there is free, except for patents that cover mutations specific to Ashkenazi Jewish women. So, in Europe, to protect Myriad's commercial interests, "by law, a doctor must ask a woman patient if she is an Ashkenazi Jew"—a question that elicits understandable unease among ethicists (Stix, "Owning the Stuff of Life," 83).

Chapter 4

1. The Einstein cat quotation is cited in Steve Mirsky, "Einstein's Hot Time," *Scientific American,* September 2002, 102. However, it's probably apocryphal. The quotation appears all over the Internet, but not in printed collections of Einstein quotes that I have been able to find.

2. Thomas Bleha, "Down to the Wire," *Foreign Affairs,* May–June 2005, 1, www.foreignaffairs.org/20050501faessay84311/thomas-bleha/down-to-the-wire.html. Note that Bleha's position is controversial—the United States does well on mobile broadband subscriber numbers and on the business and residential services that are actually delivered. See also John Markoff, "Study Gives High Marks to U.S. Internet," *New York Times,* April 9, 2008, Technology section, 9.

3. Spectrum Policy Task Force, Federal Communications Commission, Technology Advisory Council Briefing (presentation, December 2002), slide 9, www.fcc.gov/oet/tac/TAC_December_2002.ppt, cited in Thomas W. Hazlett, "Spectrum Tragedies," *Yale Journal on Regulation* 22 (2005): 242–74, at 248, fig. 1, n. 28. The horizontal axis shows the "ultra-high-frequency" (UHF) range from 300 MHz to 3 GHz. Hertz refers to the number of times per second a wave oscillates—it tells you where to tune your receiver to pick up the wave and also the information-carrying capacity of that wave. In this chart, the vertical access represents recorded emission levels or "amplitude," measured in standard decibel units (dBm). Note also that the range of "prime" spectrum can keep expanding as technologies emerge that can exploit spectrum more intensively. For an informative graphic on overuse and underuse, see Woolley, "Dead Air," 140–41, fig. "Gasping for Airwaves" (see chap. 1, n. 10).

4. For a classic exposition of these problems, see Arthur S. De Vany et al., "A Property System for Market Allocation of the Electromagnetic Spectrum: A Legal-Economic-Engineering Study," *Stanford Law Review* 21 (1969): 1499–1561, at 1504–12. See also Reed E. Hundt and Gregory L. Rosston, "Communications Policy for 2006 and Beyond," *Federal Communications Law Journal* 58 (2006): 1–35, at 12.

5. Yochai Benkler, "Overcoming Agoraphobia: Building the Commons of the Digitally Networked Environment," *Harvard Journal of Law and Technology* 11 (1998): 287–400, at 359–60.

6. Dale Hatfield and Phil Weiser, "Toward Property Rights in Spectrum: The Difficult Policy Choices Ahead" (Cato Institute Policy Analysis No. 575, August 17, 2006), 1, www.ssrn.com/abstract=975679.

7. Before we can conclude spectrum is underused, we need information not only on use levels in the other spectral dimensions but also on build-out costs for a given technology and on "the benefits accruing from bandwidth availability versus the benefits associated with alternative spectrum uses" (Hundt and Rosston, "Communication Policy," 12). Hazlett argues that "while heavy usage (in radiated power) is not synonymous with economic value obtained from radio wave use, the pattern—with wide fluctuation in wireless activity—is highly suggestive" ("Spectrum Tragedies," 248). For a description of the technological aspects of spectrum use, see De Vany et al., "Property System," 1501–5.

8. Hundt and Rosston, "Communication Policy," 3.

9. Bleha, "Down to the Wire," 5 (referring to calculations by economist Charles Ferguson).

10. Hazlett, "Tragedy of the Telecommons" (see chap. 1, n. 11).

11. Bleha, "Down to the Wire," 5.

12. Woolley, "Dead Air," 140. Note that dropped calls also result from techno-logical limits of mobile wireless, not just gridlock. Wireless design involves some trade-off between quality of service (QoS) and mobility. To get affordable mobil-ity we rationally accept QoS below that of landlines. That said, the regulatory mis-takes identified by Woolley make the underlying technological challenges more difficult to solve.

13. Quoted in ibid., 141.

14. Ibid.

15. My figure compresses down to four categories the hundreds of bands of li-censed spectrum shown in John R. Williams, Office of Plans and Policy, Federal Communications Commission, "U.S. Spectrum Allocations 300–3000 MHz: A Ver-tical Bar Chart with Frequency Bands Shown Approximately to Scale," November 2002, 15, chart, www.fcc.gov/Bureaus/OPP/working_papers/oppwp38chart.pdf. In addition to frequency space, spectrum can be allocated along a host of other di-mensions such as time, geography, direction, and power levels. The FCC produces charts of these analogous dimensions of use (and underuse), but they go beyond our cat/no-cat level of analysis.

16. Williams, "U.S. Spectrum Allocations," 15. See also Hazlett, "Spectrum Tragedies," 248.

17. Woolley, "Dead Air," 144.

18. "Airwaves Auction Sets Record, but Public Safety Network in Jeopardy," *New York Times*, March 18, 2008, Business section, 6; Richard Martin, "Public Safety Gets Lost in 700-MHz Bidding," *Information Week*, February 15, 2008, www.informationweek.com/shared/printableArticle.jhtml?articleID=206504491.

19. Quoted in Woolley, "Dead Air," 149.

20. Jerry Brito, "The Spectrum Commons in Theory and Practice," *Stanford Technology Law Review* (2007), para. 8, http://stlr.stanford.edu/pdf/brito-com-mons.pdf.

21. For example, restrictions on 30 MHZ of "U-PCS" spectrum allocated in the early 1990s meant that this unlicensed spectrum did not generate virtually any economic activity for a decade (while the neighboring 120 MHz allocated for PCS licenses carried about half of the 240 million U.S. mobile subscribers). See Thomas W. Hazlett, "Optimal Abolition of FCC Spectrum Allocation," *Journal of Economic Perspectives* 22 (2008): 103–28, at 114, 121. In addition, the 3650–3700

MHz "WiMax" band recently allocated for unlicensed use may become problematic to the extent that nonexclusive rights do not provide incentives needed to invest in necessary infrastructure (Brito, "Spectrum Commons").

22. Lessig, *Future of Ideas*, 77–78 (see chap. 1, n. 60).

23. Hazlett, "Optimal Abolition," 121–22.

24. On mobile handoffs, see Stephanie E. Niehaus, "Bridging the (Significant) Gap: To What Extent Does the Telecommunications Act of 1996 Contemplate Seamless Service," *Notre Dame Law Review* 77 (2002): 641–72, at 651.

25. See generally Lessig, *Future of Ideas*; Yochai Benkler, "Some Economics of Wireless Communications," *Harvard Journal of Law and Technology* 16 (2002): 1–59; and Brito, "Spectrum Commons," para. 10 and n. 13 (collecting sources).

26. For a brief primer on FCC spectrum management from the 1930s to the present, see Philip J. Weiser and Dale N. Hatfield, "Policing the Spectrum Commons," *Fordham Law Review* 74 (2005): 663–94, at 668–69; and Thomas Hazlett, "The Rationality of U.S. Regulation of the Broadcast Spectrum," *Journal of Law and Economics* 33 (1990): 133–75. See also Benkler, "Some Economics," 3–4.

27. Lessig, *Future of Ideas*, 76, 84, 219. See also Brito, "Spectrum Commons," paras. 10–15 (summarizing the positions of commons advocates and gathering sources). There's an analogy here to landownership: sometimes, private owners return land to the commons when the costs of maintaining private ownership come to exceed the benefits. See Barry Field, "The Evolution of Property Rights," *Kyklos* 42 (1989): 319–45, at 320–21.

28. Benkler, "Some Economics," 10.

29. See Hazlett, "Optimal Abolition," 122 (noting some of the technologies that commons advocates argue may be able to multiply the spectrum that is effectively available).

30. From J. H. Snider, "Spectrum Policy Wonderland: A Critique of Conventional Property Rights and Commons Theory in a World of Low Power Wireless Devices" (Telecommunications Policy Research Conference, George Mason University School of Law, September 30, 2006), 22, fig. 7. Reproduced with permission from J. H. Snider. Snider compiles and updates data reported in Kenneth R. Carter, Ahmed Lahjouji, and Neal McNeil, "Unlicensed and Unshackled: A Joint OSP-OET White Paper on Unlicensed Devices and Their Regulatory Issues" (OSP Working Paper Series No. 39, Federal Communications Commission, May 2003), http://hraunfoss.fcc.gov/edocs_public/attachmatch/DOC-234741A1.pdf. The Carter et al. report contains a useful glossary of technical terms used to discuss unlicensed spectrum (53–60).

31. Hazlett, "Spectrum Tragedies," 249.

32. This brief history is taken from Thomas W. Hazlett, "Is Federal Preemption Efficient in Cellular Phone Regulation?" *Federal Communications Law Journal* 56 (2003): 153–237, at 160–69.

33. Jerry A. Hausman et al., "Valuing the Effect of Regulation on New Services in Telecommunications," *Brookings Papers on Economic Activity: Microeconomics* (1997): 1–54, at 23. See also Kenneth Arrow et al., Nobelists' Report for Verizon, 10–11, 23 (unpublished manuscript, November 18, 2003) (noting that "even modest delays in new product introduction can have significant adverse effects on consumer welfare").

34. McCaw Communications assembled the first non-Bell national cellular network, and was then bought out by AT&T (Jeffrey S. Young, "Craig McCaw—The Wireless Wizard of Oz," *Forbes,* June 22, 1998, www.forbes.com/1998/06/22/feat.html).

35. Hazlett, "Spectrum Tragedies," 250. See also "Nextel History," at http://nextelonline.nextel.com/en/about/corporateinfo/company_history5.shtml.

36. Hazlett, "Spectrum Tragedies," 249. These calculations are complex and contested, but however you cut it—between producers and consumers—the surplus is a big number.

37. Ibid., 260 (the $120 billion figure includes about $88 billion in mobile phone and data service revenue, $13 billion in equipment revenue, and $21 billion in network capital expenditures).

38. John Markoff and Matt Richtel, "F.C.C. Hands Google a Partial Victory," *New York Times*, August 1, 2007, Business section, 1. There have also been many small spectrum auctions during this period. The big 2008 auction for the 700 MHz bands was "auction 73."

39. Federal Communications Commission, "In the Matter of Additional Spectrum for Unlicensed Devices below 900 MHz and in the 3 GHz Band," ET Docket No. 02–380 (released December 20, 2002), 17 F.C.C.R. 25,632 at 25,634 paras. 6–7, http://gullfoss2.fcc.gov/prod/ecfs/retrieve.cgi?native_or_pdf=pdf&id_document=6513404215.

40. For example, see Corey Boles, "Bid for Broadband Access Short-circuits in Testing," *Wall Street Journal*, February 13, 2008, B6 (describing the failure of an unlicensed wireless broadband device that would operate in the unused buffer bandwidths between television channels); "Google Plan Would Open TV Band for Wireless Use," *New York Times*, March 25, 2008, Business section, 9. See also Hazlett, "Optimal Abolition," 112 (arguing that allowing unlicensed use of white spaces would further lock in wasteful broadcast allocations, fragment rights holders, and make later reorganization even more costly).

41. Kelly Hill, "T-Mobile USA, Leap Move Closer to AWS Launches," *RCR Wireless News*, October 20, 2007, www.rcrnews.com/apps/pbcs.dll/article?AID=/20071020/SUB/71019011/0/.cms.

42. See, for example, Carey Goldberg, "It's a Control Thing: Vermont vs. Cell Phone Towers," *New York Times*, March 11, 1998, National Desk, 12; and Timothy Tryniecki, "Cellular Tower Siting Jurisprudence under the Telecommunications Act of 1996: The First Five Years," *Real Property, Probate, and Trust Journal* 37 (2002): 271–86, at 272.

43. See Om Malik, "700 MHz Explained in 10 Steps," March 14, 2007, www.gigaom.com/2007/03/14/700mhz-explained.

44. On the creation of McCaw Wireless (bought by AT&T) and VoiceStream (which was merged into T-Mobile), see Dan Meyer, "Stanton Parlayed Early McCaw Success to Wins with Western Wireless, DT," *RCR Wireless News*, May 10, 2004, www.rcrnews.com/apps/pbcs.dll/article?AID=/20040510/SUB/405100704.

45. See Malik, "700 MHz Explained" (citing figure from Aloha Partners).

46. Brad Smith, "For Sale: Wireless' Beachfront Property," *Wireless Week*, September 1, 2007, www.wirelessweek.com/Article-Wireless-Beach-Front-Property.aspx.

47. Hazlett, "Optimal Abolition," 115–16.

48. Hundt and Rosston, "Communication Policy," 12. As they point out, solutions could also include permitting "secondary use" —that is, allowing unlicensed users to make temporary use of licensed spectrum. But even with secondary use, more solutions will be required.

49. Lessig, *Future of Ideas*, 84.

50. For example, there's the high-stakes "net neutrality" debate raised by my colleague Tim Wu. See Tim Wu, "Why You Should Care about Network Neutrality: The Future of the Internet Depends on It!" Slate.com, May 1, 2006, www.slate.com/id/2140850. For a scholarly treatment, see Tim Wu, "Network Neutrality, Broadband Discrimination," *Journal of Telecommunications and High Technology Law* 2 (2003): 141–79, www.ssrn.com/abstract=388863.

51. See Hazlett, "Optimal Abolition," 109–11.

52. Ibid., 113. Note also that there are hundreds of millions of old analog televisions in homes around the country. Eliminating the usefulness of these receivers is not an insignificant step for the government to take. Congress set aside $1.5 billion for vouchers to pay for converting analog television sets to receive digital signals.

53. Hazlett, "Spectrum Tragedies," 251–53.

54. See Woolley, "Dead Air," 144.

55. William Safire, "Spectrum Squatters," *New York Times*, October 9, 2000, op-ed, 21 (referring to FCC chair William Kennard's use of the term); Office of U.S. Senator John McCain, "McCain Calls for Free TV Time from Broadcasters," press release, June 19,

2002, http://mccain.senate.gov/public/index.cfm?FuseAction=PressOffice.PressRe-leases&ContentRecord_id=51d6157c-45f5-4657-8049-319dc7a3865a&Region _id=&Issue_id=.

56. Hazlett, "Optimal Abolition," 119.

57. From Cellular Telecommunications and Internet Association, "Background on the CTIA's Semi-Annual Wireless Industry Survey" (2004), http://files.ctia .org/pdf/CTIA_Semiannual_Survey_YE2003.pdf, fig. 6. Used with the permission of CTIA–The Wireless Association®.

58. Hazlett, "Spectrum Tragedies," 257, 256.

59. John Hambidge, senior director of marketing, IP Wireless, quoted in Annie Lindstrom, "Carrying the MDS/ITFS Torch: Smaller Operators Are the Current Front-Runners Utilizing the MDS/ITFS Band, and Big Mobile Carriers Might Join the Race as Well," *Broadband Wireless Business* 40 (September–October 2003): 12–15, 29, at 12.

60. Hazlett, "Spectrum Tragedies," 258. The reasons for allowing this grid-locked system are contested. In part, it may have involved Congress and the FCC acting to protect buyers of auctioned spectrum from competition on these bands.

61. Wireless Communications Association International, National ITFS Associa-tion, and Catholic Television Network, "A Proposal for Revising the MDS and ITFS Regulatory Regime" (White Paper Submitted to the FCC on October 7, 2002), 10, www.lbagroup.com/WCA-NIA-CTN%20White%20Paper%20_final_complete.pdf.

62. Hazlett, "Spectrum Tragedies," 258.

63. Woolley, "Dead Air," 144, 149.

64. On the larger stakes, see Tim Wu, "Weapons of Business Destruction: How a Tiny Little 'Patent Troll' Got BlackBerry in a Headlock," Slate.com, February 6, 2006, www.slate.com/id/2135559. The $612 million settlement is noted at Black-berry.com, "Research in Motion and NTP Sign Definitive Settlement Agreement to End Litigation," www.blackberry.com/news/press/2006/pr-03_03_2006-01.shtml.

65. "Direct Testimony of Richard Lynch on Behalf of Intervenor Verizon Wire-less," *In re Certain Baseband Processor Chips and Chipsets, Inv.,* No. 337-TA–543 (U.S. International Trade Commission, June 2006).

66. According to Lynch, when he first committed to 3G, there was in the United States "no significant ecosystem of vendors available to support our wireless broadband network with applications, content, and infrastructure" (ibid.). Verizon Wireless's investment created "a positive feedback loop: the more bandwidth that is available, the larger the files people will upload and download over the Inter-net. . . . In short order, wireless broadband went from a 'nice to have' to a 'must have' service for wireless carriers" (ibid., 13).

67. *eBay v. MercExchange, LLC,* 547 U.S. 388, 396–97 (2006) (Kennedy, J., concurring).

68. Matt Richtel, "Patent Ruling Strikes a Blow at Qualcomm," *New York Times,* June 8, 2007, Business section, 1.

69. George Gilder, "The Wireless Wars," *Wall Street Journal,* April 13, 2007, Opinion section, 13.

70. "Smoot-Hawley's Revenge," *Wall Street Journal,* August 23, 2006, http://online.wsj.com/article/SB115629065211742815.html.

71. Lynch, "Direct Testimony of Richard Lynch," 22.

72. Ibid., 24–26.

73. "VZW Inks Broadcom Deal, Won't Fight ITC Ban," *Fierce Wireless,* July 20, 2007,www.fiercewireless.com/story/vzw-inks-broadcom-deal-wont-fight-itc-ban/2007-07-20.

74. Lynch quoted in Sue Marek, "Does Qualcomm's Workaround Work?" *Fierce Wireless,* August 10, 2007, www.fiercewireless.com/story/does-qualcomms-workaround-work/2007-08-10.

75. Lynnette Luna, "Nokia's Timing Couldn't Be Worse for Qualcomm," *Fierce Wireless,* August 20, 2007, www.fiercewireless.com/story/nokias-timing-couldnt-be-worse-qualcomm/2007-08-20.

76. W. David Gardner, "U.S. Falls Further Behind in Global Broadband Penetration," *Information Week,* April 24, 2007, www.informationweek.com/hardware/showArticle.jhtml?articleID=199201042; and Roger O. Crockett, "How to Get U.S. Broadband Up to Speed: Providers and the Feds Must Work Together to Stop the U.S. from Falling Further Behind," *Business Week,* September 8, 2003, 92–96. See also George Gilder, "Stop the Broadbandits," *Wall Street Journal,* March 4, 2004, A16. Gilder writes, "Although by conventional measures the US now ranks 11th among nations in broadband penetration, by Asian standards the U.S. has no household broadband connections at all. South Koreans and Japanese enjoy links some 10-to-50 times faster than our fastest connections to homes" (ibid.).

77. This section builds on Michael A. Heller, "The UNE Anticommons: Why the 1996 Telecom Reforms Blocked Innovation and Investment," *Yale Journal on Regulation* 22 (2005): 275–87. The FCC's unbundling mandate is at *Telecommunications Act of 1996,* Pub. L. No. 104–104, 251(d)(2), 110 Stat. 56, 143; 47 C.F.R. 51.319(a)–(g). For an introduction to some of the controversies surrounding implementation of the 1996 act, see chaps. 1 and 2 of Peter W. Huber et al., *Federal Communications Law,* 2d ed. (New York: Aspen Publishers, supp. 2004). See also John Steele Gordon, "The Death of a Monopoly," *American Heritage* (April 1997): 16–18.

78. *United States Telecom Ass'n v. FCC,* 290 F.3d 415, 427 (D.C. Cir. 2002).

79. "Letter from Twenty-two Economists to the President of the United States" (March 25, 2004) (on file with author), 2. See also Huber et al., *Federal Communica-*

tions Law, 13, 15, 118–22 (on the UNE pricing scheme), 90–91 (noting that more than 6,000 interconnection agreements had been reached between incumbents and new providers and submitted to state regulatory commissions for review under the 1996 act).

80. Shapiro, "Navigating the Patent Thicket," 1:121 (see chap. 1, n. 13). On potential anticommons dynamics in the semiconductor industry, see Bronwyn H. Hall and Rosemarie Ham Ziedonis, "The Patent Paradox Revisited: An Empirical Study of Patenting in the U.S. Semiconductor Industry, 1979–1995," *RAND Journal of Economics* 32 (2001): 101–28.

81. On a potential software anticommons, see James Bessen, "Patent Thickets: Strategic Patenting of Complex Technologies" (working paper, Research on Innovation, March 2003), www.researchoninnovation.org/thicket.pdf; James Bessen and Eric Maskin, "Sequential Innovation, Patents, and Imitation" (unpublished manuscript, revised March 2006), www.sss.ias.edu/publications/papers/econpaper25.pdf. See also Mark A. Schankerman and Michael D. Noel, "Strategic Patenting and Software Innovation" (Center for Economic Policy Research Discussion Paper No. 5701 [June 2006], available at www.nber.org/~confer/2006/si2006/prl/schankerman .pdf). For a critical view, see Ronald J. Mann, "Do Patents Facilitate Financing in the Software Industry?" *Texas Law Review* 83 (2005): 961–1030.

82. On anticommons risks in nanotechnology, see Clarkson and DeKorte, "Problem of Patent Thickets," 180–200 (see chap. 3, n. 94); and Terry K. Tullis, "Application of the Government License Defense to Federally Funded Nanotechnology Research: The Case for a Limited Patent Compulsory Licensing Regime," *UCLA Law Review* 53 (2005): 279–313. See also Mark A. Lemley, "Patenting Nanotechnology," *Stanford Law Review* 58 (2005): 601–30.

Chapter 5

1. Paul Moses, "The Paper of Wreckage: The 'Times' Bulldozes Its Way to a Sweetheart Land Deal You Will Pay For," *Village Voice,* June 17, 2002, 39.

2. See Dagan and Heller, "The Liberal Commons," 549–623, at 551, 603–9 (see chap. 1, n. 5).

3. *Hodel v. Irving*, 481 U.S. 704, 712 (1987). See also Heller, "Tragedy of the Anticommons," 686 (see chap. 1, n. 15).

4. For a usage example, see J. Matthew Phipps, "BANANA Republic," *Seattle Times,* August 23, 2003, editorial, http://seattletimes/nwsource.com.archive/ ?date=20030823&slug=satrdr23.

5. This section expands on Michael Heller and Rick Hills, "Land Assembly Districts," *Harvard Law Review* 121 (2008): 1465–1527.

6. Mike Wallace, "Eminent Domain: Being Abused?" *60 Minutes*, CBS, July 4, 2004, www.cbsnews.com/stories/2003/09/26/60minutes/main575343.shtml.

7. Moses, "Paper of Wreckage," 39. Calculating the total subsidy bestowed on the *Times* is difficult because the deal also included complex tax breaks worth tens of millions (ibid., 36–39).

8. Photos copyright © Stefan Hester, 2002. Used by permission.

9. Moses, "Paper of Wreckage," 36–39.

10. Wallace, "Eminent Domain: Being Abused?"

11. A losing landowner challenge is reported at *In re W. 41st St. Realty v. N.Y. State Urban Dev. Corp.*, 744 N.Y.S.2d 121 (N.Y. App. Div. 2002).

12. The building has its own Web site (www.newyorktimesbuilding.com) with a photography portfolio by Annie Liebowitz but no mention of the displaced landowners.

13. Elena Cabral, "A Home on the Range: In Texas Colonias, a Community Emerges One Deed at a Time" (Ford Foundation Report, Fall 2004), www.fordfound.org/pdfs/impact/ford_reports_fall_2004.pdf. See pp. 26–29. For a description of life in Texas colonias, see Lynn Brezosky, "Shantytowns Transform Themselves," *USA Today*, July 11, 2007, www.usatoday.com/news/nation/2007-07-11-2822289773_x.htm. For the state's perspective, see www.sos.state.tx.us/border/colonias/faqs.shtml.

14. For solid analyses of the relationship between bad law and poverty, see Hernando de Soto, *The Mystery of Capital: Why Capitalism Triumphs in the West and Fails Everywhere Else* (New York: Basic Books, 2000) and *The Other Path: The Economic Answer to Terrorism* (New York: Basic Books, 1989).

15. See Peter Hellman, "How They Assembled the Most Expensive Block in New York's History," *New York*, February 25, 1974, 31. See also Andrew Alpern and Seymour Durst, *Holdouts!* (New York: McGraw-Hill, 1984), 112–17.

16. There are occasional and newsworthy exceptions, such as a neighborhood in North Carolina that recently assembled itself (Michelle Crouch, "A Neighborhood in North Carolina Is Put Up for Sale," *New York Times*, August 14, 2005, Real Estate section, 8). Similarly, in Manhattan, neighboring apartment owners sometimes team up to sell for a multiple of the separate unit price (Vivian Marino, "Good Neighbors Make Good Profits," *New York Times*, February 27, 2005, Real Estate section, 1, 9). More examples are collected at Robert C. Ellickson and Vicki L. Been, *Land Use Controls* New York: Aspen Publishers, 2005), 853–54.

17. Copyright © Robert Saiget/AFP/Getty Images 2007. Used by permission. For a discussion of this example, see Howard W. French, "Homeowner Stares Down Wreckers, at Least for a While," *New York Times*, March 27, 2007, Foreign Desk, 4. Usually, in China, landowners have little ability to hold out against rede-

velopment. Wu Ping, the owner of this island in Chongqing, was a rare exception, a feat that made her one of the most popular topics on Chinese blogs, until the government decided her holdout might have political overtones, and discussion ceased (ibid.).

18. Editorial, "A Weak Court Ruling," *Brooklyn Paper,* January 18, 2008, www.brooklynpaper.com/stories/31/3/31_03editorial.html.

19. The official project Web site is at www.atlanticyards.com. The opponents maintain a Web site at www.developdontdestroy.org. Like most real estate projects, Atlantic Yards is highly sensitive to interest rates and overall market conditions. Delays are common and costly. See Charles V. Bagli, "Slow Economy Likely to Stall Atlantic Yards," *New York Times,* March 21, 2008, New York and Region section, 1.

20. Daphne Eviatar, "The Manhattanville Project: Can Columbia's Other Campus Find a Home?" *New York Times,* May 21, 2006, Magazine section, 34–35.

21. Nicole Stelle Garnett, "The Neglected Political Economy of Eminent Domain," *Michigan Law Review* 105 (2006): 101–50, at 109–10.

22. Testimony of Susette Kelo before the Senate Judiciary Committee of the U.S. Congress, review of *Kelo v. City of New London* court case on eminent domain, September 20, 2005.

23. Photos by Isaac Reese, 2004. Copyright © Institute for Justice. Used by permission.

24. *Kelo v. City of* New London, 545 U.S. 469, 489 (2005).

25. Quoted in Terry Pristin, "Developers Can't Imagine a World without Eminent Domain," *New York Times,* January 18, 2006, Business section, 5.

26. William Yardley, "Anger Drives Support for Property Rights Measures," *New York Times,* October 8, 2006, 26.

27. Previous cases in this line include *Hawaii Housing Authority v. Midkiff,* 467 U.S. 229 (1984) and *Berman v. Parker,* 348 U.S. 26 (1954).

28. See generally Robert H. Nelson, *Private Neighborhoods and the Transformation of Local Government* (Washington, D.C.: Urban Institute Press, 2005); and Robert H. Nelson, "Welcome to the New—and Private—Neighborhood: Local Government in a World of Postmodern Pluralism," *Reason,* April 2006, 36.

29. See Community Associations Institute, Industry Data: National Statistics, www.caionline.org/about/facts.cfm.

30. See Richard Briffault, "A Government for Our Time? Business Improvement Districts and Urban Governance," *Columbia Law Review* 99 (1999): 365–477, at 367.

31. See Heller and Hills, "Land Assembly Districts."

32. Ibid., 1515. Typically, with land readjustment, a government takes control of fragmented agricultural parcels on the city's outskirts, puts in roads and sewers,

and then redivides the land. Landowners get back smaller but more valuable plots because the land is better serviced and can be built on; the government keeps some land for public services and sells some to pay for the infrastructure (ibid., 1516–17).

33. This section expands on Dagan and Heller, "The Liberal Commons," 603–8.

34. For a poignant documentary film chronicling the story of black land loss, see Charlene Gilbert, *Homecoming . . . Sometimes I Am Haunted by Memories of Red Dirt and Clay* (2000). A detailed list of resources on the land-loss issue is available on the film's Web site, "Homecoming, Resources," www.pbs.org/itvs/homecoming/resources.html.

35. Dagan and Heller, "The Liberal Commons," 551.

36. Ibid., 604–5.

37. Ward Sinclair, "Black Farmers: A Dying Minority," *Washington Post*, February 18, 1986, 1.

38. Emergency Land Fund, *The Impact of Heir Property on Black Rural Land Tenure in the Southeastern Region of the United States* (Emergency Land Fund, 1980), 282.

39. Ibid., 75, 282.

40. Joseph Brooks, "The Emergency Land Fund: A Rural Land Retention and Development Model," in *The Black Rural Landowner: Endangered Species,* edited by Leo McGee and Robert Boone (Westport, Conn.: Greenwood Press, 1979), 117–34, at 121.

41. Robert S. Browne, *Only Six Million Acres: The Decline of Black Owned Land in the Rural South* (New York: Black Economic Research Center, 1973), 53.

42. Lisa Groger, "Tied to Each Other through Ties to the Land: Informal Support of Black Elders in a Southern U.S. Community," *Journal of Cross-Cultural Gerontology* 7 (1992): 205–20, at 205, 210, 217. For a discussion of the varying levels of ability of landless elders to mobilize informal support, see Lisa A. Kelly, "Race and Place: Geographic and Transcendent Community in the Post-Shaw Era," *Vanderbilt Law Review* 49 (1996): 227–308, at 243n56.

43. Dahleen Glanton, "Ex-Slave's Land Heirs Feel Island Shift," *Chicago Tribune*, July 11, 2006, Domestic News section, 5. The timeline for the effective right of first refusal is set out in S.C. Ann. § 15–61–25 (2007). See also Federation of Southern Cooperatives/Land Assistance Fund, Fighting to Save Black-Owned Land from 1967 to 2007, www.federationsoutherncoop.com.

44. Glanton, "Ex-Slave's Land Heirs," 5.

45. Heller, "Tragedy of the Anticommons," 686.

46. Map courtesy of the Office of Water Resources, Rosebud Sioux Tribe, Rosebud, South Dakota. See also Thomas Biolsi, "Imagined Geographies: Sovereignty,

Indigenous Space, and American Indian Struggle," *American Ethnologist* 32 (2005): 239–59, at 244.

47. A useful overview of checkerboarding and fractionation is available at Indian Land Tenure Foundation, Indian Land Tenure Issues Resulting from Allotment, www.indianlandtenure.org/ILTFallotment/introduction/issues.htm. The Web site also provides a succinct history of allotment and links and resources.

48. Ibid.,www.indianlandtenure.org/ILTFallotment/introduction/checkerboard ing.htm.

49. This section draws from Heller, "Tragedy of the Anticommons," 685–87.

50. Hearings on H.R. 11113 before the Subcommittee on Indian Affairs of the House Committee on Interior and Insular Affairs, 89th Cong., 2d sess., 10 (1966) (Rep. Aspinal). These remarks are cited in *Hodel v. Irving,* 481 U.S. 704, 707–8 (1987).

51. 78 *Cong. Rec.,* 11,728 (June 15, 1934) (Rep. Howard), cited in *Hodel,* 481 U.S. at 708.

52. The reforms appear in the Indian Land Consolidation Act, codified as amended at 25 U.S.C. sec. 2206 (1984), and were rejected by the Supreme Court in *Babbitt v. Youpee,* 519 U.S. 234, 243 (1997) ("The narrow revisions Congress made . . . do not warrant a disposition different than the one this Court announced and explained in *Irving.*").

53. *Hodel,* 481 U.S. 713.

54. I explain why the Court went too far in Heller, "Boundaries of Private Property," 1213–17 (see chap. 1, n. 17).

55. A comprehensive archive of documents, chronologies, and news stories relating to the Indian trust accounting case (posted by the Indian plaintiffs) is available at Indian Trust, *Cobell v. Kempthorne,* www.indiantrust.com. For an archive of the legal documents that the U.S. Department of Justice has filed in the case, see U.S. Department of Justice, Civil Division, *Cobell v. Kempthorne et al.,* www.usdoj.gov/civil/cases/cobell.

56. See Indian Trust, "*Cobell v. Norton*: An Overview," www.indiantrust.com. The contempt order was issued February 22, 1999; the "irresponsibility" statement came in a court opinion dated December 21, 1999. Both documents are available from the archive at www.indiantrust.com.

57. "The Verdict: It's Broken," *New York Times,* February 1, 2008, editorial, 24.

58. On the relationship between land fragmentation and the potato famine, see William L. Langer, "American Foods and Europe's Population Growth," *Journal of Social History* 8 (1975): 51–66, at 56–57.

59. Terry Pristin, "Large REITs Are Paring Their Noncore Holdings," *New York Times,* December 17, 2003, Business section, 6. The developers of AvalonBay, on

the Lower East Side in Manhattan, specialize in exploiting BANANA republic locations: "[They limit their] searches to 'high barrier to entry' areas, where developers encounter obstacles to construction, strict zoning limitations or community
resistance. Such projects expose the company to lengthy delays, high legal bills
and intense community opposition, but they also mean less competition from
other developers" (Nadine Brozan, "Rental Developer's Manhattan Debut: Lower
East Side," *New York Times*, January 4, 2004, Real Estate section, 1, 6). Houston, the
only major American city not to have comprehensive land-use zoning, raises different risks. As one investor notes, "There are no barriers to entry. There's tons of
supply, and you have to be very careful about how you invest in that marketplace"
(Terry Pristin, "Amid an Apartment Glut, Building Prices Move Up," *New York
Times*, June 23, 2004, Business section, 7).

60. See generally William A. Fischel, *The Homevoter Hypothesis: How Home Values
Influence Local Government Taxation, School Finance, and Land-Use Policies* (Cambridge: Harvard University Press, 2001).

61. Richard Epstein, "Tragedy Pure and Simple," *Financial Times*, April 18, 2003,
http://search.ft.com/ftArticle?queryText=epstein+tragedy&aje=true&id=03041
8005137#lessig, para. 2.

62. Greg J. Protasel and Lee Huskey, "Governing the Anticommons: Shallow
Natural Gas Leasing in Alaska" (unpublished manuscript, 2005), 1,
www.pmranet.org/conferences/USC2005/USC2005papers/pmra.protasel.huskey
.2005.pdf.

63. Copyright © The New Yorker Collection 1991 Robert Weber from cartoon-
bank.com. All Rights Reserved.

64. Protasel and Huskey, "Governing the Anticommons," 11–12.

65. Quoted in Chris Whittington-Evans, "Alaskans Deserve Better CBM Rules,"
Anchorage Daily News, January 9, 2005, www.gasdrillingmatsu.org/cweadncompass
.html. See also Protasel and Huskey, "Governing the Anticommons," 14.

66. Sarah Bartlett, "A New York Trade Thrives on Red Tape," *New York Times*,
September 13, 1991, 1. In a follow-up article, Barlett wrote, "This week it looked
as though the expediters themselves needed expediters. In order to comply with a
new law passed by the City Council, they had to register with the Building Department. But many were finding that the obstacle course the department had set up
was so convoluted that they faced the prospect, at least temporarily, of not being
able to work" ("The Day the Expediters Needed Some Expediters," *New York
Times*, New York and Region section, 5).

67. Vernon Loeb, "Delay in Issuing Building Permits Expedites a Career," *Washington Post*, May 18, 1995, District Weekly, 1.

68. Copyright © Chester Higgins, Jr./The New York Times/Redux, 1991, used by permission.

69. Rick Orlov, "Permit Reforms Ordered: Council Panel to Review Changes," *Los Angeles Daily News*, May 7, 1995, N4.

70. Daniel P. Garcia et al., *The Development Reform Committee: Permit Streamlining and Bureaucratic Reform in the City of Los Angeles: Report and Recommendations* (February 7, 1995) (transcript available at the Los Angeles Public Library), 5.

71. Kristin Hood, "Charter Reform and the Land Use Entitlement Process in the City of Los Angeles" (unpublished manuscript, Fall 2006), 37 and n. 126.

72. Stewart Sterk writes that "case law does not sufficiently capture the instances in which decisionmakers use the environmental review process to delay, recast, or kill development projects for ends unrelated to environmental goals" ("Environmental Review in the Land Use Process: New York's Experience with SEQRA," *Cardozo Law Review* 13 (1992): 2041–96, at 2055). For a brief review of literature pro and con on the effects of EIRs, see Ellickson and Been, *Land Use Controls*, 391–93.

73. Peter Applebome, "Epic Battle over Plans for Fancy Mall," *New York Times*, May 13, 2007, 24.

74. Buchanan and Yoon, "Symmetric Tragedies," 11 (see chap. 1, n. 61).

75. Jathon Sapsford, "Quake-Hobbled Kobe Shows How Land Law Can Paralyze Japan," *Wall Street Journal*, December 12, 1996, 1. I discuss the Japan case briefly in Heller, "Tragedy of the Anticommons," 684–85. For an in-depth study, see Mark D. West and Emily M. Morris, "The Tragedy of the Condominiums: Legal Responses to Collective Action Problems after the Kobe Earthquake," *American Journal of Comparative Law* 51 (2003): 903–40.

76. Sapsford, "Quake-Hobbled Kobe," 1.

77. Tsuneo Kajiura, *Shinseiki no Manshon Kyojô* [Condominium Residence in the New Century] (2001): 74–76, cited in West and Morris, "Tragedy of the Condominiums," 908n.16.

78. Sapsford, "Quake-Hobbled Kobe," 1.

79. John Gertner, "Home Economics," *New York Times*, March 5, 2006, Magazine section, 94–99, at 94.

80. On state reforms aimed at streamlining approvals, see Ellickson and Been, *Land Use Controls*, 507–8, 786–87.

81. BANANA, NIMBY, and NIMTOO are just a few of the LULU acronyms (a LULU is a locally undesirable land use). Others include GUMBY (gotta use many back yards), NIABY (not in anyone's back yard), NIMBL (not in my bottom line), NIRPBY (not in rich people's back yards), NIYBY (not in your back yard), and

NOPE (nowhere on planet earth) (Jesse Dukeminier et al., *Property* [New York: Aspen Law and Business, 2006], 917n.32).

Chapter 6

1. World Bank, *Russia, Housing Reform, and Privatization: Strategy and Transition Issues,* edited by Bertrand Renaud (Washington, D.C.: World Bank Press, 1995).

2. On Russian housing reform, see Bertrand Renaud, "The Housing System of the Former Soviet Union: Why Do the Soviets Need Housing Markets?" *Housing Policy Debate* 3 (1992): 877–99; and Alain Bertaud and Bertrand Renaud, "Socialist Cities without Land Markets," *Journal of Urban Economics* 41 (1997): 137–51, at 146–48. See also Alain Bertaud, "The Spatial Organization of Cities: Deliberate Outcome or Unforeseen Consequence?" (Institute of Urban and Regional Development, Working Paper WP-2004-01, July 1, 2004), http://repositories.cdlib.org/iurd/wps/WP-2004-01.

3. See also Shlomo Angel, *Housing Policy Matters: A Global Analysis* (New York: Oxford University Press, 2000), 260.

4. See World Bank, *Russia,* 82–90. See also Stephen B. Butler and Sheila O'Leary, *The Legal Basis for Land Allocation in the Russian Federation* (Washington, D.C.: Urban Institute Press, 1994), 102–30.

5. Although housing is often overlooked as an economic good, it rivals enterprise privatization in importance. See World Bank, *Russia,* 15–22, 27–34. See also Merritt B. Fox and Michael A. Heller, "What Is Good Corporate Governance?" in *Corporate Governance Lessons from Transition Economy Reforms,* edited by Fox and Heller (Princeton: Princeton University Press, 2006), 3–34.

6. Heller, "Tragedy of the Anticommons," 624 (see chap. 1, n. 14).

7. This section draws substantially from ibid., 633–47.

8. On the British "Right to Buy" program, see Raymond J. Struyk, "The Long Road to the Market," in *Economic Restructuring of the Former Soviet Bloc,* edited by Raymond J. Struyk (Washington, D.C.: Urban Institute Press, 1996), 1–69, at 23.

9. On one coup attempt, see Peter Galuszka, "Eyewitness to a Coup That Failed," *Business Week,* October 13, 1993, 28.

10. Heller, "Tragedy of the Anticommons," 623.

11. Heller, "Tragedy of the Anticommons," 671.

12. Ibid., 642–47.

13. Copyright © The New Yorker Collection 1993 Al Ross from cartoonbank.com. All Rights Reserved.

14. Fox and Heller, "What Is Good Corporate Governance?"

15. Heller, "Tragedy of the Anticommons," 647–48.

16. Ibid., 627–33.

17. See Cheryl W. Gray, Rebecca J. Hanson, and Michael Heller, "Hungarian Legal Reform for the Private Sector," *George Washington Journal of International Law and Economics* 26 (1992): 293–353, at 303–6. On the Soviet legal system and socialist law of property, see George M. Armstrong Jr., *The Soviet Law of Property* (London: Butterworths, 1983), 6; and F. J. M. Feldbrugge, *Russian Law: The End of the Soviet System and the Role of Law* (Boston: M. Nijhoff, 1993), 229–46.

18. The term *real estate* first appeared in post-Soviet Russian statutes in the "Law of the Russian Federation on Basic Principles of the Federal Housing Policy" (December 24, 1992). See also William G. Frenkel, "Private Land Ownership in Russia: An Overview of Legal Developments to Date," *Parker School Journal of Eastern European Law* 3 (1996): 257–304, at 287.

19. This section draws from Heller, "Tragedy of the Anticommons," 630–33.

20. Heller, "Tragedy of the Anticommons," 632.

21. See ibid., 633–42.

22. Heller, "Tragedy of the Anticommons," 638.

23. See Susan Rose-Ackerman, *Corruption: A Study in Political Economy* (New York: Academic Press, 1978), 106–07; Andrei Shleifer and Robert W. Vishny, "Corruption," *Quarterly Journal of Economics* 108 (1993): 599–617, at 615.

24. On kiosks, see Heller, "Tragedy of the Anticommons," 642–47.

25. Sergei Khrushchev, "Stands of Dirty Capitalism," *Asia, Inc.*, March 1994, 86.

26. Margaret Shapiro, "Perils of Kiosk Capitalism: Russia's New Entrepreneurs Pay for Permits and Protection," *Washington Post*, August 28, 1993, 15, 18.

27. James P. Gallagher, "Russia's Kiosk Capitalists Keep Wary Eye on Hard-Line Premier," *Chicago Tribune*, January 5, 1993, 10.

28. See de Soto, *Other Path*, 60–62 (see chap. 5, n. 14).

29. See ibid., 72, 152, 173–77.

30. See ibid., 161–63 (property registries), 163–71 (long-term contracts), 177–78 (patents).

31. Ellen Barry, "Kiosk Crackdown Yields Sidewalk Space, Bitterness," *Moscow Times*, February 14, 1995.

32. On Moscow apartments, see Heller, "Tragedy of the Anticommons," 647–50.

33. Struyk, "Long Road," 22–28.

34. See, for example, Duncan Kennedy, "Neither the Market nor the State: Housing Privatization Issues," in *A Fourth Way? Privatization, Property, and the Emergence of New Market Economies,* edited by Gregory S. Alexander and Grazyna Skapska (New York: Routledge, 1994), 253–66, at 263–64; and Duncan Kennedy and Leopold Specht, "Limited Equity Cooperatives as a Mode of Privatization," in ibid., 267–85, at 268.

35. On communal apartments, see Heller, "Tragedy of the Anticommons," 650–54.

36. Lyudmila Ivanova, "You and Me, He and She, Together a Communal Family," *Argumenty i Fakty* 26 (1995), 6, translated and condensed in *Current Digest of the Post-Soviet Press*, August 9, 1995, 10.

37. Andrew E. Kramer, "A Price Run-Up for Run-Down Communes: Office Rents Are Out of Sight in Russia, and Old Buildings Are New Real Estate Frontier," *New York Times*, December 22, 2006, Business section, 1, 4.

38. Mikhail Zoshchenko, "Nervous People," in *Nervous People, and Other Satires*, edited by Hugh McLean, translated by Maria Gordon and Hugh McLean (New York: Pantheon Books, 1963), 124–26, at 124.

39. Kramer, "Price Run-Up," 4.

40. See, for example, Celestine Bohlen, "Moscow Privatization Yields Privacy and Problems: Comes the Revolution in Apt. 26," *New York Times*, February 28, 1993, 1; Marcus Warren, "Door Shuts on a Russian Phenomenon," *Sunday Telegraph* (London), January 10, 1993, 14.

41. Malcolm Gray, "Capitalist Crimes: Swindlers Prey on Elderly Tenants of Prized Apartments," *Macleans*, January 10, 1994, 17. Gray quotes the deputy commander of Moscow's missing persons unit as saying: "Privatization of apartments started in October 1991, and it soon led to a new problem: homeowners, most of them old people, started disappearing" (ibid.). On this trend, see also Victoria Clark, "Dying to Get a Home of One's Own," *The Observer* (London), November 28, 1993, 28; and Fred Hiatt, "The Dark Side of Privatization: To Moscow Con Men, Scant Housing Is Worth Killing For," *Washington Post*, November 13, 1993, 1.

42. Kramer, "Price Run-Up," 4.

43. Ibid.

44. On the five factors, see Heller, "Tragedy of the Anticommons," 654–56.

45. See generally Merritt B. Fox and Michael A. Heller, "The Unexplored Role of Initial Conditions," in *Corporate Governance Lessons*, edited by Fox and Heller, 367–404.

Chapter 7

1. This chapter builds on Michael A. Heller, "The Rose Theorem?" *Yale Journal of Law and the Humanities* 18 (2006): 29–48, which, in turn, relies on John R. Wennersten, *The Oyster Wars of Chesapeake Bay* (Centreville, Md.: Tidewater Publishers, 1981).

2. On oyster basics, see Wennersten, *Oyster Wars*, 3–5; Robert Hedeen, *The Oyster: The Life and Lore of the Celebrated Bivalve* (Centreville, Md.: Tidewater Publish-

ers, 1986), 191–92; and Joseph Conlin, "Consider the Oyster," *American Heritage* 31 (1980): 72–73.

3. Wennersten, *Oyster Wars,* 6. In 1701, a visitor to Virginia remarked, "The abundance of oysters is incredible. There are whole banks of them so that the ships must avoid them. A sloop which was to land us at Kingscreek, struck an oyster bed, where we had to wait for about two hours for the tide" (Hedeen, *Oyster,* 6).

4. Courtesy of the Prints and Photographs Division, Library of Congress, LC-USZC4–2466.

5. Wennersten, *Oyster Wars,* 13–14 (noting the introduction of high-capacity dredges by "plundering Yankee drudgers" and a midcentury Maryland law passed in response that banned "foreign," that is, nonresident, oystering); 28–32 (describing the two types of boats and the men who operated them). See also Hedeen, *Oyster,* 158–83 (detailing procedures and tools for tonging and dredging).

6. M. J. Burns, "Working the Beds Off Annapolis," *Harper's Weekly,* January 11, 1890, 20. Courtesy of the Prints and Photographs Division, Library of Congress, LC-USZ62-103700.

7. On the racial economy of oystering, see Wennersten, *Oyster Wars,* 33–35.

8. Schell and Hogan, "Oyster Pirates Dredging at Night," *Harper's Weekly,* March 1, 1884, 136. Courtesy of the Prints and Photographs Division, Library of Congress, LC-USZ62-76144.

9. The best work on the Oyster Wars, from which this section draws substantially, is Wennersten, *Oyster Wars.*

10. See Hedeen, *Oyster,* 9. See also Wennersten, *Oyster Wars,* 46–47.

11. Wennersten, *Oyster Wars,* 47.

12. David O. Stewart, *The Summer of 1787: The Men Who Invented the Constitution* (New York: Simon and Schuster, 2007), 1–10.

13. For the New Jersey side of the story (and the best scholarly work linking oystering with law and social history), see Bonnie J. McCay, *Oyster Wars and the Public Trust: Property, Law, and Ecology in New Jersey History* (Tucson: University of Arizona Press, 1998). For an oyster history focusing on New York, see Mark Kurlansky, *The Big Oyster: History on the Half Shell* (New York: Ballantine Books, 2006). As an aside, New Jersey–New York mollusk wars continue even unto this day. See Andy Newman, "In Raritan Bay Border War Flares Anew over Littlenecks and Cherrystones," *New York Times,* July 5, 2007, New York and Region section, 1.

14. William Brooks, *The Oyster: A Popular Summary of a Scientific Study* (Baltimore: John Hopkins University Press, 1905), 76.

15. Ibid., 19 (noting that since "1820, upwards of thirty laws . . . have passed the Legislature").

16. *Oxford English Dictionary,* "over-use, *n.*" (citing an 1862 book that referred to oystering practices in the Channel Islands).

17. Quoted in Conlin, "Consider the Oyster," 73.

18. Hunter Davidson, *Report upon the Oyster Resources of Maryland to the General Assembly* (Annapolis: Wm. Thompson, 1870), 11.

19. Wennersten, *Oyster Wars,* 48.

20. Ibid., 76 (quote), 42–46 (Rice's tale).

21. Schell and Hogan, *Harper's Weekly,* March 1, 1884, 136. Courtesy of the Prints and Photographs Division, Library of Congress, LC-USZ62-76142.

22. Schell and Hogan, *Harper's Weekly,* March 1, 1884, 136. Courtesy of the Prints and Photographs Division, Library of Congress, LC-USZ62-76143.

23. Quoted in Wennersten, *Oyster Wars,* 80.

24. Wennersten, *Oyster Wars,* 83.

25. Quoted in ibid., 84.

26. See Davidson, *Report upon the Oyster Resources,* 3.

27. Brooks, *Oyster,* 3, 76–77.

28. Ibid., 132–33, 137, 139, 149.

29. *Wharton v. Wise,* 153 U.S. 155 (1894) (ruling that the Pokomoke Sound was a distinct body of water to which Marylanders had no right to access for taking oysters).

30. Wennersten, *Oyster Wars,* 95. Disputes arose over every aspect of oyster culture. Alongside the big territorial disputes, there were even judicial fights over the empty shells, the cultch. For example, the U.S. Supreme Court allowed states to require oystermen to return 10 percent of their emptied oyster shells to the bay as cultch—simultaneously a novel form of state taxation, tool for conservation, and locus for resistance *(Leonard and Leonard v. Earle,* 279 U.S. 392, 396–98 [1929]). See also Eduardo Peñalver, "Regulatory Taxings," *Columbia Law Review* 104 (2004): 2182–54, at 2210–11 (discussing cultch as a form of tax).

31. Cited in Conlin, "Consider the Oyster," 72.

32. Brooks, *Oyster,* 77.

33. Encyclopedia Britannica (1911 ed.), available at www.1911encyclopedia.org/Oyster.

34. H. M. Wilder, *Harper's Weekly,* May 28, 1887, 389. Courtesy of the Prints and Photographs Division, Library of Congress, LC-USZ62-128026.

35. Quoted in J. Rydon, *Oysters with Love,* title page (London: Peter Owen, 1968); and Hedeen, *Oyster,* 3.

36. See Conlin, "Consider the Oyster," 70. A modern record was set in the 1970s, when Vernon Bass downed 588 oysters in seventeen minutes and thirty-two seconds (ibid.).

37. Pliny the Elder, *The Natural History of Pliny*, edited by John Bostock and H. T. Riley (London: H. G. Bohn, 1855), bk. 9, chap. 79, sec. 54, "The First Person That Formed Artificial Oyster-Beds."

38. *Merry Wives of Windsor*, 2.2.2–3.

39. See Arthur Koestler, *The Sleepwalkers: A History of Man's Changing Vision of the Universe* (London: Penguin, 1959), 19–25.

40. Quoted in J. P. Hore and Edward Jex, *The Deterioration of Oyster and Trawl Fisheries of England: Its Causes and Remedy* (London: E. Stock, 1880), 6.

41. Anthony Hamilton, *The Memoirs of Count Grammont, Complete*, edited by Sir Walter Scott (1713; reprint, London: Bickers and Son, 1906).

42. The complete, searchable, and entertaining text of the *Memoirs of Count Grammont* is available online at www.gutenberg.org/files/5416/5416.txt.

43. Charles Dickens, *The Pickwick Papers* (1837; reprint, London: Collins, 1982), 300.

44. Davidson, *Report upon the Oyster Resources*, 4.

45. Writing in 1599, Henry Buttes noted, "It is unseasonable and unwholesome in all months that have not an R in their name to eat an oyster" (*Dyet's Dry Dinner* [London: Tho. Creede, 1599]). See also Hedeen, *Oyster*, 6 (noting that this health "superstition has no basis in fact"). Bonnie McCay has uncovered a 1719 act by the colonial assembly of New Jersey prohibiting oyster gathering from May 10 until September 1—one of the earliest oyster laws anywhere in America (*Oyster Wars and the Public Trust*, 8).

46. T. C. Eyton details an early-nineteenth-century treaty between Britain and France limiting methods and times for oyster harvesting (*A History of the Oyster and the Oyster Fisheries* [London: J. Van Voorst, 1858], 10–11).

47. On the Faversham charter, see Patricia Hyde and Duncan W. Harrington, *Faversham Oyster Fishery: Through Eleven Centuries* (Kent, England: Arden Enterprises, 2002).

48. Thomas C. Hayes, "Confrontation in the Gulf: The Oilfield Lying below the Iraq-Kuwait Dispute," *New York Times*, September 3, 1990, 7.

49. See Gary D. Libecap, "Unitization," in *The New Palgrave Dictionary of Economics and the Law*, edited by Peter Newman (London: Macmillan, 1998), 3: 641–44.

50. See Charles Lockwood, "In the Los Angeles Oil Boom, Derricks Sprouted Like Trees," *Smithsonian*, October 1980, 187–206; Kenny A. Franks and Paul F. Lambert, *Early California Oil: A Photographic History, 1865–1940* (College Station: Texas A&M University Press, 1985), 103–8.

51. See Gary D. Libecap and James L. Smith, "The Self-Enforcing Provisions of Oil and Gas Unit Operating Agreements: Theory and Evidence," *Journal of Law, Economics, and Organization* 15 (1999): 526–48, at 526.

52. Aerograph Co., Signal Hill, circa 1923. Courtesy of the Prints and Photographs Division, Library of Congress, Control #2007660408. For more on Signal Hill, see www.consrv.ca.gov/dog/photo_gallery/historic_mom/photo_01.htm and www.priweb.org/ed/pgws/history/signal_hill/signal_hill_1932.html.

53. For a historical perspective on exclusive economic zones, see "The United Nations Convention on the Law of the Sea: A Historical Perspective," www.un.org/Depts/los/convention_agreements/convention_historical_perspective.htm#Exclusive%20Economic%20Zone.

54. Adam Smith, *An Inquiry into the Nature and Causes of the Wealth of Nations,* edited by Edwin Cannan, 5th ed. (1776; reprint, London: Methuen, 1904), bk. 1, chap. 3, para. 8.

55. Quoted in Wennersten, *Oyster Wars,* 28.

56. *Frank Leslie's Illustrated Newspaper,* May 18, 1867, 136. Courtesy of the Prints and Photographs Division, Library of Congress, LC-USZ62-128743. The engraving above the entrance to the lunchroom reads "Oysters in Every Style."

Chapter 8

1. Michael A. Heller, "The Cutting Edge of Poster Law," *Journal of Legal Education* 49 (1999): 467–79.

2. J. P. Hore and Edward Jex, *The Deterioration of Oyster and Trawl Fisheries of England: Its Cause and Remedy* (London: Elliot Stock, 1880), 1–2.

3. Japan has a best-selling new genre of novels composed on cell phone keypads (Norimitsu Onishi, "Thumbs Race as Japan's Best Sellers Go Cellular," *New York Times,* January 20, 2008, Foreign Desk, 1).

4. See "Narita Fiasco: Never Again" (see chap. 1, n. 19).

5. For example, see Depoorter and Vanneste, "Putting Humpty Dumpty Back Together" (see chap. 1, n. 62).

6. On the use of the Bankruptcy Code, U.S.C. Section 363(f), as a solution to anticommons tragedy, see Edward Janger, "Private Property, Information Costs, and the Anticommons," *Hastings Law Journal* 54 (2003): 899–930, at 924–28.

7. Tomas Kellner, "Chop Job," *Forbes,* November 1, 2004, 83–84.

8. Ibid., 84.

9. Ibid.

10. Ibid., 86.

Index